T0345165

"Not only does the discipline of data science need this book, it holds critical insights and lessons for other facets of enterprise IT too. For the first time, the critically important ideas of emergent design practice have been weaved into the hyper-rational world of data science in an accessible and practical way. Kailash Awati and Alex Scriven have written the first data science book of its kind – a must read for anyone interested in the governance of data and the complex problems that data and analytics seeks to help solve."

Paul Culmsee, *Managing Partner, Seven Sigma Business Solutions*

"A refreshingly practical approach to success in data science and machine learning. The value of Awati and Scriven's contribution to this field is that emergent design lends to data science a coherence that previously was missed in the chasm between the promise of new tech and the organisational change required to harness it. They've bridged that gap with a highly accessible read, weaving the wealth of their collective experience with the rigour of leading researchers, intellectuals and practitioners into a lively jaunt covering the full vocabulary of concepts for leaders (from deep learning to tech stack to GDPR) that will hold 'aha' moments for even the most seasoned data and analytics professionals and (hopefully!) spawn a new generation of strategic leadership and emergent practice in this space."

Passiona Cottee, *Associate Director, NSW Government*

"If you are passionate about the successful implementation of data science and analytics strategies, then put this book on your required reading list. You will learn why and how to define a direction by finding and framing problems that matter to people across the organisation."

Zanne Van Wyk, *Worldwide Education Industry Architect at Microsoft*

"*Data Science and Analytics Strategy* covers a wide range of topics like building analytics and data science capability, building data driven culture in the organization and ethical aspects of practicing data science. It includes advice which are easy and very practical to use in real world scenarios. All in all, a great read for all those who want to setup analytics and data science practises within their organization."

Duhita Khadepau, *Director (Analytics and Data Science), Assignar*

"Succeeding with data science and analytics is no easy ride, however this book gives the reader a range of ideas and actions to combat the challenges faced by professionals in this field. Finding a path to success requires new approaches and this book provides a refreshing perspective for practitioners to consider as they strive for success."

Sandra Hogan, *Co-Founder, Amperfii*

Data Science and Analytics Strategy

This book describes how to establish data science and analytics capabilities in organisations using an evolutionary approach that increases the chances of successful outcomes while minimising upfront investment. Based on their experiences and those of a number of data leaders, the authors provide actionable advice on data technologies, processes, and governance structures so that readers can make choices that are appropriate to their organisational contexts and requirements.

The book blends academic research on organisational change and data science processes with real-world stories from experienced data analytics leaders, focusing on the practical aspects of setting up a data capability. In addition to a detailed coverage of capability, culture, and technology choices, a unique feature of the book is its treatment of emerging issues such as data ethics and algorithmic fairness.

Data Science and Analytics Strategy: An Emergent Design Approach has been written for professionals who are looking to build data science and analytics capabilities within their organisations as well as those who wish to expand their knowledge and advance their careers in the data space. Providing deep insights into the intersection between data science and business, this guide will help professionals understand how to help their organisations reap the benefits offered by data. Most importantly, readers will learn how to build a fit-for-purpose data science capability in a manner that avoids the most common pitfalls.

Kailash Awati is a data and sensemaking professional with a deep interest in helping organisations tackle complex problems. He is an Adjunct Fellow in Human-Centred Data Science at the UTS Connected Intelligence Centre and a Data and Insights Manager at a government agency. Over the last decade, he has established data capabilities in diverse organisations using the principles described in this book. In addition to his work in industry, he has developed and taught postgraduate courses in machine learning and decision-making under uncertainty. He is the co-author of two well-regarded books on managing socially complex problems in organisations: *The Heretic's Guide to Best Practices* and *The Heretic's Guide to Management*.

Alexander Scriven is a senior data scientist at Atlassian in Sydney, Australia, and has experience across start-ups, government, and enterprise building analytical capacities and executing on data science projects. He greatly enjoys teaching and mentoring and has built and delivered both master's-level university courses in machine learning and deep learning and highly rated courses for online platforms such as Datacamp. His research interests are in applying data science techniques to novel industry challenges. Alex greatly enjoys bridging the gap between cutting-edge technology and business applications.

CHAPMAN & HALL/CRC DATA SCIENCE SERIES

Reflecting the interdisciplinary nature of the field, this book series brings together researchers, practitioners, and instructors from statistics, computer science, machine learning, and analytics. The series will publish cutting-edge research, industry applications, and textbooks in data science.

The inclusion of concrete examples, applications, and methods is highly encouraged. The scope of the series includes titles in the areas of machine learning, pattern recognition, predictive analytics, business analytics, Big Data, visualization, programming, software, learning analytics, data wrangling, interactive graphics, and reproducible research.

Published Titles

Public Policy Analytics
Code and Context for Data Science in Government
Ken Steif

Supervised Machine Learning for Text Analysis in R
Emil Hvitfeldt and Julia Silge

Massive Graph Analytics
Edited by David Bader

Data Science
An Introduction
Tiffany-Anne Timbers, Trevor Campbell and Melissa Lee

Tree-Based Methods
A Practical Introduction with Applications in R
Brandon M. Greenwell

Urban Informatics
Using Big Data to Understand and Serve Communities
Daniel T. O'Brien

Introduction to Environmental Data Science
Jerry Douglas Davis

Cybersecurity Analytics
Rakesh M. Verma and David J. Marchette

Exploratory Model Analysis
Explore, Explain, and Examine Predictive Models
Przemyslaw Biecek and Tomasz Burzykowski

For more information about this series, please visit: www.routledge.com/ Chapman--HallCRC-Data-Science-Series/book-series/CHDSS

Data Science and Analytics Strategy

An Emergent Design Approach

Kailash Awati
Alexander Scriven

CRC Press
Taylor & Francis Group
Boca Raton London New York

CRC Press is an imprint of the
Taylor & Francis Group, an **informa** business

A CHAPMAN & HALL BOOK

Designed cover image: Getty Images

First edition published 2023
by CRC Press
6000 Broken Sound Parkway NW, Suite 300, Boca Raton, FL 33487-2742

and by CRC Press
4 Park Square, Milton Park, Abingdon, Oxon, OX14 4RN

CRC Press is an imprint of Taylor & Francis Group, LLC

© 2023 Kailash Awati and Alexander Scriven

ISBN: 978-1-032-19633-6 (hbk)
ISBN: 978-1-032-19632-9 (pbk)
ISBN: 978-1-003-26015-8 (ebk)

DOI: 10.1201/9781003260158

Typeset in Palatino
by Newgen Publishing UK

Kailash

For my amazing wife who steered our family through challenging times while battling a serious illness: Arati, you inspire me every day.

Alex

For Jennifer. My world.

Contents

Foreword

In my experience the ability to go from a collection of data science use cases to a full-blown capability presents a significant challenge for many organisations. Recognising that organisations have traditionally struggled with the ability to develop and execute data and analytics strategies, this book by Kailash Awati and Alex Scriven provides practical guidance for leaders who are looking to derive tangible benefits from data. Apart from covering traditional topics such as capability development, technology, and productionising data science, a novel and perhaps the most important feature of the book is its coverage of governance and ethics. Data practitioners and enthusiasts will be exposed to the key elements of data science and analytics and will learn how to apply these features to organically and sustainably grow data capabilities.

Emergent Design urges data leaders and practitioners to look beyond the technical aspects of the discipline. Organisations that fail to recognise the sociotechnical aspects of data science will struggle to develop a sustainable data capability. Whether you are setting out on your journey or refining your existing data science programmes, there is a significant benefit to be gained by adopting the approach advocated in this book. Based on evolutionary principles of change, it provides a simple and effective framework to guide you on your data journey.

In addition to challenging conventional wisdom about how to "do data", this book captures the diverse experiences of many data and analytics leaders who discuss how they have overcome the challenges associated with harnessing the growing potential of emerging data technologies in a scalable and sustainable manner. Many organisations are rightfully focussed on ensuring the interoperability of technology and establishing efficient, optimised processes. However, as this book stresses, the most critical element of success lies in building the skills and expertise of your greatest assets: the people in your organisation.

Craig Napier
Chief Data Officer, University of Technology Sydney
August 2022

Preface

As we were close to completing the book, *Harvard Business Review* published an article entitled, *Is Data Scientist Still the Sexiest Job of the 21ˢᵗ Century?*[1] The article revisits a claim made a decade ago, in a similarly titled piece about the attractiveness of the profession.[2] In the recent article, the authors note that although data science is now a well-established function in the business world, setting up the function presents a number of traps for the unwary. In particular, they identify the following challenges:

- The diverse skills required to do data science in an organisational setting
- A rapidly evolving technology landscape
- Issues around managing data science projects; in particular, productionising data science models – i.e., deploying them for ongoing use in business decision-making
- Putting in place the organisational structures/processes and cultivating individual dispositions to ensure that data science is done in an ethical manner

On reviewing our nearly completed manuscript, we saw that we have spoken about each of these issues, in nearly the same order that they are discussed in the article (see the titles of Chapters 5–8). It appears that the issues we identified as pivotal are indeed the ones that organisations face when setting up a new data science function.

That said, the approach we advocate to tackle these challenges is somewhat unusual and therefore merits a prefatory explanation.

The approach proposed in this book arose from the professional experiences of two very different individuals, whose thoughts on how to "do data" in organisational settings converged via innumerable conversations over the last five years. Prior to working on this book, we collaborated on developing and teaching an introductory postgraduate data science course to diverse audiences ranging from data analysts and IT professionals to sociologists and journalists. At the same time, we led very different professional lives, working on assorted data-related roles in multinational enterprises, government, higher education, not-for-profit organisations and start-ups. The main lesson we learned from our teaching and professional experiences is that, when building data capabilities, it is necessary to first understand where people are – in terms of current knowledge, past experience, and future plans – and grow the capability from there.

To summarise our approach in a line: *data capabilities should be grown, not grafted*.

This is the central theme of Emergent Design, which we introduce in Chapter 1 and elaborate in Chapter 3. The rest of the book is about building a data science capability using this approach.

Naturally, we were keen to sense-check our thinking with others. To this end, we interviewed a number of well-established data leaders and practitioners from diverse domains, asking them about their approach to setting up and maintaining data science capabilities. You will find their quotes scattered liberally across the second half of this book. When speaking with these individuals, we found that most of them tend to favour an evolutionary approach not unlike the one we advocate in the book. To be sure, organisations need formal structures and processes in place to ensure consistency, but many of the data leaders we spoke with emphasised the need to grow these in a gradual manner, taking into account the specific context of their organisations.

It seems to us that many who are successful in building data science and analytics capabilities tacitly use an emergent design approach, or at least some elements of it. Yet, there is very little discussion about this approach in the professional and academic literature. This book is our attempt at bridging this gap.

Although primarily written for business managers and senior data professionals who are interested in establishing modern data capabilities in their organisations, we are also speaking to a wider audience ranging from data science and business students to data professionals who would like to step into management roles. Last but not least, we hope the book will appeal to curious business professionals who would like to develop a solid understanding of the various components of a modern data capability.

That said, regardless of their backgrounds and interests, we hope readers will find this book useful ... and dare we say, an enjoyable read.

Kailash Awati
Alexander Scriven
Sydney, September 2022

Notes

1 https://hbr.org/2022/07/is-data-scientist-still-the-sexiest-job-of-the-21st-century
2 https://hbr.org/2012/10/data-scientist-the-sexiest-job-of-the-21st-century

Acknowledgements

Kailash and Alex

We would like to thank the data leaders who were beyond generous with their time, advice, and support in the course of writing this book. They are: Craig Napier, Duhita Khadepau, Firas Hamdan, Hema Prasad, Ian Jackman, Jan Lambrechts, Josh McNeil, Kumar Parekh, Dr Kobi Leins, Matt Minor, Sandra Hogan, Sonya Zecchin, Sylvia Jastkowiak, and Zanne Van Wyk. Brief biographies of these accomplished individuals are available in the following pages. We'd also like to thank Passiona Cottee for her significant contribution to the section on ethics in Chapter 8. Last, but not least, our thanks go out to George Knott for his support through the process of writing this book.

Kailash

I first encountered the concept of emergent design about a decade ago, in a conversation with my friend and longtime collaborator, Paul Culmsee. My thanks go out to him for introducing me to the idea and for many discussions about it in the years since.

Over the last many years, I have been fortunate to have had multiple opportunities to set up data analytics capabilities in diverse environments. It is these experiences that have enabled me to road-test and refine the ideas presented herein. I'm therefore indebted to numerous colleagues and workmates who travelled the road with me. In particular, I would like to call out Anusha, David Lefeve, Hendrik Mieves, Sean Heffernan, Homan Zhao, Sree Acharath, Sam Kohli, Nivi Srinivasan, Vidyalakshmi Rao, Matthew Harwood, Anita Menon, and Neil Finlay.

A huge thank you to my managers past and present – Mario Techera, Matthew Perry, Joe Helo, Yasuhiro Nishimi, Simon Buckingham Shum, Josh McNeil, and Celia Murphy – all of whom gave me the freedom to try out new ways of working within their organisations.

I am indebted to Simon Buckingham Shum who, in 2016, gave me the opportunity to teach in the Master of Data Science and Innovation (MDSI) programme at the University of Technology Sydney. A big thank you to all of the MDSI students I have had the privilege of teaching over the last five years: I have learnt much from my interactions with you all, both in and outside the classroom. I'd like to single out Chris Mahoney who supported me as a tutor through challenging pedagogical times during the height of the Covid pandemic. A special thanks to my brilliant co-author, Alex, from whom I have learnt much about the ins and outs of doing data science in different contexts. Yes, we are unlikely collaborators … but I think it works!

Finally, and most importantly, I'd like to thank Vikram, Rohan, and Arati, the mainstays of my life, without whom none of this (or anything else) would have been possible.

Alex

When Kailash and I began discussing how to paint this book on the blank canvas in front of us, it began with sharing stories: stories of success, stories of failure, funny stories, and frustrating stories. All manner of stories from the quite different paths we have walked.

It is therefore important that I acknowledge and thank everyone for the roles they played in these stories which have shaped myself and my input into this project. Firstly, a broad thanks to everyone who has been involved in working with, for, and around me during my career. Special thanks to Sally Wade, Gelina Talbot, and Jon Beard (as well as my old managers Mick G, Jen M.W, Mel B, and others) for the belief in me and opportunities they created and supported me through. To Adrian Cordiner (and the Digital Rhinos) for all our work (past, present, and future!) and his support during my studies. As well as the entire "Datanauts" crew for the projects we worked on together.

I would also like to thank the various people I have worked with on teaching and academic work across UNSW and UTS, especially Isabella Dobrescu, Alberto Motta, and my current research team (notably Bogdan, Kaska, and David). Additionally, all the students whom I have taught including those in the Master of Data Science and Innovation (MDSI) programme at the University of Technology Sydney. I still feel ongoing pride seeing all the amazing things they all continue to do.

An important acknowledgement and thanks is needed for ongoing friend and mentor figures Perry Stephenson, Tim Cubitt, and Kailash (of course, an additional thanks for being my co-author on this project) as I've wended and wound my way through my career. A special thanks to Duhita Khadepau for her ongoing friendship, mentorship, and for everything we have worked on together, including her involvement in this project.

Most importantly, the biggest thanks to my close friends, to my family, to my constant companion Alfie, and most especially to my rock, Jennifer. This project and everything that I have done which is represented here I couldn't have done without your support and care.

Contributors

Passiona Cottee is a leader at the nexus of data, automation, privacy, and ethics, drawing on over 20 years' experience across both public and private sectors. A machine learning teacher and data ethicist, she is currently setting up an AI lab function within a foresight team at the NSW Department of Premier and Cabinet and guest lectures in the University of Technology Sydney's Data Science for Innovation program.

Firas Hamdan is currently the Data Governance Lead at KPMG Australia and has over 20 years' experience working with clients assessing governance practices and creating practical programmes to build a lasting culture of governance and ethical data practices. Firas has a long history of successfully leading data analytics and governance programmes across a variety of industries including banking and financial services, telecommunication, media, retail, energy, utilities, and assets management.

Sandra Hogan is an accomplished data science and analytics leader with over 20 years' experience in building and leading analytics and data science teams and over 10 years in providing specialist consulting to many large organisations across Australia and New Zealand. In 2018, Sandra was recognised as #2 Analytics Leader in Australia by the Institute of Analytics Professionals of Australia (IAPA). She is the founder of Leap Analytics, an analytics advisory company, and a co-founder of a software company, Amperfii, helping people to collaborate and create great outcomes with data and analytics.

Ian Jackman is currently the General Manager, Data and Analytics (CDO) at Bendigo and Adelaide Bank, where he has developed and driven the organisational data and analytics strategy, embedding data governance, and a data-driven culture whilst enabling value from data through an enterprise analytics centre of excellence. He has deep expertise in analytics and technology, and has consulted to organisations across industries to derive business and customer value.

Sylvia Jastkowiak is Principal Advisor in Data Ethics and Privacy at NEC Australia where she has worked with a variety of organisations and industries. She has specialist expertise in designing privacy tools and ethical frameworks that help organisations navigate their legal and social obligations when utilising personal and sensitive data.

Duhita Khadepau is currently the Director (Analytics and Data Science) at Assignar, a construction-tech start-up in Sydney, Australia. She is a seasoned data professional with over 15 years' experience in designing and executing data strategies of organisations in India, Singapore, and Australia, across the homeware, banking, B2B SaaS, and retail e-commerce sectors. She has held pivotal roles in building data capacities across some of Australia's most successful start-ups, helping them scale and raise funds, and has held lecturing and teaching positions in data science.

Jan Lambrechts is currently a data ethics lead at ANZ with deep prior experience across both government and commercial organisations in data ethics, privacy, data governance, and overall analytics enablement. He has led teams and projects to build ethical frameworks from the ground up and top-down, and worked closely with teams to translate and embed these into everyday practice.

Kobi Leins (GAICD) is an Honorary Senior Fellow of King's College, London; Non-Resident Fellow of the United Nations Institute for Disarmament Research; Advisory Board Member of the Carnegie AI and Equality Initiative; Member of Standards Australia as a technical expert on the International Standards Organisation's work on AI Standards; co-founder of Responsible Innovation and the Life Sciences with IEEE; and Affiliate, ARC Centre of Excellence for Automated Decision-Making and Society. Leins has previously managed programmes and teams in administrative law and justice, humanitarian law, human rights law, and disarmament with the UN and the International Committee of the Red Cross and worked in two different university faculties of Engineering and Computer Science. Leins is the author of *New War Technologies and International Law: The Legal Limits to Weaponising Nanomaterials*, Cambridge University Press (2022). Further publications can be found at kobileins.com.

Josh McNeil is the Manager (Direct Marketing and Campaigns) at Cancer Council NSW and has over a decade of experience in the NFP space in using data to drive organisational outcomes and building analytics capabilities.

Matt Minor is currently the Head of Group Data and Analytics at the Blackmores group where he has built and executed on building their analytics strategy and capacity. He has deep experience building and leading analytics teams across Australia and the UK, across industries including finance, software, and health.

Craig Napier is currently the Chief Data Officer at the University of Technology, Sydney, and is the President of the Data Warehouse Institute (Australian Chapter). In 2020, he was recognised as being amongst the top three analytics leaders by the Institute of Analytics Professionals Australia (IAPA). He has led and developed analytics strategies and teams driving enterprise data initiatives at a number of Australia's top universities and held lecturing positions in business analytics.

Kumar Parekh is an experienced leader in data and AI strategy who has built data strategies and overseen implementation of analytics work across the entire business value chain. His career has included building data capabilities in major institutions across industries such as government (state and federal), mining, financial services, higher education, aged care, airlines, and property to name a few. He was at the helm of one of the earliest pioneering data teams in geocoding data in Australia.

Hema Prasad is a seasoned data and analytics executive leader with over two decades of global experience enabling large-scale business transformations via data, analytics, and business intelligence for Fortune-50 and ASX clients in USA, India, and Australia. Specialising in data strategy, data platforms modernisation, data architecture, governance, big data, cloud and platform engineering, data science, and analytics, Hema is a highly regarded and recognised data practitioner. An active public speaker, industry advisor, and mentor, she is passionate about working with students and aspiring data professionals to raise awareness on data and analytics career pathways.

Zanne Van Wyk is a data and analytics strategist with over 30 years' experience in building and executing data analytics and data science strategies across a variety of industries across the globe, with special expertise in the education sector. She is currently a worldwide education industry architect at Microsoft, developing strategies and roadmaps for a portfolio of industry partners.

Sonya Zecchin has led and built analytics capabilities across industries as varied as insurance, telecommunications, government, and logistics over the past 25 years. She has held lecturing positions on applying analytics to the business context and has been a learning content developer for IAPA. Her focus is now on supporting the development of people in analytics by delivering original and curated learning experiences.

1

Introduction

Data Science as a Sociotechnical Capability

This book is the outcome of over 35 years of collective experience gained by us, the authors, in building data capabilities in diverse organisations, ranging from large multinationals and technology companies to fast-growing start-ups and small not-for-profits. Our key message is that building an effective data capability[1] is, at its heart, a problem of organisational change. This may come as a surprise to some readers, but we suspect it will strike a chord with those who have walked the path of building such capabilities.

As noted by many researchers (e.g. Gagné et al. 2000, Peus et al. 2009), the success of an organisational change initiative depends on managing its impact on those who are affected by it. Consequently, setting up a data capability in an organisation requires a careful consideration of people, technology, and, more importantly, the interactions between the two. One could say that a data science capability is a *sociotechnical*[2] system.

The introduction of a new way of working into an organisational setting will typically trigger reactions ranging from unbridled enthusiasm to covert resistance. Often the enthusiasts (typically managers) will not understand the reluctance of the resistors (typically employees who feel threatened or undermined). These issues must be worked through collectively as the strategy is implemented. Indeed, resolving such issues is just as important as the more obvious decisions pertaining to skills and technologies.

The Fallacy of Strategic Alignment

The conventional approach to formulating and implementing a data science strategy takes a technocentric view, i.e., it focuses on:

DOI: 10.1201/9781003260158-1

a. Acquiring the appropriate technology and skills.
b. Aligning these to the business. This is sometimes referred to as strategic alignment.

Given adequate budget, technology and skills are easy enough to acquire in the market. Strategic alignment is considerably harder, and it's worth understanding why.

The notion of strategic alignment of technology can be traced back to an influential paper by Henderson and Venkatraman (1989). The paper describes the need for "aligning" the business and technology strategies of companies and details a "Strategic Alignment Model" that purports to "guide management practice" towards achieving this. Although it is acknowledged that data science is distinct from other technology capabilities, in practice much of data science strategy work takes its inspiration from this notion of alignment. For example, as Robert de Graaf notes in his book *Managing Your Data Science Projects* (de Graaf 2019):

> *It's crucial for data science teams to be able to demonstrate their value by linking their activities to their organization's mission because there will be doubters who believe that data science is a waste of time.*

And a bit later:

> *The first step in developing a [data science] team strategy that achieves alignment with the organization is a careful study of the organization's strategy document... Every organization has slightly different overall goals and mission... The challenge for the data science team is to decide how the data science team supports those goals.*

The notion of alignment assumes that data science is a capability that can be grafted on to an organisation rather than grown. This book argues the opposite: *that data science is a capability that is best grown rather than grafted.* Growing a capability is a matter of *evolution*, not alignment. Indeed, alignment of the kind de Graaf mentions is difficult to achieve because the real world has a logic of its own that tends to escape our strategy documents and plans. So, as we will discuss later (Chapter 4), your first step is not about studying organisational strategy documents as de Graaf suggests; it is about defining a direction by finding and framing problems that matter to people across the organisation. If done right, the "alignment" that strategists hanker after will come for free. Our job in this book is to show you a way to "do it right".

The notion of strategic alignment has been problematised by many academics, but none have done so as eloquently as the late Claudio Ciborra, who wrote:

> *... while strategic alignment may be close to a truism conceptually, in the everyday business it is far from being implemented. ... If alignment was supposed to be the ideal "bridge" connecting the two key variables [business and technology], it must be admitted that such a conceptual bridge faces the perils of the concrete bridge always re-designed and never built between continental Italy and Sicily, (actually, between Scylla and Charybdis) its main problem being the shores: shifting and torn by small and big earthquakes ... .*
>
> *Ciborra 1997*

The problem with the notion of strategic alignment is that it is an abstraction that is not "out there in the world" but resides in the heads of strategists and the documents they produce. Plans that attempt to realise this kind of alignment fall apart as soon as they encounter messy real-world details. This tension between plans and reality is one of the many paradoxes inherent in strategy development. We will revisit this in Chapter 3 where we describe the principles of Emergent Design. The main point we wish to make now is that it is best to avoid making detailed plans too early in the game. We realise that this may go against everything you've heard or read about strategy development, so here are a couple of stories that might help illustrate our point. Along the way, we'll also take the opportunity to introduce a few concepts that are central to the approach we advocate in this book.

A Tale of Two Databases[3]

Many years ago, Kailash joined an organisation in the throes of change. Among other things, they were in the process of replacing a venerable Lotus Notes-based system with a newer Customer Relationship Management (CRM) product. As a part of this effort, he was asked to build a system to integrate data from the CRM system with other syndicated and publicly available datasets. The requirements were complex but, fortunately, the development team and key business stakeholders were co-located on one floor. The system design evolved through continual, often animated, discussions over the entire development period, in an environment characterised by openness and trust.

The system was delivered on schedule, with minimal rework required.

Some years later, he was invited to participate in a regional project aimed at building a data warehouse[4] for subsidiaries across Asia. The initiative was driven by the corporate IT office located in Europe. This was part of a new organisation-wide strategy to harmonise a data landscape that was – to put it mildly – messy. However, the subsidiaries thought their local systems were just fine. They were suspicious of corporate motives which they saw as a power play that would result in loss of autonomy over data and reporting.

After much debate in many videoconferences, a face-to-face meeting was called to resolve the issue.

The Wickedness of Building Data Capabilities

A few weeks before the meeting, Kailash stumbled on a 1973 paper by Horst Rittel, a professor of design at UC Berkeley (Rittel and Webber 1973). In the paper, Rittel coined the phrase *wicked problem* to describe a complex situation that is perceived in different ways by different stakeholders and is therefore difficult to translate into a clear problem statement. Rittel described ten characteristics of such problems. Although Rittel was talking about problems relating to town and infrastructure planning, Kailash saw that the characteristics he described applied exactly to the problem of the data warehouse. The first column in Table 1.1 lists the characteristics according to Rittel and the second describes the relevance of the characteristic to Kailash's data warehousing dilemma.

A question: how many of the characteristics in Table 1.1 apply to complex data projects you have worked on?

When dealing with wicked problems, the trick is to find a way to surface and reconcile diverse viewpoints. One therefore needs to make multiple perspectives explicit in a manner that enables a group to develop a shared understanding of contentious issues. Done right, this can lead to a resolution of the issue, at least partially. In other words, it is about seeking diverse viewpoints on the issue with a view to finding common ground, however small. Our point in telling such a story at this early stage is to highlight the wicked aspects of building new data capabilities in organisations.

As the story about the second database illustrates, *data is invariably political.* Often, the department or function that collects or generates the data will, by default, be seen as the "owner" of the data. That is, they have the mandate to tell the story of that data and use it for reporting, forecasting, or modelling. More importantly, they determine who gets access to the data. It is important for strategists and analysts to be sensitive to potential political issues such as ownership. Data professionals who overlook this aspect of their work will come unstuck for reasons that have nothing to do with technical competence.

There is another, less obvious, political issue that is worth unpacking. It has to do with how the data is interpreted and whose interests the interpretation represents. The mainstream approach to data modelling assumes that real-world objects and relationships can be accurately represented by models. As an example, a data model representing a sales process might consist of entities such as customers and products and their relationships, such as sales (customer X purchases product Y). It is tacitly assumed that objective,

TABLE 1.1

Characteristics of Wicked Problems and Their Relevance to Data Warehousing

Wicked Problem Characteristic	Relevance to the Situation
There is no definitive formulation of a wicked problem.	The formulation of the problem – standardisation vs reporting – depended on who was asked.
Wicked problems have no stopping rule.	A data warehouse is never done; it evolves as user requirements evolve.
Solutions to wicked problems are not true-or-false, but good-or-bad.	Data architecture is an exercise in compromise – there is no absolute right or wrong.
There is no immediate or ultimate test of a solution to a wicked problem.	Since a perfect solution does not exist, there is no ultimate test of a solution.
Every solution to a wicked problem is a "one-shot operation" because there is no opportunity to learn by trial and error; every attempt counts significantly.	Though this is not always true, there are invariably some data design decisions that can be extremely expensive or even impossible to fix without redoing the entire thing.
Wicked problems do not have an enumerable (or an exhaustively describable) set of potential solutions, nor is there a well-described set of permissible operations that may be incorporated into the plan.	There are, in principle, a huge number of viable data warehouse designs.
Every wicked problem can be considered to be a symptom of another problem.	There are fundamental principles of data warehouse design, but each data warehouse is unique, reflecting the unique requirements and technology choices of the organisation.
The existence of a discrepancy representing a wicked problem can be explained in numerous ways. The choice of explanation determines the nature of the problem's resolution.	The discrepancy here was that we had two conflicting approaches to designing the data warehouse. However, this was a political issue, not a technical one, and the politics itself was due to differences in perception of the situation.
The planner has no right to be wrong.	The database designer would be held responsible for the consequences of design decisions that were made. The decision itself was about steering a narrow course between the Scylla of subsidiaries and the Charybdis of corporate.

bias-free models of entities and relationships of interest can be built by asking the right questions and using appropriate information collection techniques.

However, things are not quite so straightforward: as data professionals know, real-world data models are invariably tainted by compromises between rigour and reality. This is inevitable because the process of building a data model involves at least two different sets of stakeholders whose interests are often at odds – business users and data modelling professionals. The former are not interested in the purity of model; they care about how well it supports their business processes. The interests of the latter, however, are often the opposite. And if that wasn't enough, there is the interest of the customer as well – for example, about how their data is protected from unauthorised access and the potential for misuse. We'll discuss these issues at length in Chapter 8.

The above reveals a truth about data modelling that is not fully appreciated by practitioners: that it is a process of negotiation and ethics rather than a search for a true representation of business reality. In other words, it is a sociotechnical problem that has wicked elements. This point has been highlighted in a brilliant paper by Heinz Klein and Kalle Lyytinen (1992). The key takeaway from the paper is that a data model is but one possible interpretation of reality. As such, there are many possible interpretations of reality so the "correctness" of any model hinges not on some objective truth but on a negotiated, best-for-group interpretation. This necessarily implies that a well-constructed data model "fuses" or "brings together" at least two different interpretations – those of users and modellers.

The mainstream view of data is that it asserts a truth and that data models reflect that truth. The view we are describing here, however, makes us aware that *data models are built in such a way as to support particular agendas.* Moreover, since the people who use the model are not those who construct it, *a gap between assumed and actual meaning is inevitable.* Indeed, even meaning evolves over time as the design evolves. It has been noted that a good design not only implements current business processes but also facilitates change (Dorst 2019). This necessarily implies that the design itself should be capable of evolving as the group's understanding of context evolves.

It is worth pausing here to think about the implications of the above. The example we have discussed deals with a technical matter – the design of a data warehouse. Even so, we see that there are wider issues that need to be addressed before the technologists can get to work. The point we want to emphasise here is that *social and political considerations permeate the entire spectrum of data capability building, from the technical to the organisational.*

The Notion of Emergent Design

Some years after the data warehousing story related above, Kailash found himself in a more senior role in the same organisation, a role in which he had responsibility for data-related work across a geographic region.

When Kailash was promoted to the new role, his boss asked him to explore the possibility of setting up a regional development centre for analytics that could serve the entire organisation. There was a clear cost argument in favour of such centre. However, given the sharply divided opinions around offshoring, the public airing of such a proposal would cause all kinds of reactions, many of which would be negative. The first problem was to address those upfront.

Kailash talked to the usual suspects, a few big outsourcers and consultancies, but soon realised that their aims were not congruent with his. Everything the outsourcers said pointed to high costs and potential conflicts down the line, such as vendor lock in and expensive contract variations.[5] As we will elaborate later in Chapter 6, the hidden costs of outsourcing are much too high. This was the second problem.

Oh, and if that weren't enough, there was another catch: the boss told him that there was zero budget for this at the time as it was not an official project. Moreover, since the initiative did not exactly have backing from corporate, it was unlikely to be supported in the near future. This was problem number three.

It was around that time that Kailash came across the notion of *Emergent Design* (Cavallo 2000a, 2000b), the key theme behind this book. The essential idea is to start from where people are and take small steps, each of which leads to demonstrable improvement. This generally requires some trial and error, but since the investment at each step is small and the benefit is demonstrable, it is not hard to convince the folks who sign cheques. Moreover, this enables one to continually adjust one's approach based on feedback from the previous step, much like nature does in the process of evolution. Actions are based on a given context, but the context itself changes because of the action and thus necessitates recalibrating subsequent actions.

At this point you might be thinking "this is exactly the same as an Agile approach – such as Scrum". That is not so. The key difference between Agile and Emergent Design is that in Agile, the endpoint of a sprint (or whatever else it is called in your favourite flavour of Agile) is well defined; in Emergent Design, it isn't. In the latter, we set out in a particular direction but without a well-defined endpoint. Indeed, there is no endpoint because new horizons open up as one proceeds, leading to new goals. This is exactly what one wants from a good strategy; a strategy that cannot evolve is worthless.

We'll say more about Emergent Design and how it was used to address the above challenge in Chapter 3. For now, we will make the observation that the way a problem is *framed*[6] – be it building a data warehouse or a data capability or anything else – is based on a range of implicit assumptions about the underlying nature of the problem. Most often the assumptions are based on conventional wisdom or "best practice" thinking, which leads to canned solutions that are rarely suited to the context at hand. Indeed, every organisation is unique in its details, so canned or one-size-fits-all approaches are unlikely to work well. Finding the right solution is a matter of taking small steps, each of which makes a tangible difference to the business. This is a process of *wayfinding* – setting out in a direction and working one's way to a destination, with details of next steps becoming apparent only as one progresses. This is not to say that one is proceeding blind. The metaphor we like to use is that it is akin to finding one's way through a thick fog; you need to focus on the immediate next step because your visibility is limited. Conventional strategies assume that one has a clear view of the future. In reality, the future is always foggy, which is why we advocate Emergent Design.

Given that data is political and developing a strategy is a process of wayfinding, one is inexorably led to the conclusion that *building new data capabilities in an organisation is an emergent process.* A technocentric approach that focuses largely on technical aspects such as technical knowledge, standards, and infrastructures exclusively will lead to disappointment. This is not to say that these are unimportant. Rather it is that they must be decided based on a deep understanding of the wider organisational context in which they will be implemented.

What to Expect from This Book

Given the above introduction, you're probably wondering what *actionable* advice you are going to get from this book. It should be clear that we are not going to provide you with a formula complete with templates and roadmaps based on "best practices" that you can copy-paste to your situation. Indeed, our intention is the opposite: to emphasise that there are no best practices … but there are good practices. So, what is a good practice?

In the context of building a data capability, good practice lies in:

1. Understanding the current state of your organisation from the perspective of how data is currently used and how it could be used.

2. Using the understanding developed in (1), to formulate high-level aspirational goals that set a direction rather than an objective. It is trivially true that you cannot foresee the future in all its detail. If this is so, then you cannot know upfront where your organisation is going to end up, so it is pointless to try and articulate that objective at the start. *Focus on the journey instead.*

3. What does "focusing on the journey" entail? Essentially it means eschewing big changes in favour of incremental and adaptive improvements.

4. Above all, putting people at the heart of what you do.

The value of a strategy is not in the strategy itself but in the process of strategising – thinking about where you are right now and (keeping that in mind) what should your next move be. By the end of this book, we hope to convince you that not only is this a practical approach, but is one that is superior to the conventional approach to developing data or any other sociotechnical capabilities.

The Structure of the Book

Since the approach we propose is novel, we will shift between theory and practice. As you go through the book, you will notice the chapters will (sort of) alternate between the two. That said, even the theoretical chapters are grounded via real-world examples and case studies. We hope these will help clarify what Emergent Design is and why we think it is the best way to go about building sociotechnical capabilities. Here's a brief summary of the structure of the book.

Chapter 2 is an introduction to data science for managers. Chapter 3 provides readers with a detailed introduction to Emergent Design. Chapter 4 describes the first – and most important – step in formulating a data science strategy based on the principles of Emergent Design. Chapters 5–8 cover in detail various aspects of the strategy including capability and culture (Chapter 5), technical matters (Chapter 6), an end-to-end view of the data science workflow (Chapter 7), data & AI governance, ethics, and privacy (Chapter 8), and finally a closing chapter to summarise the key points and offer some tips on selling the approach to your executives (Chapter 9).

Throughout we provide a number of vignettes based on our experiences of building data capabilities in diverse organisations and, more importantly, those of accomplished data leaders whose biographies appear in the front matter. It should be noted that not all the elements discussed in this book will be relevant for your situation. Feel free to pick and choose the bits you think will be useful in your context. Akin to evolution, Emergent Design is ultimately about doing what helps you make progress, however small.

We hope the stories related in this chapter and the commentary around them illustrate the limitations of the conventional, technocentric approach to building data capabilities in organisations. Along the way, we have also taken the opportunity to introduce a couple of concepts that are key threads that run through the book: *wicked problems* and *Emergent Design*. Our aim was to give you a sense of the approach advocated in this book. If you're browsing this chapter in your local bookstore, library, or online, we hope what you have read so far has piqued your interest enough to take this book home and read further.

Notes

1 Note that we will use the phrases *data capability* and *data science capability* interchangeably in this book as we will cover both. However, our primary focus is on building a *modern* data capability, which is necessarily about data science and analytics.
2 The term "sociotechnical system" came from the work done by Eric Trist and Ken Bamforth in the 1940s and 1950s, on the interactions between workers and technology in coal mines in the UK (Trist and Bamforth 1951). A brief account of the early history of the term can be found at: https://eight2late.wordpress.com/2015/04/07/from-the-coalface-an-essay-on-the-early-history-of-sociotechnical-systems/. In recent years, the term has been picked up and used in myriad other contexts (see Jasanoff and Kim 2013, for example).
3 This section and the following one are adapted from Awati (2021).
4 We will explain this term in Chapter 2. For now, think of it as a database that integrates data from several different systems.
5 https://eight2late.wordpress.com/2016/05/03/the-hidden-costs-of-it-outsourcing/
6 Problem framing is about defining or extracting a problem from a business situation. We'll say more about this at various points in this book.

References

Awati, K. (2021), "Software development as a wicked problem", *Increment*, Issue 19. Available online at: https://increment.com/planning/software-development-as-a-wicked-problem/

Cavallo, D. (2000a), "Emergent design and learning environments: Building on indigenous knowledge", *IBM Systems Journal*, Vol. 39 No. 3–4, pp. 768–781.

Cavallo, D. (2000b), *Technological Fluency and the Art of Motorcycle Maintenance: Emergent Design of Learning Environments* (Doctoral dissertation, Massachusetts Institute of Technology). Available online at: https://dspace.mit.edu/bitstream/handle/1721.1/9135/45233377-MIT.pdf

Ciborra, C. (1997), "De profundis? Deconstructing the concept of strategic alignment", *Scandinavian Journal of Information Systems*, Vol. 9 No. 1, pp. 67–82.

de Graaf, R. (2019), *Managing Your Data Science Projects*. Apress, Berkeley, CA.

Dorst, K. (2019), "Design beyond design", *She Ji: The Journal of Design, Economics, and Innovation*, Vol. 5 No. 2, pp. 117–127.

Gagné, M., Koestner, R. and Zuckerman, M. (2000), "Facilitating acceptance of organizational change: The importance of self-determination", *Journal of Applied Social Psychology*, Vol. 30 No. 9, pp. 1843–1852.

Henderson, J. and Venkatraman, N. (1989), "Strategic alignment: A framework for strategic information technology management", MIT Centre for Information Systems Research, Working Paper No. 190. Available online at: https://dspace.mit.edu/bitstream/handle/1721.1/49117/strategicalignme00hend.pdf

Jasanoff, S. and Kim, S. H (2013), "Sociotechnical imaginaries and national energy policies", *Science as Culture*, Vol. 22 No. 2, pp. 189–196.

Klein, H. K. and Lyytinen, K. (1992), "Towards a new understanding of data modeling", in Floyd, C., Zuellighoven, H., Budde, R. and Keil-Slawik, R. (Eds), *Software Development and Reality Construction*, Springer Verlag, Berlin, pp. 203–219.

Peus, C., Frey, D., Gerkhardt, M., Fischer, P. and Traut-Mattausch, E. (2009), "Leading and managing organizational change initiatives", *Management Revue*, Vol. 20 No. 2, pp. 158–175.

Rittel, H. W. and Webber, M. M. (1973), "Dilemmas in a general theory of planning", *Policy Sciences*, Vol. 4 No. 2, pp. 155–169.

Trist, E. and Bamforth, K. (1951), "Some social and psychological consequences of the longwall method of coal-getting: An examination of the psychological situation and defences of a work group in relation to the social structure and technological content of the work system", *Human Relations*, Vol. 4 No. 2, pp. 3–38.

2

What Is Data Science?

The Data Analytics Stack

Before beginning any discussion of the *what*, *how*, and *why* of data science, it is necessary to set the scene for *where* it sits within traditional data-related functions. Data science itself is not new; many old and well-established analytical techniques have been rebranded as data science or machine learning techniques.[1] Be that as it may, there is a general perception that when problems become sufficiently complicated or difficult (both, indeed, quite subjective terms), it is appropriate to label what is being done as being *advanced* and thus worthy of being called *data science*. This is why we will avoid defining the term and instead discuss what data scientists do, where data science fits into the modern organisational landscape, and the elements that are needed in order to do data science.

In this book we will use the term *data analytics stack* to describe both the functional and technical elements that are required for data science (see Figure 2.1).

The bottom half of the figure deals with matters such as data ingestion (acquisition), storage, and access. These are foundational elements of the stack. The top half deals with the things one needs to do in order to extract business value from the data. This includes *data analytics*, (which refers to traditional data analysis work that involves data exploration, analysis, and reporting), *business intelligence (BI)*, and data science. We'll discuss data analytics in relation to BI and data science later in this chapter. For now, we'll simply note that data analytics refers to a broad range of tools and techniques that help provide insights into organisational performance. We will defer a detailed discussion of the topmost element of the stack, MLOps (Machine Learning Operations), to Chapter 7 which will also include a more detailed outline of how data science projects can be undertaken in a considered and collaborative fashion. For now, we simply note that it refers to the things one needs to do in order to make the products that data scientists build available to the business in a reliable and repeatable way.

The present chapter is an overview of topics that we cover in much greater detail in the latter half of the book (Chapters 5–8). Our primary aim here is

DOI: 10.1201/9781003260158-2

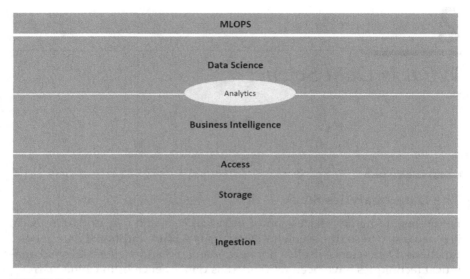

FIGURE 2.1
The data analytics stack.

to prompt readers to think about how/where a data science capability might fit within their organisations. We'll start from the bottom of the stack and work our way up (with the caveat noted above about MLOps). Although the chapter is written for those who are new to data strategy and building data capabilities, it may also serve as a review for those who are experienced in these areas.

Data Ingestion

Organisations collect data for various purposes. Typically, this data exists in diverse systems that clients, employees, and other stakeholders interact with. In each of these systems, data is structured and stored in a manner that serves the operational purposes of those systems, which may support specific business functions such as finance, marketing, or sales. An example is a customer relationship management (CRM) system that stores customer interactions across the organisation (sales, marketing, support, and so on). Typically, those who design the databases underlying these operational systems rarely pay attention to analytical requirements; their immediate interest is in supporting business or operational transactions (such as sales or employee information updates) rather than analysing data. The data residing in these systems therefore needs to be extracted and stored elsewhere in order to be available for analytical purposes. As part of this process, it is also typically cleaned and transformed along the way. This Extract, Transform and Load process (ETL as it is often referred to) is the domain of *data engineering* which we will say much more about in Chapter 6.

Why do we store this data, intended for analytics, separately from the operational systems? There are two reasons for this:

1. In order to avoid directly accessing source systems when doing analytical or reporting work. The storage structures in source systems are typically optimised for transactional work (like registering customers, processing financial transactions, etc.) but are not optimised for reporting and analytics. We discuss this further in the section on storage in this chapter.
2. To combine multiple data sources in order to open up new analytical opportunities. For example, the software used by the sales team likely contains a username or ID for each employee working in that system, however all HR details related to the employee likely reside in a separate HR system. Therefore, to answer questions related to understanding sales rep performance patterns by unit or region, these two datasets need to be integrated. Pushing data from one transactional system into another can quickly become unwieldy when you have multiple systems that need to be linked for analytical purposes. Moreover, the transactional systems are typically provided by external vendors so you will not have unfettered access to their datastores. In particular, you will not be allowed to modify their databases to store the data from other systems. Hence, the most effective way to proceed is to extract data from multiple systems and store it in a dedicated analytics datastore over which your organisation has full control.

When ingesting data, there are a host of considerations that one must think through. The most important one is: *when to perform the extraction?* In most cases, it is reasonable to do a bulk extraction of data sometime in the early hours of the morning when the source systems are least likely to be used. This process, often called *batch processing*, will grab all data or new and updated data since the last refresh, depending on whether the analytical datastore is to be fully or incrementally refreshed each day. In the former case, the entire history is reloaded each day; in the latter, only new data is loaded and modified data updated. A full refresh, though technically simpler, is difficult to implement in a timely manner when the data volumes involved are large. An incremental refresh, on the other hand, is technically harder, but easier on computing resources as it includes only new and modified data (since the last refresh). Regardless of which option is chosen, the analytical datastore is up to a day behind the transactional systems because the extraction is performed each night.

There are real-time/streaming options that address this deficiency. These transfer data from operational systems to analytical datastores as the data is inserted or updated in the former. A number of popular technologies exist for this such as Apache Kafka[2] and the offerings from the three big cloud providers[3] (AWS: Amazon Kinesis Firehose,[4] GCP: Google Cloud Dataflow,[5] Microsoft: Azure Event Hubs[6]). Needless to say, the engineering effort and cost associated with real-time data as compared to batch processing is an order of magnitude greater and so should not be undertaken unless absolutely necessary for the business. A principle that has served us well is that the ingestion currency requirements should match those of the analytical function. In other words, you should pursue this option only if you have people who use real-time dashboards to perform analyses that materially affect *important* business decisions. If this is not the case, we would strongly advise against implementing real-time data ingestion.

That said, we should note an important caveat here in relation to aligning ingestion frequency with analytical needs. There are many operational (as opposed to analytical) situations in which alerts relating to data streams are important. As an example, within the manufacturing sector there is an increasing use of IOT[7] (Internet of Things) to monitor system performance in real time. Examples of these include various sensors that monitor events as they occur such as weight, pressure, and operational metrics for mining equipment or machinery in a manufacturing factory. In this case, live streaming of data is a critical operational (rather than analytical) requirement to ensure the smooth functioning of the system and is therefore justified on business grounds. It is worth keeping in mind that such real-time data collected for operational reasons might also provide you with an opportunity to illustrate the value of data science. For example, sensor data from machinery in a manufacturing plant could be used to build a model to predict potential failures before they occur. Such a situation is a genuine instance of real-time analytics.

Technology vendors will always endeavour to sell you their premium offerings with real-time data processing capabilities. Before signing up, ask yourself … or better, ask potential users of the offering whether they really need it. Better still, start with the simpler option and consider upgrading only when a genuine requirement presents itself. Indeed, such an approach would be consistent with the core philosophy of Emergent Design, which is to start simple and enhance your technology stack as the organisation's needs grow and, perhaps more importantly, as your understanding of the organisation's needs grows.

Storage

Once ingested, the data must be stored somewhere. There is much debate and discussion within the analytics community about approaches to designing an analytical storage solution so we will restrict our comments to a few time-tested principles that have served us well. Firstly, we would strongly advise against following the latest trend as that invariably leads to sub-optimal solutions that have not been widely trialled and tested. New technologies should be given time to mature before they are considered seriously , particularly when they involve a major change such as moving the entire data storage system of an organisation. In our experience, the benefits of "early adoption" in such cases are grossly overstated.

A concept that has survived the test of time is that of the *data warehouse* – a term we mentioned without introduction in the first chapter. A data warehouse is a repository that is structured in a way that integrates data from multiple systems for purposes of reporting and analytics. It is typically composed of a number of *data marts*, smaller repositories that are focused on specific business areas such as finance, sales, and marketing. Each of these data marts focus on *facts*: events or objects that are important to a business area. For finance, a fact could be a financial transaction, for sales, it could be a customer order, and for marketing, it could be a customer profile update. Each of these facts can be analysed ("sliced and diced") in a number of different ways. For example, financial transactions can be reported by year, month, day, business unit, customer, etc. Each of these ways of "slicing and dicing" the data are called *dimensions*. The trick in data warehousing is to find a set of *common dimensions* that apply to facts from across the entire business. Examples of such dimensions are *date* and *region*, both of which are often used to analyse data pertaining to sales, orders, and other business-relevant facts.

This kind of modelling results in a data mart design consisting of a central fact table connected to several dimension tables – a structure that is often referred to as a *star schema*. A star schema is the most common design paradigm for an *enterprise data warehouse*, which is a centralised, aggregated, and integrated collection of data marts that enables analytical work. An enterprise data warehouse consists of several data marts which can be connected via common dimensions. We won't say much more about data warehousing in this book as our focus is on strategy rather than technology. However, if you want to know more about "the facts of data warehousing", we recommend the highly readable classic by Ralph Kimball and his collaborators (Kimball and Ross 2011).

An enterprise data warehouse requires considerable design and programming work. Building a good data warehouse requires deliberate, planned, and conscious effort. It involves iterative design based on continual discussions between business stakeholders and data modellers. As a counterpoint, the notion of a *data lake* has become quite popular in recent years. In contrast to a data warehouse, a data lake requires much less design upfront. In its simplest and most unsophisticated avatar, a data lake consists of datasets from diverse source systems, transferred with minimal transformation or cleansing. The onus for cleaning and structuring the data is on the analyst who wishes to use the data.[8] Those who promote this approach note, quite rightly, that there is significant saving in terms of effort and cost (compared to data warehouses) because there is little or no design or transformation work required upfront. This is therefore a much quicker and flexible approach compared to the considerable process and design-heavy work associated with data warehousing. However, beyond a point, the lack of structure in a data lake can be a hindrance because it results in a motley collection of data sets that have no relationship to each other.

The hybrid *data lakehouse* approach seems to be a result of the recognition of this limitation. As the name suggests, the lakehouse approach attempts to strike a balance between the design-centred philosophy of data warehousing and the laissez-faire approach of the data lake.

There are a number of other technical considerations within the storage layer. These include the patterns of storage: relational[9] vs non-relational databases[10] and big data storage. To dive too deep into these would turn this chapter into a data engineering textbook. However, it is worth briefly noting the considerations in evaluating these technologies for use. The driving forces behind choices here should be the *size* and *type* of data being processed. Here are the main considerations:

- Structured Query Language (SQL) databases are for data that can be stored in a tabular format. Each table represents an entity (such as a customer) and tables are related to each other via columns they have in common. Relational databases have been around since the 1980s and remain the storage workhorse for most organisations. Moreover, most software applications (whether locally installed or in the cloud) tend to use relational databases as their primary datastores.

- Columnar databases are structured with access available via "columns" rather than rows so common analytical queries that require aggregations can simply retrieve the relevant column rather than bringing in the entire record. The choice here depends on the specific queries that your analytical team will typically run.

- NoSQL (non-relational) databases store data as documents and keys with no explicit relationships defined between documents. NoSQL databases are good choices for storing unstructured data (such as text documents or video) or large volumes of data. These technologies are noted for their ability to scale well as volume increases (in comparison to SQL-based databases).

- "big data" tools such as Hadoop[11] and Spark[12] are typically relevant to NoSQL technologies, particularly for terabyte-range storage. Due to advances in storage and computing technologies in the last decade, what was "big" ten years ago is no longer so. Whilst not clearly defined, what may seem as "big" – hundreds of thousands of rows of data, even millions in some instances – can be easily handled by modern relational (i.e., SQL-based) cloud infrastructure options without the need to implement relatively expensive big data infrastructure. Keep in mind, too, that SQL and relational database skills are easier to find than NoSQL skills (more about that in capability building which we cover in Chapter 6).

There are newer services being offered today that question the need for a database itself. Data storage in flat files seems a retrograde solution from decades ago when relational databases were yet to go mainstream. Yet, providers such as AWS allow files stored in their cloud storage buckets to be queried using SQL as if in a database ... and with reasonable performance to boot. This can be an extremely cheap, fast solution to temporary analytical storage needs before your data warehouse or data lake is built. It is a great way to implement proof-of-concept solutions in a short time.

Our treatment of data storage is brief, but the point we really wish to make is that there are many choices available to you. Moreover, in this day and age where platforms and infrastructure are available as pay-as-you-go services, there is ample scope for trialling different options via proof-of-concept projects. The idea is to start simple and move to more sophisticated architectures as you learn what works for you. As we will see in the next chapter, this is very much in line with the philosophy of Emergent Design.

Access

Whilst we will say more about data privacy, security, and access principles later in this book (Chapter 8), it is proper for us to mention access here as it is an important consideration when building your data analytics stack. As mentioned in Chapter 1, access to data is often tied to ownership. Typically, the functional area that collects the data is considered to own it. For example, the HR department is functionally charged with the recruitment, retention, and performance management (among many other things) of staff. Therefore, data related to employees and their activities is often considered to be "owned" by them and hence, by implication, so is all the associated reporting and analytical infrastructure. However, data science models often depend on merging data from multiple functional systems and thus require access to datasets that are owned by different groups.

The first issue here is to work through the politics of data ownership. This may require discussion and negotiation with the affected functional groups regarding what data is needed, who will have access to it, and how it will be used. It is important to note that this issue can be deeper than just ownership politics. For example, marketing may want to build a model to predict the performance of sales representative. Such a model will likely benefit from HR data. However, the HR department may, quite rightly, raise concerns as this is personal data. The data science team must be able to provide good reasons for why this data should be provided and the measures that will be taken to ensure that legislation around personally identifiable information[13] (PII) will be complied with. With data access comes data responsibility; gone are the days when one could be cavalier about how data is used and for what purpose.

These matters come under the purview of *data governance*, which is defined by The Data Management Association (DAMA) (a global leader in data governance certification) as *"planning, oversight, and control over management of data and the use of data and data-related sources"* (DAMA 2017). We discuss data governance in greater depth (including its relation to AI governance and ethical data practices) in Chapter 8. However, for now we simply note that as data moves from functional silos to an enterprise-wide store, the function of enterprise data governance becomes critically important, especially with increasing legislation around what can and cannot be done with personal data. Establishing data governance principles at an appropriate level of the corporate hierarchy is a critical element of establishing a data science function. In addition to access and privacy, this function deals with issues pertaining to ethics, bias, and fairness in data science work. We'll say much more about these issues in Chapter 8, including the relationship between data governance, AI governance, and ethical data practices.

BI vs Analytics vs Data Science

BI has been a standard element of the data analytics stack for more than a couple of decades. What is BI? In brief, it is about *reporting business performance across the entire organisation*. Note that in this section we are primarily discussing the craft of BI, analytics, and data science. We expand on this in Chapter 5 where we discuss the various roles that support these crafts. However, there is value in discussing these briefly here to set the scene.

First up is BI. There are a plethora of BI tools in the market – some of the more popular ones are Power BI,[14] Tableau,[15] QlikView,[16] Business Objects,[17] etc. Most of these have excellent visualisation capabilities and the flexibility to create dashboards that integrate and visually display information from different domains.

In situations where the BI team has an organisation-wide remit, as is often the case, the data used by the team is generally sourced from an enterprise data warehouse. Indeed, the BI team is often responsible for guiding and informing the design, maintenance, and enhancement of the enterprise data warehouse. Their function also requires them to become familiar with third-party software and tools and be competent in SQL so that they can query databases directly if needed. Often though – and more so in recent years – business requirements or even plain curiosity prompts individuals in these teams to explore advanced statistical learning techniques and tools, nudging them towards the world of data science. Later we will comment on the similarities and differences between BI and data science and why we placed the analytics oval where it is in Figure 2.1. However, continuing our journey "up" the stack, we'll first describe what BI is in more detail so we can differentiate it from the other two areas.

Much of what BI professionals do relates to extracting, analysing, and presenting useful performance-related information from data. Depending on the specifics of their role, they probably do one or more of the following:

- Work with business users to understand *reporting* needs.
- *Identify* data required to fulfil those needs.
- Use SQL to *manipulate (or wrangle)* and *analyse* data.[18]
- Build *reports* for business users using spreadsheets or reporting tools such as Power BI and Tableau.

BI primarily focuses on *reporting* key business *activities that have already occurred*. For example, how much product was sold in the last year, and how well sales are tracking against budget. Such information is useful because it helps decision makers understand how their business is performing and take corrective action if needed. This kind of reporting is so useful that BI professionals are sometimes the first hires when an organisation is building a new analytics function. However, since the technical expertise required for BI work can often be picked up by people who have an analytical bent and/or are able to work with spreadsheets, it is also the case that BI talent can be found within the organisation. The HR team will need to analyse and report on staffing levels, annual leave balances, and recruitment activities in order to ensure capacity for key business activities. *Someone* has to be doing this already, so it is often the case that there are highly local hotspots of analytical activity in business units, even in the absence of a formal organisation-wide analytics function. It should be clear that one of the first steps of your strategy development effort is to scan your organisation for such individuals. In addition to their analytical mindset and keenness to learn new skills, they typically have deep domain expertise and are potential recruits (or allies) for your efforts in establishing and growing a data capability. We will say much more about this in the capability building sections of Chapter 5.

With that said for BI, let's move on to data science. If you use your favourite search engine to look up definitions of data science (and you may want to do so now), you will see that it takes a much broader view of data than BI does. Rather than dwelling on definitions, we think it is more useful to highlight what data scientists do, so that you can compare and contrast it with the more familiar BI function:

- Work with business users to *frame* the *problem*.
- *Identify* data required.
- *Explore* the data relating to the problem using a variety of data *manipulation* (wrangling) and *visualisation* techniques.
- Build, test, and refine models to *solve* the problem.

In brief then, BI focuses on reporting, while Data Science focuses on problem-solving. Note our use of the word "frame" – it is a term that will crop up at various points in this book, emphasising an oft overlooked truth that one is rarely (never?) presented with readymade problems. One has to frame or extract problems from situations that one is presented with. We'll say more about this later in this section; for now, let's continue with the distinctions between BI and data science and analytics.

It is often said that the key difference between BI and data science is that the former is backward-looking in that it focuses on what happened in the past, whereas the latter is forward-looking – that is, it concerns itself with what is going to happen in the future[19]. This is an oversimplification. The problems data science deals with can vary widely, ranging from things like predicting sales, prices, or loan defaults to automatically finding patterns in data (customer segmentation being a classic example). The last is about finding hidden patterns in the data rather than prediction. So, although much of the hype around data science is about predictive models, there is much more to it than just that. Prediction is a fine thing, but insight is often more useful – for example, your marketing manager may want to know which potential customer she should target, but it's likely she will also want to know *why*. Indeed, one without the other feels empty and you will often hear data scientists talk of the tension of insight vs predictive power, especially in contexts relevant to business stakeholders.

As shown in Figure 2.2, although data science requires a deeper knowledge of certain areas (such as statistics and programming), there are a number of skills that it has in common with BI.

Let's now turn to data analytics by asking: where does *analytics* fall in Figure 2.2? It is important to preface the following discussion with the note that these generalisations should be qualified because they depend on the size and analytical maturity of the organisation. Such is the nature of specialisation that with a smaller team, people are more likely to wear many different hats. Indeed, as we can attest to from our own experience, the first data science or analytics hires in an organisation can (will!) spend significant time doing what is more conventionally considered data engineering, BI, or analytics.

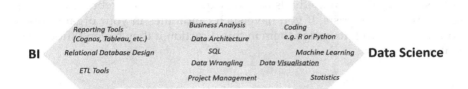

FIGURE 2.2
Skills required for BI and data science.

The distinction between BI and analytics is best clarified through a concrete example. The sales department may wish to set up a dashboard to be able to monitor sales across time, by organisational unit. A BI analyst would be able to connect to the relevant corporate datastores and build the relevant line/pie/bar graphs. However, such dashboards can answer only questions that they were designed to. The manager of the sales unit may ask the analyst to conduct an analysis on the top-selling products, where they are sold, and highlight any interesting patterns in the data. Answers to such questions necessitate exploratory analyses that go beyond standardised dashboard reports. We emphasise here that, if the stakeholder had simply asked for the top products to be included in the dashboard, this would be an enhancement that the BI function could provide. However, looking for drivers of sales, what characterises a top customer or what products are purchased together requires exploratory analyses rather than canned reports based on simple queries. This is the domain of analytics. Of course, it should also be noted that such analytical work, when found to be valuable, often ends up being operationalised in BI reports. Analyses that are useful invariably end up becoming "business as usual".

It should be clear from the above example that the line between BI and analytics is a blurry one. However, if one wishes to make a distinction nonetheless, BI is about reporting what happened and analytics is about figuring out why. One can go a step further and use machine learning to build predictive models. In the latter case, one is squarely in the domain of data science.

We emphasise that it is important not to be overly concerned about these distinctions as they are far from clear cut. For example, what if one is doing traditional statistics such as forecasting or hypothesis testing? Statistical tools are an important part of a data scientist's kit. However, we also see many analysts with statistical training employing them (for example A/B testing[20] has been around for years). Many of these analysts have learnt or are learning programming languages such as R and Python that enable them to utilise the vast libraries of statistical tools that those languages offer. As a result, it is not uncommon to see adventurous analysts doing fairly complex statistical analyses. If so, these individuals would be quite justified in rebranding themselves as data scientists. If you have such candidates in your organisations, you would do well to nudge them in this direction if they haven't thought of it already.

Are You Ready for Data Science?

Before we move to the top layers of the analytics stack, it is worth reflecting on the topics and concepts introduced above and thinking about how they relate to your organisation. Whilst there are a number of detailed analytical maturity models from the likes of Gartner,[21] Mckinsey,[22] and many others[23] (and you are certainly encouraged to look up a few), our take is based on a set of specific questions that will help determine the analytical maturity of your organisation. Here we go:

1. For reporting:
    a. Do business units read/download reports from within their operational datastores (i.e., finance accesses reports from the accounting system, HR accesses reports from the HR system)?
    b. Do individual units download data from these systems and use spreadsheets to build reports?
    c. Are there dashboards that source data from multiple systems?
    d. Is there an ingestion and storage pipeline into a Data (warehouse/lake/lakehouse) from multiple sources?
        i. Does this support a dashboarding/reporting layer?
        ii. Does this support direct access for deeper analysis?
2. For analysis:
    a. When additional questions are asked beyond the existing reports, how are these answered? *Can* they be answered?
        i. Is there a dedicated team/function to answer such questions?
        ii. Does this capability sit within functions or is it a standalone unit that is available to all?
    b. How fast are these questions answered?
        i. If not fast enough, is the bottleneck related to data issues or lack of skills?
3. Looking forward:
    a. Are there any forecasting or predictive activities?
        i. Are these carried out by individuals on their computers?
        ii. Or, are these deployed centrally and updated automatically as the source data is updated?

4. Organisationally:
   a. Are there centralised data functions (architecture or analysis)?
   b. Are there localised data functions (e.g., an analyst within the HR team)?
   c. Is there an executive portfolio or position related to data?
      i. Does their mandate relate to only BI and reporting?
      ii. Does their mandate include finding and answering analytical questions?
      iii. Does their mandate include data science?

These questions can provide a high-level overview of your current level of analytical maturity.

It is important to note that it isn't mandatory to have an analytics stack set up before one establishes a formal data science function. Indeed, it generally makes sense to work towards it gradually as one progresses. However, although you can do analytics and data science without having the entire stack set up, you cannot productionise or scale your efforts without a complete stack. Here's why:

- Firstly, there won't be efficient use of analytics resources to deliver value to business stakeholders. Consider, for example, a data scientist who has been hired to forecast sales in different stores. If there is no database set up, they will have to export files from a number of systems, write code to join them together, and clean them prior to building a forecasting model. When presenting the results of their model to the sales manager, the conversation may go something like this:

  DS: Here, you can now forecast the sales in any given store for the next 6 months.
  Sales: That is great! However, can I see the sales for the previous 6 months? I need to know how we are trending year-on-year and where we are getting the most sales.
  DS: Sorry, this only looks forwards. I could build you something, but that will take a while …

  Now our keen data scientist will spend a fair bit of time building an ad-hoc data stack to answer the questions posed by the sales manager. However, because their work is geared to answering a specific question, they will likely end up building something specific to their project. Building data pipelines is too important to be driven by a single project, so it is a good idea to start thinking about your analytics stack from an organisation-wide perspective sooner than later.

- Secondly, in order for data science to live "in the wild", a robust and performant data architecture is needed. All the data wrangling and munging the data scientist does when they are building a model will need to be productionised. This often means writing SQL, ensuring the correct data is gathered from the right sources, and integrating the data into structures that are optimised for retrieval of information. Of course, this could be done on a case-by-case basis for every model, but writing custom data pipelines for each model is setting yourself up for a maintenance nightmare.

The point is this: once a trained model is ready for deployment, it is akin to a software product. Your users will expect it to function reliably, be up to date and available when needed. Without a proper supporting data architecture, it will be difficult to move data science projects off the laptop of the data scientist to a product that can be relied on for business decision-making. We will say much more about this in Chapter 7 where we talk about MLOps.

The Data Science Process

Having said what data science (generally) is, how does one actually go about doing data science? What is the process? A good place to start is with Figure 2.3, taken from one of the slides in the introductory data science course that we have designed and taught at the University of Technology Sydney (UTS).

We think it presents a nice high-level overview of the key considerations when doing data science in business environments. In the next few pages, we will walk you through these. If you are wondering why we are doing this instead of diving straight into the nuts and bolts, this common scenario – which you may well have encountered – might help explain why.

You wake up one morning with stiff shoulder and decide to get an expert to fix the problem. So, you make an appointment to see your doctor at the local

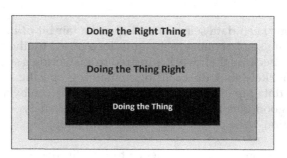

FIGURE 2.3
The data science process summarised.

clinic. She begins by asking a series of diagnostic questions – did you stress the joint in any way? Do you have aches or pains in other joints? Are you able to raise your hand above your head? And so on. Based on your responses, she may ask further questions or stop; she may even order some imaging.

Hopefully the result of her analysis is that you are suffering from a shoulder strain due to over-exercise. She prescribes avoiding the gym for a few days and taking an over-the-counter painkiller to ease the discomfort.

But what if your doctor had jumped to her conclusions without asking the diagnostic questions? Or worse: rushed you off to invasive surgery to fix your shoulder? The questions the doctor asks are designed to narrow down possibilities so that she can reach a diagnosis. A good diagnostician not only listens carefully to the reported symptoms, but also makes their own investigation either via direct observation (is there bruising in the area of the pain? Is the patient able to move their shoulder? Do they have pain elsewhere?) or using instruments (do tendons in the area respond to a reflex hammer?). The responses received from you and the data gathered by observation prompt further questions that continually narrow the possible treatment options.

This story has a direct analogue in the world of data science. Good data science practice means that you don't just jump in and start throwing a bunch of math, code, and the latest "cool" techniques at a problem in the hope something will work. That would be akin to a doctor who prescribes a cure without taking the time to diagnose the illness. This is a waste of time and effort and will not help in building credibility of your nascent data science capability.

Doing the Thing

Most technical books on data science practice tend to focus heavily on teaching techniques that can be used to manipulate, explore, and build models using data. In doing so, they gloss over a critical data science skill that's hinted at in our parable about the doctor's visit.

In real life you are never presented with a readymade problem. Instead, you are presented with a situation from which you must *extract* or *frame* a problem. This is analogous to the process of diagnosis. To best understand the process of data science, we'd like to provide you an insight into how good data scientists approach this. Here's why:

> *An organisation almost **never** gives data scientists a data science problem to work on. They will be given a business situation and it is up to them to frame the problem and then (and only then) select appropriate data science tools to solve it.*

Like any meeting of disparate minds (in this case, the domain knowledge experts and data science practitioners), the more either side can develop an understanding of the other, the greater the chance of a successful partnership. Although data scientists do often build domain knowledge over time, they are also quite likely to encounter new, domain-specific challenges on a regular basis. Therefore, learning the language, high-level terminology, and processes associated with one's industry domain can greatly assist in facilitating the collaboration between business and tech and thereby help data scientists frame meaningful problems.

The framing process sits between the business domain and the data science capability.

If you've had any experience at all with BI or traditional analytics, there is a good chance we're telling you something you already know. You likely have already framed problems from business requests by translating as in the examples below:

- *Stakeholder statement*: "I would like all my data in one place"
  - *Framed as a technical problem*: build a data warehouse and ETL pipeline, likely refreshed overnight
- *Stakeholder statement*: "I want to be able to visualise key KPIs easily"
  - *Framed as a technical problem*: build a visualisation layer connected to the necessary data source (perhaps the above data warehouse, with batch data extracts or live connections built with Tableau, Power BI, etc.)

Framing data science problems starts with similar, but possibly more specific statements such as, "I want to know which customers are likely to default". As discussed briefly earlier in our doctor's visit example, such problem statements need to be unpacked and interpreted correctly. Only once the problem is unambiguously defined can one apply machine learning techniques to solve it. And that is a good segue into our next topic: a brief look at the kinds of machine learning problems typically encountered in business.

Machine Learning Problem Types

The first step in building a common vocabulary that can help in translating a business situation into a data science problem is recognising what *kind* of data science problem you might be dealing with. Understanding this helps the data scientist figure out which techniques might be useful.

At a high level, we could classify the world of machine learning as shown in Figure 2.4.

The first split above depends on whether your data is *labelled* or not – that is, whether the target variable (the one you want to predict) is known. For example, a set of credit history data from which one wishes to predict whether a customer would default would be considered labelled if there is a column that tells you whether the customer did indeed default or not. All this means is that *we have historical data for the attribute that we wish to predict*.

At this stage it is useful to pause and clarify some terminology before we continue. In the literature, you will hear the words *target* and *label* used

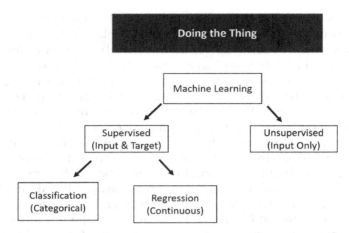

FIGURE 2.4
Machine learning problem types.

interchangeably along with some other less common terms *outcome, y-variable,* or *dependent variable.* The remaining attributes in the dataset (the ones other than the target) are called *variable, independent variables, attributes, predictors,* and *features* among others.

As noted above, your first key consideration is whether there is a clearly defined target column available. If there is, we are working in the realm of *supervised* machine learning. If not, the problem at hand is *unsupervised.* Unsupervised learning is where there is no label or target defined and is therefore about finding structure and patterns within the data itself. The distinction is sometimes not so clear as there are problems that can be framed as either supervised or unsupervised, or even use elements of both at different stages of the project. Don't worry about these situations for now; the point to note is that there is usually more than one way to solve a machine learning problem.

The majority of commercial work in machine learning falls under the supervised category: most business stakeholders have an idea of what they would like to know (i.e., the target variable) and often have historical data for which those outcomes are known (i.e., labelled data). Predictive models are *trained* (built) on labelled historical data.[24] When applied to new data for which the outcome (label) is not known, the model can then predict the label.

Although not as common, a couple of unsupervised learning techniques are used from time to time in the commercial world: these are *dimensionality reduction* and *clustering.* We will provide a brief overview about these below before moving on to a more detailed discussion of machine learning types.

Dimensionality reduction is a technique that is used to reduce the number of variables (predictors) in a dataset. It can be helpful in situations where you have a large number of variables and you wish to compress the information contained in these into a smaller set of variables. Reducing the number of variables results in some loss of information, but the reduction is done using mathematical techniques that minimise this loss. Why would you want to reduce the number of variables? The first reason is that it might make the dataset easier to visualise. The second is that it can sometimes make the dataset easier to work with. The danger, however, is that some of the information lost might be important from a predictive perspective.

Clustering is a more commonly used unsupervised technique. It is essentially used to find groups in data. An example familiar to marketers is that of customer segmentation. Historically, this is typically done by using rules to categorise people into groups. The rules are usually based on a handful of dimensions (variables) such as age and gender. For example, one might create two categories of Child (<18) and Adult (>18). Or a more complex grouping into four categories as Child + Female, Child + Male, Adult + Female, Adult + Male. In clustering, instead of using rules, you would use algorithms to automatically find segments (groups) in your data. As the algorithm does the work, you can, in principle, add a number of other variables such as behavioural data on how users interact with your website, sales figures, demographics and geographics, and any other data you may have. The algorithms will tell you whether there are distinct groups of users based on all the variables you choose to include and will also tell you which group each user belongs to. This is a case of unsupervised learning as you are not providing any labels or classification criteria. The downside is that the clusters the algorithms find are based on mathematical relationships between variables that may or may not have business significance. As a result, this area of data science involves a great deal of interpretive work after the clustering is completed.

With that said for unsupervised learning, we will move on to discuss supervised learning in more detail. Let's look at two of the commonly encountered types of problems encountered in supervised learning. The distinction between them is best explained through an example. Imagine that you are attempting to predict the *price* of a house, given the number of bedrooms, house type, and whether it has a pool or not. A typical row in your data might look something like in Table 2.1.

In contrast, if you are attempting to predict whether the house has a *pool*, given the price and the other previously mentioned factors, you might have something like in Table 2.2.

In both cases, the target variable is known, so it is a supervised problem. However, the two problems are qualitatively different. In the first case you are attempting to predict a number that can take on any positive value (price), whereas in the second case you are attempting to predict a discrete category (does it have a pool? Y or N). The first scenario is referred to as *regression* and the second is called *classification*. The difference between the two lies in whether your target variable is continuous (regression) or categorical

TABLE 2.1

A Row of Data in a House Price Dataset with Price as a Target Variable

Features			Target
Bedrooms	House Type	Pool (Y/N)	Price
4	Apartment	Y	$450,000

TABLE 2.2

A Row of Data in a House Price Dataset with Pool as a Target Variable

Features			Target
Price	House Type	Bedrooms	Pool (Y/N)
$450,000	Apartment	4	Y

(classification). You may also see a sub-classification of the latter into *binary* or *multiclass* classification. This relates to whether the categorical output has only two possibilities (Y/N, 1/0, etc.) or three or more possibilities (high-medium-low, for example).

The above has practical implications for the framing of data science problems in your organisation. When framing challenges that might be amenable to predictive modelling, here are some preliminary questions to consider:

1. Do you have data that is clearly *labelled* (you have a target variable available for every "row" of data)?
2. Do you have a set of features that are *likely to be predictive* of the target variable? Domain experts will usually have a sense for which variables are important in this respect.
3. More broadly, can you think of some candidate use cases that may be classification or regression types of problems?

To let the above knowledge really sink in, let's do a small fun test of knowledge with some common, real-world examples.

Test Your Knowledge

How would you classify the following problems in terms of whether they are supervised or unsupervised **and** classification or regression?

1. Detecting if an email is spam?
2. Predicting if a customer will "churn" (cancel their account) from an online software product?

3. Predicting what "band" a student's marks will fall into based on previous academic performance and demographic factors?

4. Predict whether a piece of machinery will fail in the next month?

5. Predicting a person's income?

6. Discovering if there are groupings of wines based on their chemical properties?

7. A recommendation engine?

Take a moment now (don't look ahead!) and have a think, write down your response before continuing (answers in Table 2.3).

How did you do? We are sure you aced this exercise. Although it seems trivial, the ability to speak this core common language with data scientists will greatly aid in your efforts towards building a data science function. At any given time, there are likely many projects that your data science function can work on. Prioritising potential work should not only be based on business value and priorities, which we discuss more later, but also the ease with which the scenario can be cast into a familiar machine learning problem type as noted above. Nothing like a quick win to gain credibility for your efforts (and yes, we discuss how to find quick wins in Chapter 4!).

You're probably wondering about our use of the word "cast" – is the type of problem up to the problem framer?

Short answer: sometimes! Here's an example:

You may have noticed that we omitted the answer to the last question in the exercise above (recommendation engine). Why was this? Every

TABLE 2.3

Answers to "Test Your Knowledge" Quiz

Business Problem	Machine Learning Type
1. Detecting if an email is spam?	Supervised, (binary) classification
2. Predicting if a customer will "churn" (cancel their account) from an online software product?	Supervised, (binary) classification
3. Predict what "band" a student's marks will fall into based on previous academic performance and demographic factors?	Supervised, (multiclass) classification
4. Predict whether a piece of machinery will fail in the next month?	Supervised, (binary) classification
5. Predicting a person's income?	Supervised, regression
6. Discovering if there are groupings of wines based on their chemical properties?	Unsupervised, clustering
7. A recommendation engine?	**Discuss!**

time we include this example in our introductory machine learning class, we get a variety of answers. Did you say it was classification? Or regression? Perhaps you even said unsupervised and included clustering in your answer?

The answer is that it depends on the specific situation at hand.

Are you trying to predict a rating that someone will award a book or movie? If so, is the scale continuous (regression) or discrete (classification)? On the other hand, perhaps you are trying to predict whether someone will like/not-like or purchase/not-purchase (binary classification) the product. Perhaps there is an implicit clustering of related products, for example, in the way to select them? Or may be a 1–10 rating scale can be transformed into 2 or more classes (8 + is "love" and < 7 is "not-love" a product).

Indeed, all these are valid responses depending on the situation, and the one you choose depends on the business context and the question that needs to be answered. The takeaway at this point is that business problems can be framed in a number of different ways. We mention this here because we want to emphasise that *data science at its best is a creative endeavour that just happens to use code and algorithms to paint a picture of what is going on.*

What about AI?

The term AI (artificial intelligence) is one that has a much broader definition than what is commonly discussed in the media and data science circles today. It has a history[25] dating back to the 1950s and 1960s and stretches from sub-fields such as search strategies, knowledge representation, and philosophical considerations about what constitutes cognition. These days, when the media discusses AI, it often is an example of *deep learning* in action. We won't discuss this topic at length; however, a brief note is worthwhile as you are likely to come across this in your data science capability journey if you haven't already.

Deep learning is, at its heart, a set of algorithms based on "neural networks"[26] that enable data scientists to deal with problems that are difficult for traditional machine learning methods. As you can see in the example of predicting house prices above, the features are structured (i.e., in tabular form) and numerical (or binary). However, what if the question was to predict the house price based on *images* of the house? Or if you wanted to base your prediction on a textual description in the listing? It is not immediately apparent as to how one could represent these data types (images, text) in the traditional columns-and-rows representation of data that is used in relational databases. Deep learning algorithms enable data science practitioners to turn text, images, video, sound, and other tricky data types into forms that can be used to build predictive models.

Just a few years ago, deep learning was a specialist skill, but in the last couple of years it has become more mainstream due to the availability of comprehensive (and open source) software libraries that enable non-specialists to use these algorithms without a detailed knowledge of the intricacies of the algorithms. That said, whilst the capabilities of deep learning are impressive, they are only necessary if you are dealing with unstructured data such as text, images, and video. In fact, some recent studies challenge the view of these algorithms as the silver bullet for all problems. They find that for tabular data,[27] and time series,[28] classical machine learning techniques tend to perform better or no worse[29] than deep learning approaches. An added limitation of deep learning models is that it tends to be hard to understand how the models arrive at their predictions. This has implications for explainability and defensible data science practices (more about these topics in Chapters 7 and 8). With these limitations in mind, if your organisation is not using images, video, sound, or other non-tabular data, then a data scientist well versed in "classical" machine learning (i.e., everything excepting deep learning) will be all you need.

Great Power, Narrow Focus

We should point out that although the neural networks that underpin deep learning are "loosely modelled on the human brain", they are very far from it in terms of flexibility and adaptability. Deep learning models, as useful as they are in answering the specific questions that they are designed to, are actually "dumb and brittle" compared to the general intelligence that humans display. This is true of all machine learning models. It is therefore worth making a brief, but important, note about the way in which machine learning produces answers to questions.

Machine learning is currently able to (in specific contexts) provide predictions for questions that would be difficult for humans to answer in a scalable way. That can be due to the complexity of the question (e.g. considering the ways different house features affect pricing in many different suburbs at different times of the year), or due to the complexity of the data source (pulling meaning from images, text, videos, etc.) or the speed at which predictions can be made. Even if a single human develops a knack for pricing houses, the person is limited by the processing capabilities of the human brain. So, a predictive model that can provide results almost instantaneously and at scale can be of great business value. However, it is critically important to keep in mind that machine learning models have a very narrow focus. A model that is built to predict the price of a house **cannot** predict the price of a car. A model that can recognise the make and model of cars from images **cannot**[30] recognise different articles of clothes. See this[31] humorous case in point for a modern example using deep fakes. So, it is important to be aware that, despite the great power of machine learning models, they have major limitations. The concept of AGI or "Artificial General Intelligence", whilst an active area of research, is still nowhere near being realised and is a long way off from the generally accessible (and still very useful) models available for business use today.

Doing the Thing Right

After this excursion into "doing the thing", it is time to return to our diagram and explore the next point: *doing the thing right* (see Figure 2.3).

In a nutshell, this is about using *good practices* when doing data science. There is a popular industry framework for data science: CRISP-DM (The Cross-Industry Standard Process for Data Mining) – see Shearer (2000) for more. The process within the framework, and the connections between them, is summarised in Figure 2.5.

The somewhat dated reference to data mining is due to the fact that CRISP-DM was formulated more than 20 years ago, well before "data science" emerged as a distinct field. Despite its age, CRISP-DM is still a decent starting

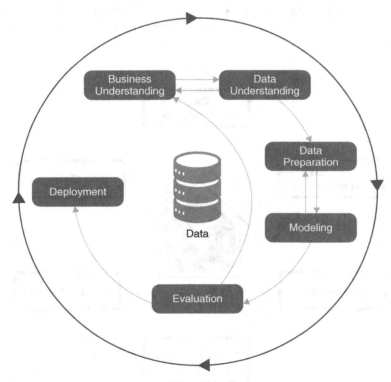

FIGURE 2.5

The CRISP-DM process. Credits: Wikimedia (https://commons.wikimedia.org/wiki/File:CRISP-DM_Process_Diagram.png).

point for systematic machine learning practice.[32] That said, our experience has taught us that the framework, as useful as it is, is not a completely accurate depiction of how things work, or even *should* work, in real life. The diagram suggests that data is at the centre of the process. We propose an alternate view (Figure 2.6) that puts the *business* at the front and centre of the process because the reality is that the data science team should have strong communication channels with the business stakeholders at every stage of the process.

The CRISP workflow (Figure 2.5) starts with business understanding. In reality, however, the initial business problem statement almost always tends to be vague; there is always a problem lurking in it, but it is not necessarily what the stakeholder says it is at the start. Therefore, to give data science projects a good chance of success, there should be discussions with business stakeholders to develop a shared understanding of the situation so that you can frame an appropriate problem. This is necessarily an iterative process that takes place at various stages of the solution process – you will never learn enough in the "Business Understanding" phase to frame the problem perfectly. Our modified version of CRISP-DM (Figure 2.6) takes this into account by allowing for stakeholder interactions at every stage of a project.

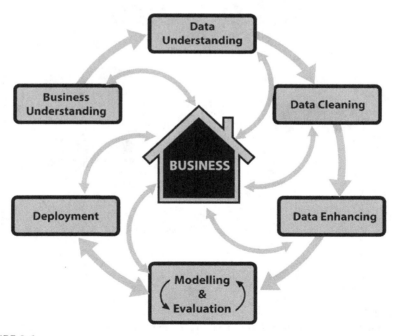

FIGURE 2.6
The modified CRISP-DM process. Diagram created by Alex Scriven (author).

It is important to note that both CRISP-DM and our modification of it miss a key element of the modern machine learning – putting models into production and monitoring/maintaining them. We will cover this aspect in detail in Chapter 7 where we present a modern Machine Learning Workflow (MLWF). However, there is value in discussing the CRISP models here as they cover all aspects of exploratory and proof-of-concept projects that you are likely to do in the early stages of setting up your data science capability.

So, what specifically are the benefits of leveraging a process such as CRISP-DM to start with (and adapting to your own context)?

1. To avoid shortcuts: as trite as it may sound, the biggest benefit of the process is that it serves as an excellent checklist of the things that should be considered in a project as it progresses. Among other things, this puts in place checks to stop the eager data scientist from skipping the "boring and tedious stuff" such as data exploration (often called exploratory data analysis or EDA) and jumping straight into modelling. Those who skip straight to modelling without undertaking good EDA or following a step-by-step process will generally end up with flawed models based on questionable assumptions that could have been validated via a quick conversation with a domain expert.

2. To maximise the chance of business success: It is naïve to expect that the business stakeholder will be able to provide data scientists with all the needed information upfront. More often than not, useful information and clarifications that inform analytical work come in at various stages of the project, typically in response to interactions aimed at showing stakeholders work in progress. So, it is vital that data science projects are set up to follow this process of *continuous translation* throughout the entire project. Moreover, this has the invaluable benefit of involving the business stakeholder (who is, after all, funding the work) in the project, thus giving them an understanding of what is happening.

   Let us be quite explicit here:

   The **worst** thing a data scientist can do is take the data and brief, disappear for three months, and come back with their *final* report. If they do this, they are likely to be working off a bunch of questionable assumptions based on an initial meeting or two. Indeed, you may want to put in place checks that explicitly prohibit this.

3. To stand up to Quality Assurance (QA): some of the frustrations in this field come from the fact that there is no single way to solve a business problem. Indeed, any problem can be framed in multiple ways, each of which may entail the use of very different machine learning techniques. It is never the case that "if you have problem X in industry Y you must use algorithm Z". Although there are algorithms that have worked well

across a variety of industries and problems, the very nature of machine learning, where the algorithm learns from *your data*, means that you cannot know *apriori* which algorithm will perform best.

Given that problems can be framed in multiple ways, it becomes important to ensure that the thinking and assumptions of the data scientist regarding modelling choices are recorded. This becomes critical during QA, not only from the perspective of technical soundness, but increasingly as a means to ensure *compliance with internal and external regulations regarding privacy and fairness.* The latter comes under the banner of governance, which we will say a bit more about below and then cover in detail in Chapter 8. Your organisation, especially if it is consumer-facing, may be called upon to explain *why* you did or did not do something. Good procedures and notes from different points in a considered process will come in very handy then.

Additionally, it is worth noting that following the above approach means the project has continually kept key business stakeholder in the loop; the project *has* been doing informal, *continuous QA* all along. These check-ins allow the project team to immediately explain any decisions, confront issues, and move on.

As your data science capability matures and takes on more projects, your team will develop a technical understanding and "modelling toolkit" that is appropriate for your industry, and company. The key takeaway for now is that skipping the problem-framing steps and going straight to the latest cool algorithm is setting this function up for failure.

Doing the Right Thing

At the highest (and therefore all-encompassing) level we have "doing the right thing" – this is essentially a statement about doing the right thing, i.e., being aware of the ethical implications of the work being undertaken. These will vary hugely from industry to industry, job to job, and even project to project. However, it is important to give these very careful consideration as you develop the data science function. At the most basic level, many of the problems your analytics function tackles will involve data about people, so there are issues around data privacy. In addition, though, it is quite possible that the models being built will affect peoples' lives in myriad ways from whether or not they get screened out for health insurance by a predictive model or screened in by facial recognition software for an additional security check. Even if your organisation is not on the front line of ethically sensitive fields such as healthcare and law enforcement, it is very likely that your organisation will handle data on or about humans.

You may find yourself in a situation where you are gathering use cases from business stakeholders and see opportunities to apply this technology to a problem in which there are potential rewards to be gained via simple and straightforward modelling. However, before you jump in, you should ask yourself the question:

Should we, just because we can?

If you don't ask the question, you may find yourself in a situation where you create "Frankenstein solutions" that affect people in negative ways. Some examples of such deeply flawed (and failed) examples include: detecting sexual orientation in photos[33] and "criminality through facial analysis".[34] Such examples do a disservice to the field of machine learning and certainly do not help the reputation of the researchers who put out such studies. Be aware that your choices in this regard can have consequences for the reputation of not only your data science function, but also your entire organisation.

At this stage of the book, we simply note that issues pertaining to ethics and privacy must be "baked into" your data science processes. It should be a part of your data governance framework. Indeed, as the field of data science matures, the industry, not to mention the general public, is expecting more out of the emerging leaders in terms of how they understand and respond to ethical and privacy-related issues. Data governance and ethics are becoming less of a "nice to have" and more of a "must have". We'll cover these in much greater detail in Chapter 8.

In Closing

This chapter, though long, is a brief introduction to the different elements of a data analytics stack. In keeping with a sociotechnical perspective, our interpretation of the stack includes infrastructural elements as well as those relating to organisational reporting and analytical capabilities. When it comes to infrastructure, these days it is easy to experiment with and pilot different options to see if they work for you. Indeed, one is spoilt for choice because of the plethora of options on offer. We'll cover these in detail in Chapter 6 where we talk about technical choices. For now, we simply note that the basic principle here is to stick to time-tested technologies that have been proven to work. These tend to be more robust. Equally important, it is easier to find people who have the skills to work with these technologies. A good rule here is to start building your stack by using technologies from vendors that your organisation is already familiar with. Indeed, a key element of Emergent Design is to start from where the organisation is, both in terms of technologies and capabilities, and move gradually in the desired direction. That's a topic we will cover in the next two chapters.

Notes

1 An example that may be familiar to the reader is linear regression (the problem of finding a line that best fits a set of point), which has been around for more than two centuries. This is often the first machine learning technique that is taught in introductory courses.
2 https://kafka.apache.org/
3 We'll say more about the major cloud technologies and providers in Chapter 6.
4 https://aws.amazon.com/kinesis/data-firehose/
5 https://cloud.google.com/dataflow
6 https://azure.microsoft.com/en-us/services/event-hubs/
7 https://en.wikipedia.org/wiki/Internet_of_things
8 Also see Chapter 5 for more information on roles pertaining to data lake environments.
9 https://en.wikipedia.org/wiki/Relational_database
10 https://en.wikipedia.org/wiki/NoSQL
11 https://hadoop.apache.org/
12 https://spark.apache.org/
13 www.oaic.gov.au/privacy/guidance-and-advice/what-is-personal-information
14 https://powerbi.microsoft.com/en-au/
15 www.tableau.com/
16 www.qlik.com/us/products/qlikview
17 www.sap.com/australia/products/bi-platform.html
18 There are, of course, a number of tools that BI professionals use to transform and load data. Commercial examples include Informatica, DataStage, Alteryx amongst many others. Most use SQL under the hood to transform data despite having a point-and-click UI.
19 See, for example, www.ibm.com/blogs/insights-on-business/retail/is-the-same-bi-and-analytics/
20 https://en.wikipedia.org/wiki/A/B_testing
21 www.gartner.com/en/documents/3136418/itscore-overview-for-bi-and-analytics
22 www.mckinsey.com/business-functions/mckinsey-digital/how-we-help-clients/digital-2020/our-assessments/analytics
23 https://michaelskenny.com/points-of-view/measuring-your-big-data-maturity/
24 As part of this process, models are *tested* using labelled historical data that is not used in training. This is done to gauge the performance of the model.
25 www.coe.int/en/web/artificial-intelligence/history-of-ai
26 Modelled loosely on the human brain, a neural net consists of thousands or even millions of simple processing nodes that are densely interconnected. (Source: https://news.mit.edu/2017/explained-neural-networks-deep-learning-0414)
27 See https://arxiv.org/abs/2207.08815
28 See https://arxiv.org/abs/2101.02118
29 See https://arxiv.org/abs/2110.01889

30 This isn't to exclude transfer learning, though this is typically found in the realm of deep learning and can only be stretched so far. See https://ieeexplore.ieee.org/abstract/document/9134370/ for more.
31 https://metaphysic.ai/to-uncover-a-deepfake-video-call-ask-the-caller-to-turn-sideways/
32 We will present a more modern model called the Machine Learning Workflow (MLWF) in Chapter 7.
33 https://callingbullshit.org/case_studies/case_study_ml_sexual_orientation.html
34 https://callingbullshit.org/case_studies/case_study_criminal_machine_learning.html

References

Dama International (2017), *DAMA-DMBOK: Data Management Body of Knowledge.* (2nd ed.). Technics Publications, LLC, Denville, NJ.

Kimball, R. and Ross, M. (2011), *The Data Warehouse Toolkit: The Complete Guide to Dimensional Modeling.* John Wiley & Sons, Indianapolis, IN.

Shearer, C. (2000), "The CRISP-DM model: The new blueprint for data mining", *Journal of Data Warehousing*, Vol. 5 No. 4, pp. 13–22.

3

The Principles of Emergent Design

The Origins of Emergent Design

Both of us teach data science classes to professionals from diverse, non-technical backgrounds. When teaching a practical course focused on techniques that students can apply immediately, it is easy to fall into the trap of covering only the technical aspects of the discipline. However, as we gained experience, we learnt that "less is more" in the sense that focusing less on technical matters and more on context (What are some common applications of these techniques? How might you adapt them to your context? How do you frame good problems? How do you solve challenging data modelling issues?) led to better learning outcomes. For example, in a deep learning course that Alex teaches, one of his assignments asks students to discuss a deep learning architecture and show how it can be applied to solve an industry problem, along with a justification of why this technology should be employed to solve this particular problem. When asked such questions, students are more engaged with the material because they can see potential applications in their own work contexts. Indeed, some of our proudest moments are when students tell us how they applied machine learning techniques, addressed complex data modelling challenges, or used problem framing approaches that we talk about in our classes to tackle problems they encountered in their own work.

The notion that learning a new technical skill is not an end in itself ought to be obvious. However, the hype surrounding new data technologies, amplified by aggressive marketing from education providers and "experts" touting their skills on social media platforms, tends to stoke the fear of missing out. This triggers one of two distinct responses: (a) giving up altogether because it is much too hard or (b) attempting to become an expert by attempting to learn as much as one can without any consideration of why. Needless to say, neither response is likely to lead to a good outcome. Strangely enough, organisational responses tend to be similar. They will either: (a) stick with doing data analytics the same way as they have been doing in the past or

DOI: 10.1201/9781003260158-3

(b) buy technology and expertise without regard to the context and culture of the organisation. Again, the outcomes are usually less than optimal.

Is There a Better Way?

The answer to the question posed in the section heading is "yes", and the details lie in the idea of Emergent Design (Cavallo 2000a, 2000b). In his doctoral thesis, wonderfully entitled, *Technological Fluency and the Art of Motorcycle Maintenance*, Cavallo notes that:

> The central thrust of this thesis is the presentation of a new strategy for educational intervention. The approach I describe here resembles that of architecture, not only in the diversity of the sources of knowledge it uses but in another aspect as well - the practice of letting the design emerge from an interaction with the client. The outcome is determined by the interplay between understanding the goals of the client; the expertise, experience, and aesthetics of the architect; and the environmental and situational constraints of the design space. Unlike architecture where the outcome is complete with the artifact, the design of [such initiatives] interventions is strengthened when it is applied iteratively. The basis for action and outcome is through the construction of understanding by the participants. I call this process Emergent Design.

There are a couple of apparent incongruities that may jump out at the reader here. Firstly, Cavallo is referring to educational interventions rather than data strategies. Secondly, the approach, unlike most conventional strategies, is inherently open-ended and iterative. It is therefore worth spending some time explaining why Emergent Design works well in the context of a strategy that involves technology.

The first point we'd like to make is that doing strategy in a meaningful way involves a lot more than setting up a team or implementing a technology; it requires the entire organisation to change the way it thinks about and approaches problems. This is a matter of learning at the organisational level, and hence the connection to Emergent Design. Secondly, the approach is inherently evolutionary in that the strategy is about *defining a direction* rather than a detailed goal. Indeed, the goal is an aspiration that one works towards via an accumulation of small wins and benefits that emerge as the organisation gets first-hand experience with the new capability.

Emergent Design, Evolution, and Learning

We'll start with a brief introduction to the origins of the term *Emergent Design*. In the 1990s, David Cavallo, then a PhD student at MIT, worked on a multi-year project to introduce new learning approaches based on computing technologies to students in rural Thailand. The work he did is documented in detail in his thesis, which is well worth a read (Cavallo 2000b). In the early stages of the project, it became evident that standard approaches to teaching computing would not work for such students. This was not because of a lack of ability on their part, but due a lack of context: Cavallo's students could not see the relevance of the technology to the day-to-day problems they faced in their villages. Faced with this impasse, Cavallo and his colleagues decided to turn the standard approach on its head: they started with the practical problems the villagers faced – such as building a dam to store water – and showed how the new technology could help them solve these problems. This shift in approach made all the difference: once students saw the relevance of the technology to their lives, they took to it with great enthusiasm and application.

When introducing a new capability into an organisation, there is often a focus on implementing a cool new technology and training people on it. Cavallo's experiences suggest that instead, one should focus on solving problems that matter to the organisation. This will not only demonstrate the usefulness of the cool new technology but also drive demand for learning and using it. Rather than "build it and they will come", it is more a matter of "demonstrate its relevance and they will come".

It is important to note that term *emergent* does not imply lack of structure or coherence. As he notes:

> *The emphasis on emergence as the guiding principle does not imply that this is an anything goes environment reacting to the whims of the participant[s]. [On the contrary, it uses] a very disciplined set of principles, methodologies, tools, activities, models, and exemplars … .*

Although the "tools, activities, models and exemplars" that Cavallo refers to may be domain-specific, the "principles" are of sufficient generality so as to be useful in diverse domains. We'll focus on describing the principles in this chapter and demonstrate their practical implications for setting up a data capability via specific examples in this and later chapters.

Although Cavallo's work is about technology-focused educational reforms, the principles he describes apply to any type of sociotechnical change. As a reminder from Chapter 1, the term *sociotechnical* serves to remind us that any technical initiative has social dimensions which, if neglected, will lead to suboptimal outcomes. Indeed, in his thesis, Cavallo (2000b) describes his own experience in managing a technology project in a healthcare organisation as being illustrative of the approach. Further examples of emergent sociotechnical change from other areas are not hard to find. A sample of these include information systems development (Luna-Reyes et al. 2005), software process improvement (Allison and Merali, 2007), and workplace technologies

(Baptista et al. 2020). That said, a recognition that sociotechnical change can be emergent is very different from managing such change using an emergent approach. The latter is what makes Cavallo's work uniquely interesting from a practitioner perspective.

Emergent Design is a principled way to achieve sociotechnical change; *principled* because it is based on how change occurs in nature. The central idea is simple: when building a new sociotechnical capability in an organisation, it is important to introduce it gradually, in a way that builds on local knowledge and interests. We'll say more about how to embark on this journey in the context of data science in the next chapter. For now, we note that establishing a sociotechnical capability, such as data science is a process of *evolutionary* rather than revolutionary change, and look at some of the implications of this view.

Firstly, evolution is not a one-way affair: as a new capability is introduced, the organisation changes too and the capability must then adjust to these new changes. The situation is better described as a *co-evolution* of the capability and its environment, the organisation being the environment in this case. A key aspect of Emergent Design is that the strategy is always subject to change, but the changes must be in response to a need rather than a blind implementation of industry "best practices" or "operating models".

Secondly, abrupt (or revolutionary) change is counterproductive because there is too much of a gap between the organisation's current capability and the newly introduced one, thus resulting in a mismatch that is difficult to adapt to. In contrast, gradual change, as advocated by Emergent Design gives the organisation and the new capability an opportunity to co-evolve and adapt to each other over time.

Thirdly, evolution is a process of trial and error by which nature figures out what works and what doesn't. In other words, it is a process of *learning*. As noted by the anthropologist Gregory Bateson (1979), there are deep parallels between the processes of evolution and those of learning. In particular, the evolution of a collective requires that individuals comprising it learn to adapt to changing conditions. Learning is an individual process that enables the collective to adapt to a changing environment.

So, establishing a new sociotechnical capability is a process of organisational learning. Therein lies a problem because the objectives and plans are typically set out by those who run the organisation but the details of figuring out of what to do and how to do it – i.e., the actual learning – occurs at the coalface, mostly by those who have little or no say in formulating the strategy. The two groups will have very different perspectives on what needs to be done and how it should be done. This is the root of many tensions or paradoxes that an emergent approach must reconcile. Here are some of the common ones that you will encounter in organisations (adapted from Cavallo):

1. **Top-down versus bottom-up emergent goal setting**: in many organisations, goals are set by management without adequate input

from lower levels. In Emergent Design, management sets high-level aspirational goals, with the details of how to progress towards them being left to those at the coalface.

2. **Control versus autonomy**: typically, management will want to retain oversight and control of what's happening but, ironically, the best results occur when management steps back and delegates decision-making to those who actually do the work. In Emergent Design, the job of management is to create the conditions and set boundaries within which people have the autonomy to make decisions relating to their work. Seen in this light, even traditionally "control focused" areas like data governance can be seen as enablers rather than means of control. We'll say more about this at various points in the book and Chapter 8 in particular.

3. **Strict versus flexible planning**: managers like plans that offer certainty; people who do the work need flexibility. The trick is to steer a course that balances the two, offering flexibility with reasonable, negotiated boundaries. Emergent Design eschews detailed roadmaps upfront, allowing details to emerge as strategies and high-level plans unfolds. In Emergent Design, roadmaps are guides that keep people from straying into danger territory, rather than rigid routes that stop them from exploring potentially interesting features they see along the way. Indeed, it is often the unplanned detours that one makes along the way that make a journey memorable. This is often true of data science projects as well. Serendipity *is* a thing in this domain.

4. **Abstractions versus actions**: plans are abstractions, actions are concrete. The difference between plans and actions is akin to the difference between a map and the territory. A map will always miss important details of the territory, and it is never clear upfront as to which details are important. Therefore, rather than following a predetermined route on a map, Emergent Design advocates small-scale actions and proof of concept projects to probe and understand the territory as one proceeds. We discuss this in detail in Chapter 4.

5. **Legacy versus new technology**: people will default to using familiar legacy technologies unless they are convinced that the new technologies confer substantial benefits. Learning a new technology is hard work. When introducing one, the compelling case to be made is not so much to convince management, but to convince those who will work with it. Emergent Design advocates introducing new technology in a way that builds on tools and ways of working that people are already familiar with. We'll say more about this in Chapter 6 where we talk about technical choices.

6. **Buy versus build**: is it better to build data capabilities by hiring data professionals or upskilling internal staff or outsourcing or some combination thereof? The answer, as always, is: it depends! In Emergent Design,

this decision is made as the need arises, but always with a view to building on what is already in place. We'll say more about this in Chapter 5.

7. **Entrained thinking patterns versus new ways of thinking**: it is extremely difficult for humans to break old thinking patterns and think in creative new ways. A detailed strategy roadmap precludes new thinking. In contrast, Emergent Design, with its high-level aspirational goals, leaves a lot to be worked out by those who implement the strategy, thus encouraging employees to think in new ways.

The paradoxes listed above are *dialectical tensions* – systemic contradictions that employees experience in the workplace. They are what makes the work of introducing a new sociotechnical capability a wicked problem (see Chapter 1). Conventional approaches to data strategy tend to overlook these entirely, jumping to plans, actions, and technology without so much as pausing to consider the impact of these hidden tensions. Taking an emergent design perspective will enable you to identify these within your organisation and design approaches that acknowledge and take them into account. The remainder of this chapter is about equipping you with the skills to do that.

Uncertainty and Ambiguity

A common myth about strategy development in organisations is that it is largely a rational process. The term *rational* refers to methods that are based on the following broad steps:

1. Identify available options.
2. Develop criteria for rating options.
3. Rate options according to criteria developed.
4. Select the top-ranked option.

Although this appears to be a logical way to proceed with strategy development, it is often difficult to put into practice because of uncertainty about the future.

It is ironic that the term *uncertainty* is itself vague when used in the context of strategy. There are at least five distinct senses in which it could apply:

1. Uncertainty about strategic options.
2. Uncertainty about one's (or rather, the organisation's) preferences for those options.

3. Uncertainty about which criteria are relevant to evaluating the strategic options.
4. Uncertainty about what information is needed to make a decision – i.e., select a strategy (information relevance).
5. Uncertainty about the information itself (information accuracy).

Uncertainty about information accuracy (item 5 above) is very different from uncertainty regarding decision criteria (item 3). Information accuracy can potentially be improved by research or statistical analysis, whereas the decision criteria may vary from group to group (shades of problem wickedness!). Put another way, item 5 is essentially about verifying facts, whereas item 3 is a broader issue that may have social, political, and even behavioural dimensions. For example, when dealing with an issue of rising crime, questions pertaining to the veracity of the figures can be checked by going back to the source (this item 5), but issues concerning what should be done about the issue is a question that cannot be answered by data alone.

In what follows, we'll refer to issues that can be resolved by scientific approaches (research, statistical analysis, data science!) as *uncertain*, whereas those that cannot as *ambiguous* (Culmsee and Awati 2016). In other words, *uncertainty* can be resolved by recourse to facts or numbers, whereas the resolution of *ambiguity* requires debate and discussion. An example might help clarify the difference between the two.

The Covid pandemic has had consequences for all of us. Most of the negative consequences depend on the transmissibility of the virus and the severity of the disease. Although both these factors can, in principle, be determined through scientific studies, there are a number of practical considerations that make this difficult. For one, it is difficult to run controlled experiments on a virus that's already out in the wild. Another is that the virus – like many viruses – tends to mutate rather rapidly, with some mutations being more transmissible and consequential (in health terms) than others. The point is: although we know we could quantify transmissibility in principle, there are practical considerations that prevent us from doing so. However, determining transmissibility, even if only approximately, is a worthwhile endeavour. So, many scientists have used *Monte Carlo simulations*[1] to determine factors that affect transmission (Xie 2020, Maltezos 2021). Monte Carlo simulation is a technique that generates multiple histories of events (such as outbreaks) by drawing random samples from probability distributions that describe the events. In other words, the technique enables one to simulate events of interest thousands of times based on known patterns and then make statistically robust estimates based on the simulations. Note however, that (a) the results are probabilistic and (b) they depend critically on the accuracy of the data that is fed into the simulation and *this data comes from various on-the-ground sources of varying reliability*. With that caveat in mind, quantifying these uncertainties using Monte Carlo enables scientists to model the dynamics of transmission of the virus.

The important point to note from this example is that when confronted with an uncertainty, scientists attempt to deal with it using quantitative analyses. Once we quantify the uncertainty, we feel that we understand the uncertainty and are therefore able to control it better. Indeed, that is the whole point of quantitative modelling of uncertainty.

This is fine as it goes, but the problem is that there are several different transmission models, each with its own set of assumptions. At any given time, there is no way to determine which model is the best. So, when it comes to determining a strategy on how to respond to the virus, *decision makers have to rely on advice that goes beyond the numbers because the numbers themselves are not known with certainty.* They are dealing with ambiguity rather than uncertainty.

With that for an example to illustrate the distinction between uncertainty and ambiguity, consider the (much less consequential!) problem of developing a data science/analytics strategy. The strategist (you!) is faced with a range of questions such as:

1. Why do we need a data science/analytics capability?
2. Is it better to develop skills in-house or hire talent?
3. What is the best technology choice?
4. How do we set up an ethical data practice?

Each of these questions is *ambiguous* because the answer depends on one's perspective. Depending on who you ask (senior management, HR, IT), you are likely to get a range of different responses. The ambiguity inherent in these issues cannot be addressed using facts and numbers because one can find "evidence" for whatever approach one might want to justify. If you think about it, this is no different from the situation of making a policy decision regarding Covid in the face of conflicting evidence from different models. And, yes, it is exactly the notion of wickedness we touched upon in Chapter 1.

When confronted with ambiguous situations, we tend to react emotionally rather than rationally. This is because such situations defy logical analysis, and we therefore feel unable to understand or control them. This causes anxiety. The introduction of a new data capability is an example of this. Within the organisation, there will invariably be mixed feelings about the new function – techies might welcome it as an opportunity to further their technical skills but others may feel threatened; marketers with quantitative skills might embrace the new capability but more traditional ones may be less enthusiastic not only because it could render their existing models and approaches obsolete, but also because the new technology seems to take human agency out of the decision-making process (and we'll say much more about this in Chapter 8). It is easy to see that different people may hold different views about the benefits of the change. One of the key challenges for the strategist is to channel the enthusiasm of the enthusiasts while also addressing the anxiety of the anxious. This *enthusiasm vs anxiety* is another of those dialectical tensions we discussed in the previous section.

In the next section, we'll discuss some ways to deal with the anxieties of those who might be concerned about the impact the new capability will have on their roles and relevance.

Guidelines for Emergent Design

From the foregoing discussion, it should be evident that an emergent design approach to strategy development is very different from conventional approaches. Consequently, it requires a very different mindset, one that is able to deal with ambiguity and is also sensitive to others' anxieties about the changes that the strategy may entail. The following guidelines, based on our collective experience, research, and conversations with data leaders, may help point the way towards cultivating that mindset through practice.

Be a Midwife Rather than an Expert

As we noted in the first chapter, strategic issues relating to data invariably display elements of social complexity. As Horst Rittel (the man who coined the term "wicked problem") noted, *"you do not learn in school how to deal with wicked problems [because] expertise and ignorance [are] distributed over all participants"* (Rittel 1972). His point here is that to make progress on wicked problems, one has to act as a facilitator rather than an expert. In practical terms, this involves having conversations with key people in business units across the organisation, with the aim of understanding their pressing problems and how data might help in solving them (we'll elaborate on this in Chapter 4). The objective at this early stage is to find out what kind of data science function your organisation needs. Rather than deep expertise in data science, this requires an ability to listen to experts in other fields, and translate what they say into meaningful problems that can potentially be solved by data science. In other words, this requires the strategist to be a midwife rather than an expert.

These conversations are also the first step towards building relationships with potential users of the new capability across the business, which brings us to the next point.

Use Conversations to Gain Commitment

In their ground-breaking book on computers and cognition, Winograd and Flores (1986) observed that "organisations are networks of commitments" between people who comprise the organisation. It is through conversations that commitments between different groups of stakeholders are established and subsequently acted on.

A few tips we have found useful in initiating conversations that can help gain commitment:

- Use open questions to understand others' viewpoints and find common ground: asking questions such as "what should we do about X?" is a good way to start understanding what people think about the issue under discussion. The main objective here is to try to look for common ground that can open up ways to involve them in the proposed changes.
- Offer a clear "what's in it for you": Often times the benefits of the strategy are not clear to some stakeholders. When talking to such people, it is important to be able to articulate a few clear benefits for them.
- Don't push your agenda: In conversations to gain commitment, it is important to listen and respond to what people are saying instead of pushing your own agenda.

The basic idea in the above is to encourage people to say what they really think, rather than what they think you want them to say. Keep in mind that people may be unwilling to engage with you because they do not understand the implications of the proposed changes and are fearful of what it might mean for them.

Understand and Address Concerns of Stakeholders Who Are Wary of the Change

As noted earlier in this chapter, when confronted with ambiguous situations, we tend to react emotionally rather than rationally. Much of the pushback to organisational change arises as a consequence of these emotions. To address this issue, one has to identify stakeholders who might be uneasy about the proposed change, and understand and alleviate their concerns. Culmsee and Awati (2016) provide advice on how to do this in specific contexts using what they call "management teddy bears". These involve offering reassurance, advice, or opportunities that reduce anxiety, very much akin to how one might calm anxious children by offering them teddy bears or security blankets.

Here are a few examples of such teddy bears:

- A common fear that people have is that the new capability might reduce the importance of their current roles. A good way to handle this is to offer these people a clear and workable path to be a part of the change. For example, one could demonstrate how the new capability (a) enriches their current role or (b) offers opportunities to learn new skills or (c) enhances their effectiveness. We could call this the *"co-opt teddy bear"*. In Chapter 7, we offer concrete ways to involve the business in data science projects in ways *that makes the projects theirs*.

- It may also happen that some stakeholder groups are opposed to the change for political reasons. In this case, one can buy time by *playing down* the significance of the new capability. For example, one could frame the initiative as a "pilot" project run by the current data and reporting function. We could call this the *"pilot teddy bear"*. See the case study towards the end of this chapter for an example of a situation in which we used this teddy bear.

- If you want to gain, buy in for an idea that might feel risky to senior management, try (a) framing it as an initiative that, if successful, could help raise their profile; we call this the *"crowning achievement teddy bear"* or (b) demonstrating that others (preferably with some serious credibility) have endorsed the idea. For obvious reasons, we call this the *"Nobel Prize teddy bear"*.

- As a final example, if a senior executive is sceptical about the usefulness of a data science capability, one could try finding an example of a similar organisation that has derived benefit from setting one up, and telling them about it. This often nudges them in the direction of "we need to do this too". Accordingly, we call this the *"FOMO teddy bear"*.

Frame the Current Situation as an Enabling Constraint

In strategy development, it is usual to think of the current situation in negative terms, a situation that is undesirable and one that must be changed as soon as practicable. However, one can flip this around and look at the situation from the perspective of finding specific things that you can change with minimal political or financial cost. In other words, you reframe the current situation as an *enabling constraint* (Kaufman and Garre 2015). Indeed, this is exactly how evolution works: organisms adapt to changes in their environment via small incremental adaptations using the resources and capabilities that are at hand.

Kaufman and Garre (2015) offer the following amusing but instructive example of enabling constraints:

> *Consider the metaphor of improvisational comedy. The first rule is: Each member must accept the line given to her by the earlier member and build on it in a comedically appropriate way in the comedic adjacent possible. Here is the first line: "Jack, here is a silver platter with a steaming pile of horse ..." Jack cannot say, "Take the platter back!" He can say "Oh! Where did you hide my cookie cutter?" This improvisation continues until the troupe creates a skit that none could have pre-stated. In the improvisational comedy case each line is an enabling constraint that creates the comedic next adjacent possible.*

The example highlights the key message of this guideline. The starting point is well defined, but there are an infinite number of possible next steps. Although the actual next step cannot be predicted, one can make a good enough next step by thinking about the current situation creatively in order to explore what Kauffman (2014) calls the *adjacent possible* – the possible future states that are within reach, given the current state of the organisation. You may have to test a few of the adjacent possible states before you figure out which one is the best. This is best done via small, safe-to-fail proof of concept projects (more on this in Chapter 4).

The metaphor of a strategy as a map leads one to think of implementation as navigating a predetermined route from a known starting point to a fixed destination. From an evolutionary perspective, however, one finds one's way by actively engaging with the immediate environment, looking out for and testing possible next steps. Rather than fixing your position on a (road)map, you want to understand where you are and – based on that - where you could go next. As Chia and Holt (2009) note, this is a process of *wayfinding* rather than navigation. Proofs of concept projects are an ideal approach to wayfinding (more on that in Chapter 4).

Finally, another important implication of the evolutionary perspective is that it encourages us to view problems through a systemic lens – i.e. the problem *and* its context – rather than a narrow perspective that is focused solely on the problem. The latter approach often ends up creating more problems than it solves. This brings us to the next point.

Consider Long-Term and Hidden Consequences

It is a fact of life that when choosing between different approaches, people will tend to focus on short-term gains rather than long-term consequences (Dallas 2011, Davies et al. 2014). Indeed, one does not have to look far to see examples that have global implications (e.g., the financial crisis of 2008 and climate change). However, as Laverty (2004) has noted,

> *firms are less likely to undervalue the long term when they are able to manage tradeoffs between short-term and long term results, and create a climate of trust that allows individuals to weather the short-term setbacks necessary to achieve long term results.*

Valuing long-term results is difficult because the distant future is less salient than the present or the immediate future. A good way to look beyond immediate concerns (such as cost) is to use the *solution after next* principle proposed by Gerald Nadler and Shozo Hibino (1990). The basic idea behind the principle is to get people to focus on the goals that lie *beyond* the immediate goal. The process of thinking about and articulating longer term goals can often provide insights into potential problems with the current goals and/or how they are being achieved. We'll say more about this approach in the next chapter.

Another popular facilitation technique that can help surface potential unforeseen issues is the *project pre-mortem* first proposed by Gary Klein (2007), and now part of the broader Agile toolkit. The basic idea is simple: the facilitator starts the session by telling the team of analysts that he has foreseen the future and knows that the modelling project that they are about to undertake has failed spectacularly. He then asks the team to independently come up with reasons for the failure. Research has shown that framing the pre-mortem as an analysis of a project that has already failed (rather than one that might) tends to prompt people to be more thorough in their consideration of what has (could have) gone wrong. Though the project pre-mortem is broader than the solution after next method, both methods help surface outcomes that are not immediately obvious at the start.

Create an Environment that Encourages Learning

Emergent Design is a process of experimentation and learning. However, all learning other than that of the most trivial kind involves the possibility of error (Bateson 1972, p. 291). So, for it to work, one needs to create an environment of psychological safety – i.e., an environment in which employees feel safe to take risks by trialling new ideas and processes, with the possibility of failure (Edmondson 1999).

A key feature of learning organisations is that when things go wrong, the focus is not on fixing blame but on fixing the underlying issue and, more importantly, learning from it so that one reduces the chances of recurrence. It is interesting to note that this focus on the system rather than the individual is also a feature of high reliability organisations such as emergency response agencies (Reason 2000).

Beware of Platitudinous Goals

Strategies are often littered with buzzwords and platitudes – empty phrases that sound impressive but are devoid of meaning (Barabba et al. 2002, Culmsee and Awati 2013). For example, two in-vogue platitudes at the time this book was being written are *digital transformation* and *artificial intelligence* (discussed briefly in Chapter 2). They are platitudes because they tell you little about what exactly they mean in the specific context of the organisation.

The best way to deconstruct a platitude is via an oblique approach (Kay 2012) that is best illustrated through an example.

Say someone tells you that they want to implement *artificial intelligence* (or a *digital transformation* or any other platitude!) in their organisation. How would you go about finding out what exactly they want? Asking them what they *mean* by *artificial intelligence* is not likely to be helpful because the answer you will get is likely to be couched in generalities such as *data-driven decision-making* or *automation*, phrases that are world-class platitudes in their own right! Instead, it is better to ask them how *artificial intelligence* would make a difference to the organisation. This can help you steer the discussion towards a concrete business problem, thereby bringing the conversation down from platitude-land to concrete, measurable outcomes. Indeed, it may even turn out that they do not need artificial intelligence to achieve what they wish to.[2]

Just to be clear, it is fine to include such phrases in your strategy *providing you also spell out what exactly they mean in your context.*

Act So as to Increase Future Choices

This is perhaps the most important point in this list because it encapsulates all the other points. We have adapted it from Heinz von Foerster's ethical imperative which states that *one should always act so as to increase the number of choices* in the future (von Foerster 2003). Keeping this in mind as you design your data science strategy will help you avoid technology or intellectual lock in. As an example of the former, when you choose a product from a particular vendor, they will want you to use their offerings for the other components of your data stack. Designing each layer of the stack in a way that can work with other technologies ensures interoperability, an important feature of a robust data technology stack (more on this in Chapter 6). As an example of the latter, when hiring data scientists, hire not just for what they know now but also for evidence of their curiosity and proclivity to learn new things – a point we elaborate on in Chapter 5.

You might be wondering why von Foerster called this an ethical imperative. An important aspect of this principle is that your actions should not constrain the choices of *others*, and hence the ethical angle.

Putting Emergent Design to Work – An Illustrative Case Study

The principles described in the previous section are general, i.e., they apply to any kind of strategy. Indeed, the beauty of an emergent approach is that it can be applied to pretty much any initiative in work or in life. That said, since conventional strategies tend to follow plan and purpose-driven approaches, it might be difficult to see what an emergent design approach looks like in practice. In this section, we will walk you through the key differences and then present an illustrative case study of the approach.

The main differences between conventional and emergent design approaches are summarised in Table 3.1

TABLE 3.1

The Main Differences between Conventional and Emergent Design Approaches to Building Sociotechnical Capabilities

Conventional Approach	Emergent Design
Prescriptive	Non-prescriptive
Plans over learning	Learning over plans
Technology-driven	Context-driven

Unlike conventional approaches to strategy development, Emergent Design does not offer a "canned approach". One cannot set out detailed steps for what you should do in your specific situation. Instead, Emergent Design is about *defining a direction* towards an *aspirational goal* but *without mapping out a complete route to achieving it*. This gives implementers the freedom to develop the capability in a way that is suited to the culture and context of the organisation. Part of the trick is also to recognise and take advantage of opportunities that arise in the course of implementation – the *adjacent possible* that we mentioned in the previous section. This requires a degree of familiarity with the internal culture of the organisation, which enables the strategist to understand what is possible and what is not. Kurtz and Snowden (2003) use the Welsh word *Cynefin* to describe this "sense of place".

Since organisational change is a process of learning, Emergent Design focuses on:

- Making the connections between the proposed new technology and current capabilities explicit (see Chapter 6).
- Creating an environment in which employees can experiment with the new technology by using it in projects that matter (see Chapter 7).
- Providing employees opportunities for formal or on the job training (see Chapter 5).
- Developing proof of concept or pilot projects that can be scaled up depending on how well they work, both in terms of costs and benefits (see Chapter 4).

In contrast, standard approaches to developing sociotechnical capabilities tend to focus solely on the technology without adequate attention to building connections to the current capabilities of the organisation.

In summary, the main difference between Emergent Design and a conventional approach to strategy is that the former pays due attention to unique features of a particular organisation, whereas the latter tends to be based on what is common across many organisations. We realise all this might sound abstract or even vague, so we now describe a case-study in which one of us (Kailash) established an analytics development centre for a large multinational.

Alex will step back as Kailash tells the story in first person.

Background

In 2012, I was promoted to a management role as Head of Service Development for the Asia-Pacific (APAC) region. For political reasons, the multinational had IT development centres in Argentina and Spain but none in the APAC region. Suffice to say, establishing a centre in the APAC region was not on the cards. Any request for permission to explore the possibility would have been met with refusal.

The Regional CIO, who I reported to, saw this as an anomaly and wished to do something about it. One day, he casually mentioned that I should explore the possibility of setting up a centre in Singapore (where the APAC office was located). When asked for details about the rationale, the CIO mentioned the following points:

- Capability augmentation
- Cost reduction/offshoring
- Having an Asia-based centre made more sense than having one in Europe or South America (from a skills availability, timezone, and cost perspective)
- A strategic move to increase the visibility of the APAC regional office

He said these were just ideas and it was for me to figure out which ones made sense for the organisation and the region. Crafting a coherent strategy around this would be the first step as it could then be used to make an argument for funding. However, this would not be straightforward because of the politics.

The Route to Emergent Design

At that time, I knew nothing about setting up a new organisation from scratch; it therefore seemed prudent to get advice from experts. I had conversations with several well-known consulting firms. They assured me that they had done this kind of thing many times before and, more importantly, they quoted costs that sounded very reasonable. It was very tempting to outsource my problem.

Not long after my conversations with the consulting firms, I came across Oliver Williamson's Nobel Prize winning work on transaction costs (Williamson 2010). The arguments presented therein drew my attention to the hidden costs of outsourcing. In brief: the consultants I had spoken with included only upfront costs, neglecting the costs of coordination, communication, and rework. Even worse, any contractual arrangement would require the services to be specified in great detail, leaving ample opportunity for the outsourcer to add on additional charges via contract variations that could not be foreseen upfront. Although I was not aware of Emergent Design at that time, I felt that specifying this level of detail upfront would not be wise ... and indeed, not even possible.

The mistake in my thinking was related to Whitehead's (1925, p.75) *fallacy of misplaced concreteness*: I had been thinking about the development hub as a well-defined entity rather than an idea that needed to be fleshed out. Moreover, given the possibility of pushback from powerful stakeholders, it was important for me to understand the organisational landscape better than I did at the time. I had to find a way to frame the development centre as a natural next step. It thus became clear to me that it would be safest to start quietly, without drawing much attention to what I was doing. This would enable me to test assumptions, gauge the organisation's appetite for the change, and, most importantly, learn by trial and error.

The ideal way to start, it seemed, would be to engage a small number of people to do specific things that delivered immediate value to the wider organisation. The trick was to find an opportunity to do so.

A Pivotal Conversation

By that time, I had already spent quite a few years in the organisation and had worked on a few global projects via which I had built an informal network of people whose judgement and discretion I trusted. As it happened, a few weeks after, my conversations with the consulting firms, one of people in my trusted network – let's call him Dave – called to catch up.

During the conversation, Dave complained about how hard it was to find database skills at a reasonable cost (Dave was located in Europe). I asked Dave what he considered to be a "reasonable cost". The number Dave quoted in reply was considerably more than one would pay for those skills at my location.

I saw that this presented an opportunity. I suggested that I could hire a developer to help his team. The developer would be located in Asia (at my office) but would be dedicated entirely to working with Dave's team. I also suggested a six-month trial period, thereby reducing Dave's risk.

Dave was interested but concerned about the administrative details regarding hiring, equipment, workspace, etc. I assured him that I would look after these and charge costs back to his cost centre. Together, we also decided to keep this quiet for the time being, following the adage that it is easier to beg forgiveness than seek permission.

Reflecting on this later, I realised that the conversation with Dave was about forging a way forward by solving a problem that mattered to someone else. Indeed, as my goal was not properly defined, that was the only way forward at that time.

First Steps

There was a fair bit of administrative work that needed doing: sorting out HR issues, a workspace, and the mechanisms for charging costs back to Dave. However, these were all matters for which there were well established processes, so it was simply a matter of talking to the right people. The trickier issues were around organisational culture and politics. For example:

- The idea of a development hub had not yet been socialised within the local organisation. Although the local CIO had mentioned the plan to the local CEO, it was not expected to happen so soon.
- More importantly, they would have to deal with the political fallout of setting up a centre in Asia, given that there were already well-established centres in Europe and Latin America.

Apart from articulating benefits, it was important to address anxieties around these issues. The obvious way to do this was to position this as a strategic initiative that would increase the relevance and importance of the local office within the wider organisation with minimal cost or headcount implications. The Regional CIO and I made a presentation to the local executive emphasising the following aspects of the initiative, which serve to illustrate a few of the principles we mentioned earlier:

- The centre, when fully staffed, would result in increased visibility and importance of the local operating unit. This is an example of handing out a teddy bear (can you figure out which one? Answer in the endnote.[3]).
- We also emphasised that the gradual approach would enable us to identify and address any unforeseen issues early – again focussing on a key concern we knew they would have.
- There were no additional headcount or cost implications for the local operating unit as the developers would be hired as contractors, paid for entirely by other operating units. This addressed the big question that was on the executives' mind: how much was this going to cost them?
- The staff in the centre would augment local capabilities thus offering a cost-effective way to ramp up staffing of regional projects as needed. Given that projects were chronically understaffed, it was anticipated that this benefit would be welcomed by the executive.

The problem of pushback from executive management at head office was a more complex issue because of the politics. We decided to deal with it later, after the initiative had gained some momentum and could be presented as a fait accompli, but one that benefited the entire organisation. Accordingly, I asked Dave to keep the plan quiet, reiterating that I'd take the blame if there was any fallout.

That done, I went ahead with hiring the developer.

Integrating the New Capability

The new developer – let's call him Raul – started work about a month and half after the initial conversation with Dave. It had been agreed that Raul would start and finish later in the day so that he could have a greater overlap with European time zones.

That was the easy bit.

The harder part was to address concerns that Dave's Europe-based team members would have regarding hiring developers in Asia. They would naturally see this as a move to outsource their jobs. Dave and I had already discussed how he would address this. Specifically, Dave would emphasise that hiring Raul was a trial arrangement to see if an Asia-based team could help augment the capability of the overstretched team in Europe – taking care to emphasise the word "augment". In line with the augmentation argument, he would also take other actions to allay any residual concerns by ensuring that all projects would be led by his team in Europe. In particular, he would involve them in decisions regarding what work Raul would be given. Once again, these "teddy bears" served to allay the anxieties of the Europe-based team.

Raul proved his worth within the first few weeks and, more importantly, he got along well with individuals in the Europe-based team who began to appreciate the value he provided. Dave was so happy with the arrangement that he began to tell others in European locations about the "Asia Development Centre". Although the centre was not established, the phrase began to be used in conversations across the organisation. This normalised the idea of an Asia-based centre making it *seem* like an already established part of the organisation. This was an important to lesson to me: a key aspect of building a new capability or function is *to get others to evangelise it* in their conversations with diverse stakeholders across the organisation. A good way to get organisational commitment for what you are doing is to have others to do the selling for you!

The "Pilot" Project

As was bound to happen sooner or later, important people in headquarters got wind of the initiative. Soon enough, a senior IT executive from headquarters visited the Asia-based subsidiary. He cornered me and asked, in fairly strong terms, about the new development centre and whether it had approval from the proper channels.

I realised instinctively that much hinged on what I said and – more import-antly – how I said it. The executive was clearly upset, so the response had to be framed in a way that would not infuriate him further. On the other hand, the response had to be convincing because the executive had the power to stop the fledgling project in its tracks with a word or two in the right ears.

"There is no plan to set up a development centre", I replied, looking the executive in the eye. "All we have done is hire one or two people here to help with the workload at headquarters".

"Who has requested help?"

I said it was Dave; the executive knew him well.

"Where do you plan to go from here?" the executive demanded.

"Like I said, there is no plan", I replied. "This is just a pilot to see if we can help improve productivity. The idea is to free people in headquarters so that they can focus on the strategic stuff".

"Just make sure it doesn't turn into something bigger".

"Absolutely", I responded, mustering what I hoped was a reassuring smile.

"OK", nodded the executive and walked out.

This is an example of a "pilot teddy bear" mentioned earlier: by emphasising the small and exploratory nature of the arrangement, I framed the initiative as temporary rather than permanent, thus buying myself some time to pay greater attention to the politics of the project over the coming weeks. At the same time, it was clear I would have to scale up quickly if I wanted to make the argument that the centre was a worthwhile initiative, a dilemma illustra-tive of the wickedness of strategy problems.

Scaling Up

Dave's evangelising was bringing in a few more short-term hires, but the numbers were still too small to make a strong case for the centre. As it happened, one of my local colleagues had received funding for several business intelligence and analytics projects. The colleague – let's call him Edwin – was relatively new to the organisation. Although Edwin was aware of what I was doing for Dave and others, he did not seem interested in being a part of the fledgling centre.

Up until that time, I had not asked Edwin to get involved because there was no rush. However, given the situation that had developed, it was clear that it was critical to get Edwin's support sooner than later. Realising that the best way to do this would be to (a) understand what Edwin needed, (b) shape the centre around his requirements, and (c) ensure that he got the credit for scaling up, I approached Edwin suggesting that the initiative would be framed as a "centre of excellence for business intelligence and analytics" and be dedicated primarily to making his projects happen. In addition, I assured him that he would get the credit for enabling the scale-up of the centre.[4]

At the same time, in order to avoid over-dependence on a single source of funding, I developed marketing material including brochures and even a short video extolling the qualities of the location. The marketing material framed the initiative as helping managers meet their KPIs – yes, one could call this a KPI teddy bear! A subtle point was that the marketing material did not talk about cost per se, the focus was on KPIs. This enabled me to use the obvious elephant in the room to my advantage – i.e., framing the initiative as being about business outcomes rather than cost although I knew that most managers would sign up because of the cost advantage.

The Official OK

To deal with politics, I started to put together a cost-benefit analysis based on figures from Edwin, Dave, and other Europe-based managers regarding the costs versus benefits of having an Asia-based capability. However, as I built the analysis, I realised that executive management would not necessarily be swayed by the KPI and centre of excellence arguments. They were bound to ask why I had chosen to set the centre up in a relatively high-cost Asian country (Singapore) rather than outsource it to an external provider in, say, India or Philippines or even next-door Malaysia.

To address this concern, I added an analysis based on Oliver Williamson's Nobel Prize winning work on transaction costs that we mentioned earlier in this chapter (Williamson 2010). The analysis demonstrated that the hidden costs of search, coordination, communication, and potential rework would easily swamp any upfront cost advantage offered by lower cost locations. I wrote up a paper making the case using transaction cost theory with the intent of presenting it to executives from headquarters when they visited the region.

The presentation was well received and I finally got the official blessing to continue. It turned out that transaction cost analysis, because of its Nobel credentials, gave the case study a degree of legitimacy and authority that it would not have had otherwise (an example of the use of a "Nobel Prize teddy bear").

The other points I emphasised were:

1. The approach was flexible and could be adjusted as the organisation learnt what worked and what didn't, in line with von Foerster's (2003) ethical imperative, *"act so as to increase future choices"* (the last of our principles outlined earlier).

2. The emergent design approach, which focused on solving existing problems, ensured that the centre would remain aligned to the needs of the organisation. However, this did not preclude the possibility of innovations from the centre being fed back into the organisation. Indeed, the whole point of an evolutionary approach to developing a new capability is to ensure that the capability offers an advantage that was not available before.

In under two years, the development centre grew to over 50 professionals who supported business intelligence and analytics projects across the region and beyond. More than half of these were hired through Edwin's projects but there were a number of others as well. The centre had diverse capabilities that were being employed in numerous projects across the globe. Through Emergent Design, it had evolved into a full-fledged unit in its own right.

Lessons Learnt

It was somewhere in the middle of all this that I first came across Cavallo's (2000a) paper on Emergent Design. Although the context Cavallo worked in was very different from mine, I realised that the approaches were philosophically very much aligned in that the focus was on building on what was already present in a gradual manner that enabled adaptation of the new capability to the local culture rather than the other way around. As Cavallo noted:

> ...*rather than having the one best way there can now be many possible ways. Rather than adapting one's culture to the approach, one can adapt the approach to one's culture.*

Indeed, the error that many other approaches to sociotechnical strategies make is that they attempt to force the capability onto a culture without making connections to it. It is important to note that as the new capability takes shape and gains traction, people will get used to new ways of working and the culture of the organisation will change too. As the capability evolves, so does the organisation.

It is important to point out that although Emergent Design does not involve detailed plans, the *process of planning* – thinking about what to do next is critical. Each step one makes should move one closer to achieving the big, aspirational objective. Conventional strategies have to be continually monitored for unforeseen risks that could derail the initiative entirely as well. Reality invariably holds surprises, so it seems obvious to us that any practical approach to strategy development and implementation must explicitly take into account the unexpected. The emergent design approach to planning is better suited to dealing with surprises because it is based on a just-in-time philosophy that embraces the flexibility of adaptation over the rigidity of long-term planning. Over the years, since my first encounter with Emergent Design, I've found a rich literature on oblique approaches to strategy design and implementation that emphasise the importance of an adaptive mindset. A particularly good reference on this is the book, *Strategy Without Design*, by Robert Chia and Robin Holt (2009). The following quote from the book may help explain the importance of leveraging what is at hand:

> ...*in an inherently chaotic and complex world, the idea of controlling and managing happenings in the world through some grand pre-designed strategy and oversight is patently unworkable. Instead of interfering with the world at a*

*general or macro level we should, rather, concentrate upon the immediate, prac-
tical situations we encounter and recognize these as the originating source of our
strategic adaptability...*

We reiterate that this does not mean that anything goes. When setting up
the development centre, we had a goal in mind as well as an approach that
would achieve it in an emergent manner. What we did not have was a detailed
roadmap. Indeed, even if we had one, it would have been rife with incorrect
costs and assumptions that would have come back to bite us later. In the next
chapter, we show you how to chart a course that has a clear direction but
leaves the details to be specified as they emerge.

The development centre had many wicked elements – lack of a clear mandate and politics, for example. These were tackled by building the case for
the centre via a proof of concept and pilot, and growing the capability in
an incremental manner that demonstrated clear value to the organisation at
every step. Our first steps gave us opportunities to test out what would work
and what wouldn't. Equally important, it enabled us to work out HR issues,
cost chargebacks, and all those minutiae that go with this kind of initiative.

Summarising

Although there is no prescriptive formula for Emergent Design, there are
principles that offer concrete guidance along the way. Our aim in this chapter
was to describe these principles along with a case study that demonstrates
how Emergent Design works in practice. It is our belief that Emergent Design
offers a safe route to building robust data capabilities because it builds on
local knowledge and culture, rather than following templatised approaches
that overlook subtle contextual factors that make organisations unique. In the
remainder of this book, we hope to show you how you can do this.

Notes

1 Monte Carlo simulation is a general analytical technique that can be applied to any
   decision problem that can be broken down into components for which it is possible to derive or estimate probability distributions. An elementary introduction
   is available at: https://eight2late.wordpress.com/2018/03/27/a-gentle-introduct
   ion-to-monte-carlo-simulation-for-project-managers/
2 https://eugeneyan.com/writing/first-rule-of-ml/
3 The "crowning achievement" teddy bear.
4 The "crowning achievement" teddy bear, yet again!

References

Allison, I. and Merali, Y. (2007), "Software process improvement as emergent change: A structurational analysis", *Information and Software Technology*, Vol. 49 No. 6, pp. 668–681.

Baptista, J., Stein, M. K., Klein, S., Watson-Manheim, M. B. and Lee, J. (2020), "Digital work and organisational transformation: Emergent digital/human work configurations in modern organisations", *The Journal of Strategic Information Systems*, Vol. 29 No. 22, pp. 1–10.

Barabba, V., Pourdehnad, J. and Ackoff, R. L. (2002), "On misdirecting management", *Strategy and Leadership*, Vol. 30 No. 5, pp. 5–9.

Bateson, G. (1972), *Steps to an Ecology of Mind*, University of Chicago Press, Chicago, IL.

Bateson, G. (1979), *Mind and Nature: A Necessary Unit*, Dutton, New York, NY, p. 4.

Cavallo, D. (2000a), "Emergent design and learning environments: Building on indigenous knowledge", *IBM Systems Journal*, Vol. 39 No. 3–4, pp. 768–781.

Cavallo, D. (2000b), *Technological Fluency and the Art of Motorcycle Maintenance: Emergent Design of Learning Environments* (Doctoral dissertation, Massachusetts Institute of Technology). Available online at: https://dspace.mit.edu/bitstream/han dle/1721.1/9135/45233377-MIT.pdf

Chia, R. C. and Holt, R. (2009), *Strategy without Design: The Silent Efficacy of Indirect Action*, Cambridge University Press, Cambridge, UK.

Culmsee, P. and Awati, K. (2013), *The Heretic's Guide to Best Practices: The Reality of Managing Complex Problems in Organisations*, iUniverse Star, Indianapolis, IN.

Culmsee, P. and Awati, K. (2016), *The Heretic's Guide to Management: The Art of Harnessing Ambiguity*, Heretics Guide Press, Marsfield, Australia.

Dallas, L. L. (2011), "Short-termism, the financial crisis, and corporate governance", *The Journal of Corporation Law* Vol. 37, p. 267.

Davies, R., Haldane, A. G., Nielsen, M. and Pezzini, S. (2014), "Measuring the costs of short-termism", *Journal of Financial Stability*, Vol 12, pp. 16–25.

Edmondson, A. (1999), "Psychological safety and learning behavior in work teams", *Administrative Science Quarterly*, Vol. 44 No. 2, pp. 350–383.

Kauffman, S. (2014), "Prolegomenon to patterns in evolution", *Biosystems*, Vol. 123, pp. 3–8.

Kauffman, S. and Garre, A. (2015), "Beyond Descartes and Newton: Recovering life and humanity", *Progress in Biophysics and Molecular Biology*, Vol. 119 No. 3, pp. 219–244.

Kay, J. (2012), *Obliquity: Why Our Goals Are Best Achieved Indirectly*, Penguin Books, Reprint Edition, London, UK.

Klein, G. (2007), "Performing a project premortem", *Harvard Business Review*, Vol. 85 No. 9, pp. 18–19.

Kurtz, C. F. and Snowden, D. J. (2003), "The new dynamics of strategy: Sense-making in a complex and complicated world", *IBM Systems Journal*, Vol. 42 No. 3, pp. 462–483.

Laverty, K., (2004), "Managerial myopia or systemic short-termism? The importance of managerial systems in valuing the long term", *Management Decision*, Vol. 42 No. 8, pp. 949–962.

Luna-Reyes, L. F., Zhang, J., Ramon Gil-Garcia, J. and Cresswell, A. M. (2005), "Information systems development as emergent socio-technical change: A practice approach", *European Journal of Information Systems*, Vol. 14 No. 1, pp. 93–105.

Maltezos, S. and Georgakopoulou, A. (2021), "Novel approach for Monte Carlo simulation of the new COVID-19 spread dynamics", *Infection, Genetics and Evolution*, Vol. 92, p. 104896.

Nadler, G. and Hibino, S. (1990), *Breakthrough Thinking*, Prima Publications and Communications, Indianapolis, IN.

Reason, J. (2000), "Human error: Models and management", *British Medical Journal*, Vol. 320 No. 7237, pp. 768–770.

Rittel, H. W. J. (1972), "On the planning crisis: Systems analysis of the first and second generations", *Bedriftsokonomen*, Vol. 8, pp. 390–396.

von Foerster, Heinz (2003), "Ethics and second-order cybernetics", in *Understanding Understanding*. Springer, New York, NY, pp. 287–304.

Whitehead, A. N. (1925), *Science and the Modern World: Lovell Lectures*, Macmillan, New York, NY.

Williamson, O. E. (2010), "Transaction cost economics: The natural progression", *American Economic Review*, Vol. 100 No. 3, pp. 673–690.

Winograd, T. and Flores, F., (1986), *Understanding Computers and Cognition: A New Foundation for Design*, Ablex Publishing, Norwood, NJ.

Xie, G. (2020), "A novel Monte Carlo simulation procedure for modelling COVID-19 spread over time", *Scientific Reports*, Vol. 10 No. 1, pp. 1–9.

4

Charting a Course

Introduction

It may seem obvious that to create a data science strategy, one needs to have a clear objective. However, from what you have read so far about Emergent Design, it should be apparent that this is not so: what one needs at the start is a *direction* rather than a detailed end state. Indeed, fixating on an end state is a recipe for failure because it distracts from the immediate obstacles on the road to building a sustainable data capability. These obstacles tend to be part of the culture of the organisation and are therefore not immediately obvious. Among other things, they are the taken-for-granted ways of working that are deeply embedded in organisations and therefore rarely questioned. Consequently, any approach to strategy development and implementation must initially focus on barriers to change rather than the change itself.

This brings us to an important feature of Emergent Design. Although it is an evolutionary approach to planning and implementing sociotechnical change, it differs from other evolutionary approaches (such as the various flavours of Agile) in an important way. Most other approaches tend to focus on how an organisation should change in order to adapt to survive and thrive. However, in doing so, they overlook an important aspect of evolution which is to *ensure that adaptations do not unduly disrupt the organisation*. Evolution has two aspects to it: the first is outward-facing, geared towards adapting to the external environment; the second is inward-facing, ensuring that the adaptations made are not disruptive to the organisation as a whole. To adapt, there must be change; to survive, there must be a degree of continuity. Since survival is a prerequisite for adaptation, it should be clear that any strategy for change must pay due attention to ensuring continuity. Emergent Design addresses the continuity issue by treating the existing situation as a condition that constrains the set of viable strategic options.

The main upshot of the above is that the strategist must select the direction of change based on what the organisation will benefit from and tolerate. To this end, there are two distinct situations that a data science strategist will be presented with:

DOI: 10.1201/9781003260158-4

1. The C-suite is aware of the potential of data science and is open to making data/evidence-based decision-making a pillar of the organisation's strategy.
2. Executive awareness of the transformative potential of data is low and there is not much support for building a data capability.

Our objective in this chapter is to provide you with advice on how to deal with these two situations. As we'll see, the actions you need to take are largely the same in both cases.

Tackling the Corporate Immune System

A key challenge in human organ transplants is the problem of rejection. This happens when the immune system of the host treats the transplanted organ as a foreign body and triggers a response that leads to the destruction of the organ. A similar "corporate immune system" operates in organisations (Birkinshaw and Ridderstråle 1999). This is the tendency to reject innovative ideas that come either from within the organisation or outside and continue to do things in established but suboptimal ways.[1]

Overcoming the corporate immune system is a challenge for the data science strategist. Rare is the case where you will get an opportunity to build a data capability from scratch. You will invariably have to begin with an existing landscape – data, technology, people, and processes – over which you have little control. Indeed, the technology and process landscape of any large organisation is a palimpsest, overwritten many times but always retaining traces of what came before. This results in innumerable and undocumented kludges and workarounds that become a part of the "way things are done around here". Once established, the inertia can be hard to overcome, particularly if the proposed change is perceived as being too radical.

Fortunately, Emergent Design can help you deal with this issue in a natural way because it starts from the local culture and capability of the organisation and makes incremental changes, each of which have demonstrable value. As exemplified in the case study presented in the previous chapter, it advocates starting small and addressing issues in a way that builds on existing capabilities, avoiding large scale reengineering of processes or technologies, at least in the early stages.

Indeed, one could say that the approach you want to start with is one of stealth, not unlike the way in which certain viruses trick the human immune system.[2] You need to build credibility amongst the organisational rank and file before you make your efforts visible to all. This is best done by addressing problems that matter to people on the ground, often far removed from the boardroom where a strategy is typically signed off. Working through such problems is a far better way to understand the gaps in your organisation's capabilities than a formal "gap analysis": it ensures that you will be solving problems that matter, rather than building "solutions in search of problems". Technology vendors almost always do the latter. This is understandable because their success is measured by how much you buy from them, not how much they actually help you; their success metrics are not the same as yours.

The following remarks from Sandra Hogan (Founder of Leap Analytics and Amperfii) are relevant here.

> *"I feel like these data science technology companies are trying to take a sledge hammer to a nail. When they come to sell me something, I tell them, maybe digital native companies are ready for that and may use it on a day-to-day basis. But I can tell you now even banks, I think, kid themselves that they're ready for it. When it comes down to it, they are still doing the basic things that we're trying to do at our company that's just starting out. A lot of these software vendors keep going to our CEO, and he keeps sending them to me. And I keep saying to him, 'don't worry about it, we don't need it'. Our problem is not technology, my guys can build it. The issue is the business is not ready for it. The problem for us, in the first instance, is finding problems that matter to people."*

By finding and solving problems that matter to people, you are minimising the chances of rejection by the corporate immune system. More importantly, by doing so, you are also developing an understanding of the context within which your fledgling data science capability must function and thrive. Indeed, as we will see later in this chapter, an approach that starts with problem finding automatically addresses many other aspects of data strategy.

Finding Problems

Those who design information systems know from experience that the worst way to figure out what users want is to ask them a direct question about what functionality the new system should have. Instead, it is more informative to ask them about important things that they are unable to do using their current systems. Following Culmsee and Awati (2014), we call this the *"What keeps you up at night?"* question. Such questions tend to elicit rich responses that can be expanded on by asking for elaborations or clarifications of specific points. It is an approach that is as useful for strategising as it is for designing new data capabilities. The reason this question works is that its phrasing implicitly prioritises problems over processes. This is important because your strategy will not fly if those who are at the receiving end of its consequences do not perceive it as addressing problems that matter to them.

Accordingly, you should start by having conversations with people across the organisation with the aim of gaining an understanding of their data pain points. The people you talk to should cover all the major departments of the organisation such as sales, operations, HR, etc. A good way to do this – if you have the blessings of the executive – is to start right at the top and work your way down. This way you get the boss' perspective first and can then ensure that you keep it in mind when talking to others. The objective is to get an understanding of your organisation's current data capabilities. From an emergent design perspective, the aim is not only to look for gaps, but also to (a) develop a good understanding of current capabilities that can be leveraged in your strategy and (b) build relationships that can be used to gain support for projects and new initiatives down the line. This was the approach taken by Sandra Hogan in her first few weeks in a new organisation:

> *"Well, the first thing I did was to meet with the CEO and try to understand a bit more from his perspective. What was his vision for the organization? More importantly, what did he see as the main areas that the organization was lacking in? I used his answer to the second question to drive my discussions with the CEO's direct reports – the broad functional heads. Note that at this level we weren't necessarily talking about data and analytics, or data science; what I was talking to them about is their business problems, the things that they saw as issues. If I got an opening, I did ask about how they were leveraging technology in their different business units and what they would like to do but could not due to the lack of technology or knowledge. Some of them were curious enough to ask me a lot of questions. Some had done some homework before talking to me, but some hadn't. It didn't matter either way because my intent was more about understanding them and building relationships."*

Apart from building relationships, conversations at this level will give you a number of additional leads which, when followed up, will help you build a picture of the data-related work currently taking place in the organisation. As she recalled:

> *"Those high-level conversations gave me a lot of leads and contacts which I followed up in the following weeks. This led to a good understanding of who was doing data-related work, who was already doing reporting, who was creating their own databases, who was already doing something along the lines of data science, even though it might not have been called that. So, I took a good look around to see what was there because I strongly believe that you should leverage what you've already invested in."*

How many people should you talk to? Answer: as many as you possibly can:

> *"In every conversation I would ask who they believe in their areas I should speak to. In the first three months I identified and spoke to probably eighty people across the organisation."*

In the course of speaking to so many people, you will invariably come across groups doing interesting work. This is exactly what happened:

> *"[In the course of these conversations] I came across a lot of interesting work that was already taking place within the organisation. IoT[3] is something that was quite interesting. It was used in various pockets across the organisation, but in complete isolation of each other. So, there was one team that had done something really clever in some of our sites with IoT. And straightaway, I could see that it would be a wonderful use case to quickly transition to an actual analytics outcome. The data was flowing in, but they were only using it for alerts and monitoring, not for predictive asset maintenance. This was a perfect situation to demonstrate a quick win and also demonstrate how data analytics could then play out in the company and provide value."*

In the absence of a centralised data or data science function, it is not uncommon for organisations to have multiple but unconnected pockets of data excellence. This is something that we have noticed through our own experiences as well as those of other data leaders we spoke with. We discuss this more in Chapter 5 in relation to building a data culture and capability, acknowledging that there are likely elements of this that already exist in your organisation today. This in itself is a compelling argument for having an organisation-wide data science (or data analytics) strategy and a centralised data function. More importantly, as in the case above, such situations can present opportunities for setting up *proof of concept* (POC) demonstrations of the value of data science.

Unlike the above situation, you might not have access to senior executives in the organisation. However, this does not matter as your primary objective is to get an understanding of the landscape and look for opportunities to demonstrate the value of building a data science capability. This can be done by having conversations at *any* level in the organisation, from departmental managers to individual contributors. This is reminiscent of the approach taken by Kailash in the mini case study discussed in the previous section. In any case, regardless of whether you start at the top or not, the information that is immediately actionable will invariably come from the people who are closest to the actual work – frontline managers or team leaders and their direct reports. It is from such conversations that an execution plan will emerge. Indeed, as Sandra Hogan noted later in our conversation with her:

"So, the execution plan that emerged was around a couple of areas. Initially, it was actually two areas. One was the platform, because what I'd found in my conversations was that there was no consistent approach to collecting, maintaining and sharing data or leveraging data. Some people had an on-premise server, some had their data on AWS.....one, I kid you not, had a server under their desk. We had 14 distinct reporting applications being used - everyone just did their own thing with no coordination. So, I thought it would be good to coalesce these activities around a central platform that we could grow and scale. The second thing was use cases: we identified and agreed as a leadership team on eight use cases we would start with, and they were the eight that we would establish the platform with."

Note that she determined that setting up a central platform was one of the priorities. It is invariably the case that technical gaps and needs will come up during these conversations. We will talk about broader considerations around technology choices in Chapter 6.

It is important to note that the "what keeps you up at night?" question is universal; it works in contexts ranging from large organisations to start ups. As Duhita Khadepau, Head of Data at Assignar (a construction software start-up), mentioned to us:

"One of the first things I do when I get hired is to take some time to talk to the leaders within the business to understand what their pain points are. The things that keep them awake at night. Meeting their KPIs is a big one. For example, a Customer Success Manager in an organization I worked for said, 'Oh, my KPI is basically to keep the churn as low as possible, it is what keeps me awake.' What I then did was to examine their customer lifecycle to see what could be improved using data? Is there anything I could do, using the data we already had, to make their lives a bit easier. So typically, that is where I focus my initial conversations. Not talking about strategy, but staying focused on how data could help them solve their problems ... which in this case was keeping churn as low as possible."

So, regardless of your specific organisational context, the responses you receive to the "What keeps you up at night?" question will give you well-defined problems that, when solved, will demonstrate the value of data to the organisation.

When asked specifically about the prioritisation of POCs over strategy formulation, Duhita's response was crystal clear:

"If I spend my first three months just building a strategy, there's going to be nothing to justify it. If I start with small projects, and POCs, I can quickly show-case the value that it brings, or the value that my team and I can bring to the table. And as a result of this everyone gets more excited about investing in the data team and their work."

You need to demonstrate the value of a data science capability via POCs before formulating a strategy. Indeed, as we will see, the strategy will emerge from the POCs.

Demonstrating Value

Before undertaking a POC, you should be clear about why you are doing it. In particular, the POC should be aimed at demonstrating a clear value for the organisation. What this means is that you will often end up tackling a small sub-case of a much larger problem. Take, for example, rather than tackling the (rather big) problem of building a customer segmentation model[4] you might look at the smaller problem of understanding which products to display to a particular online customer based on their browsing and purchasing history. This is what Duhita did in one of her earlier roles as a Data Science Lead at an online fashion retailer:

> *"... start with a small sub-case. Say, for example, when I worked with marketing at [company name], they wanted to do customer segmentation. That was a huge problem, so I tried to scope it down by asking for a specific problem they had at that moment. They said, they had this problem of what online users should see when they come to the company website The aim was to minimize the scrolling they would have to do to get to the products they were interested in. So, we built this model based on customer history, which used the same principles one would use in a customer segmentation model, but the difference was that this was to solve a specific problem so it was considerably simpler. It was also easy to demonstrate the value of the model. I could actually demonstrate that instead of spending X dollars on say Facebook or you know, some sort of other target marketing strategy on a recurring basis, [it was better to] invest that money in technology and data instead."*

Sometimes business leaders may have a high-level objective that they want you to explicitly address in your strategy. Such objectives can usually be broken down into distinct elements that can be achieved independently of each other. Each of these elements can then be tackled using a POC that can be productionised (if the POC has demonstrated value). This is the approach that Kailash took when he started working at a not-for-profit organisation. Just before he joined, the organisation had started implementing a donor-centric approach to fundraising. A key element of this was to figure out the specific fundraising events and campaigns that potential donors were likely to respond to and approach them only for those. In marketing parlance, this is called a Next Best Action[5] approach. Clearly, building a model that predicts the best offer across all products is a big task; a programme rather than a project. So, what Kailash did was to start working with historical data on the organisation's most important campaign to see if it would be possible to figure which donors in the database were most likely to participate in the campaign. This is clearly not a Next Best Action model, but a first step towards one.

From his previous experience, Kailash was aware of potential scepticism and pushback from within the organisation. Historically, the marketing team had been using a traditional RFM (Recency, Frequency, Monetary Value) approach to determining which donors to target for specific campaigns. The approach, though extremely time consuming and labour intensive, was quite successful. It was therefore important to demonstrate that the new approach would do at least as well, if not better than the old one.

Here's how Josh McNeil (Direct Marketing and Campaigns Manager at Cancer Council NSW) summarised the approach to achieving this strategic objective:

> *"… one of the key [strategic] priorities is to give donors the offer that is best suited to them at the best time … a next best action approach. But within that, there's lots of smaller models that are required. So, we looked at the calendar of activity and historical data to determine which campaign we would tackle first. Once we identified the specific campaign, the data scientists within the team worked alongside other analysts who did business as usual [built RFM models]. Because the marketing people still had the familiar way of doing things in tandem with the new approach, it ensured that there would be no disruption for them. More importantly, it provided us the ability to validate, after the campaign, whether the new way would work better than the old way, or at least be no worse. And then if it did that, there's one piece of the bigger puzzle that's completed and can form a part of the Next Best Action model."*

It is important to keep in mind that the benefits of POCs cannot always be monetised. Indeed, more often than not, their value lies in the unexpected issues that are surfaced while designing and implementing them, and the learnings that follow as a consequence. This is exactly what happened in Kailash's project. When building the first predictive model, a number of duplicates were found in the database – i.e., several donors had been entered into the database multiple times, often with variations in names (e.g., K. Awati and Kailash Awati) and addresses (Unit 4, 23 Warren St and 4/23 Warren Street). Such data quality issues had to be addressed prior to building a predictive model, so the team spent a fair bit of time figuring out how best to address this issue[6] and implemented a solution based on it.

Identifying data gaps is another example of a common non-monetary benefit of POCs. The following story from Craig Napier, about one of his early POCs at the University of Technology Sydney, is a case in point:

> *"Historically we have a number of different support structures in place to assist students who have failed [subjects]. This is fantastic, but it brings up a question: is it better to identify students who are struggling and provide them the right support when they need it? So, we are really talking about a pre-dictive model that can identify some signs that indicate that a student might be struggling before they submit assignments or sit exams. A lot of it is around interactions, and we identified that we had some data gaps in relation to that.*

For example, just because somebody doesn't engage with the online material on our LMS (Learning Management System) it doesn't mean they are struggling. Conversely, high engagement with the material doesn't mean they're going to succeed, it just means that you know they are interacting. What seems to be the case is that students will stop engaging when they fall behind. We are trying to understand what other data points we need and whether we can collect them via the LMS or other avenues. These are the things that we're trying to explore [through POCs]. We weren't asking these questions previously. We were reactive."

Indeed, it is rarely the case that you will have all the data you need at hand or that it will be perfectly clean. There are almost always gaps that will need to be filled or data quality issues that need to fixed before you can start moving from reporting to predicting. Understanding and dealing with these early is an important part of capability building.

To close this section, we would like to emphasise that despite its name, a POC should be done not to prove an idea, but to prove value. This point is best made by Craig Napier (Chief Data Officer at University of Technology Sydney), who said:

"But as we [have these conversations] we often find we don't have the technology to support some of the new capabilities we need. Historically, I think we've overused the "proof of concept" approach. It's my very strong view that we really shouldn't be proving a concept, we should already know the concepts we'll work with. We should change [our mindset] to proof of value. A big part of my role is to show people where we need to go. If we're spending all their [and our] time in proving concepts, that's all we'll do. We'll never overcome the challenge of moving a concept to production. And that's a waste of effort, a waste of time. So, let's invest our effort and time in proving business value [of things we propose to do]."

Asking open-ended problem seeking questions is the most direct route to formulating POCs that have clear business value.

Additional Benefits of "Problem Finding"

As we have seen asking questions such as "what keeps you up at night?" opens doors to finding problems that can form the basis of POCs. These POCs will address problems that matter to people who matter in the organisation. In other words, they are the first steps towards enhancing the data capabilities of the organisation in a meaningful way. However, there's a lot more that can be gleaned from the conversations. In particular, we would like to draw your attention to three things that you should listen out for:

1. People who work with data.
2. Technologies used.
3. Important data sources.

When people talk about their data "pain points" or the kinds of analyses that would help them meet or exceed their KPIs, they will invariably mention the reports, analyses, and data they currently rely on, if only to point out the shortcomings in them. These are cues for you to ask further questions about these:

1. Who creates and maintains the reports? Who performs the analyses?
2. How are the analyses performed and presented? Who do they matter to? What decisions and actions do they inform?
3. Where is the data stored? How often is it refreshed?

If your interviewees are senior management or executives, they may not have all the answers. However, they will be able to direct you to someone who will have them. Following up on these pointers will help you get a sense for the following important aspects of your strategy:

1. The skills currently available within the organisation.
2. The data landscape.
3. The technologies used.

To be sure, the picture built will be an incomplete one. However, when you're starting out, it is far more helpful to identify the above elements using this seemingly informal approach rather than a formal data, technology, and skills mapping exercise. Why? Because the elements you identify are tied to a specific business context – in other words, in addition to knowing what exists, you will understand why it exists. This seemingly random approach is far more useful than going through a separate data, technology, and skill mapping exercise.

Many years ago, Kailash did an organisation-wide data and technology mapping exercise to identify all data sources across the organisation, the data flows between them, technologies used and the analysts and end users who consumed the data. The exercise took a couple of months and helped identify data systems that were badly in need of an upgrade and even some that could be retired. However, from a strategic perspective, the exercise was of limited value because it was framed around maintaining the status quo rather than enhancing it. Ever since then, he has eschewed organisation-wide data and capability mapping exercises in favour of finding the ones that really matter – and he found that these are best surfaced indirectly, by asking the "what keeps you up at night?" question.

Powerful Questions

The "what keeps you up at night?" question that we have used at length in this chapter is an example of what we have referred to as *powerful questions* elsewhere:

> *Organisation-land tends to be full of people who ask questions based on man-agement models they have learnt in business school or read about in Forbes or Harvard Business Review. These include questions such as "What should our vision be?", "What should our data strategy be?" and "What are your reporting requirements?" While these sorts of questions are very important and definitely need to be answered, asking them at an early stage, usually elicits less than useful answers unless the problem is very well defined. When the problem is ill-defined (and strategy is an ill-defined problem) people often struggle to give meaningful answers and those given tend to be formulaic, missing important points that become obvious only in hindsight.*
>
> *Culmsee and Awati 2016, p.166*

In contrast, a question like "what keeps you up at night?" elicits responses that matter to individuals rather than organisations ... and indeed, one may well ask if anything can matter to an organisation in the same way as it might to a human. Such questions, therefore, indirectly get at concrete things that you can do that will make a difference to someone. And if you do those things, you will have gained a supporter. As we noted in Chapter 3, Emergent Design practitioners use conversations to gain commitments, and that is exactly what you are doing here.

There is another powerful question that can be useful in clarifying vague requirements that come up in the context of data capability building. The question and its utility are best illustrated by example:

As a part of enhancing organisational data capabilities, you may be asked to develop and implement a *data governance* framework.

The problem with a term like *data governance* is that it is hard to pin down because it is interpreted differently by different people in the organisation. We discuss data (and AI) governance in greater detail in Chapter 8, but here is a possible powerful question to unpack what the term means in the specific context of your organisation:

> *How would things be better if we had a data governance framework in place?*

This question forces people to think in terms of concrete improvements rather than abstractions. It works best when used in group settings in which the group is composed of stakeholders from different branches of the organisation – e.g., IT, marketing, and finance. A question like, "How would things be different (or better) if we successfully implemented a data governance framework?"

    a. Refocuses the group's attention on the desired end state rather than the means to get there.

    b. Is not bound by any governance framework imposed up-front.

    c. Fosters a shared understanding of the current situation by eliciting multiple viewpoints, thus building an appreciation of the specific context surrounding the issue of data governance.

    d. Invites answers like "Increased X", "Eliminating Y", or "Decreasing Z". These are useful because it gives insight into potential ways in which one can measure success. Further, this provides an excellent segue into other activities that are aimed at defining key performance indicators (KPIs) to quantify successful governance (something which is traditionally hard to pin down!).

Such questions mitigate blind reliance on formal frameworks because a working model has been constructed by the group. That said, once you have constructed a working model you should sense check it against a canned framework to ensure that you have not missed anything important. You may also consider having a look at the canned framework beforehand so that you can nudge attendees to think about issues that are not raised in the course of the discussion. The strange thing is that if you read the fine print on any popular framework, such as those proposed in the DMBOK,[7] they were only ever intended to be used this way – i.e., as a basis for constructing your own.

We'll talk about data governance in much more detail in Chapter 8. As we will see, you cannot plonk a canned framework on your organisation and expect it to work. Success depends on your implemented processes and structures making life easier or better for people in your organisation. Questions such as the ones above will help you figure out how to do that.

Designing for the Future

When designing POCs, it is important to think about their longer term consequences. Even with a well understood POC, it can be easy to fixate on the short term as it presents the most pressing and concrete problems. However, you want to be thinking about what Nadler and Hibino (1990), who we met briefly in Chapter 3, called the "solution after next" – what problems could this POC lead to and how are we going to address them? This is all about longer term vision. In a sense, it is an attempt to gaze into a crystal ball and see what the future consequences of a solution might be. It stimulates the exploration of future scenarios with a view to providing insight into solutions currently being considered by the group. Some of the considerations that might be important are:

1. Does the proposed solution have any downsides? If successful, will the solution have any consequences that are not immediately obvious? Chapter 8 offers an ethical lens on this question.

2. Are we thinking broadly enough? What are the directions in which this solution might be generalised? Are there other branches of the organisation that might have use cases that can benefit from similar approaches, techniques, or technologies?

3. Are the technologies we propose to use in this solution limiting in any way? In particular, can they interoperate with other technologies?

Answering these questions may entail taking an "outside view" – i.e., consulting individuals from groups/departments other than the one that will benefit from the solution.

In closing this chapter, we would like to reiterate an important aspect of Emergent Design that we have discussed in this and earlier chapters: when designing solutions, it is important to keep in mind that in real life *problems are never given, they have to be taken*, i.e., they have to be formulated from business situations. In other words, it is the situation that is given, not the problem. The problem that one extracts from a situation depends a lot on how one frames the situation … and there are many different ways in which a situation can be framed. For example, a solution that optimises an outcome for a particular business unit might do so at the expense of another unit. This happens when multiple business units share the same customer base. What is important, therefore, is to seek as broad a consensus as one can for one's POCs as they will likely determine the support you get for your strategy.

Notes

1 Note that this is distinct from rejection of an idea due to the fear of the changes it entails. We have discussed the latter at length in the previous chapter.

2 https://eight2late.wordpress.com/2013/07/03/overcoming-the-corporate-imm une-system-some-lessons-from-the-dengue-virus/

3 IoT = Internet of Things: https://en.wikipedia.org/wiki/Internet_of_things

4 A customer segmentation model groups customers into categories that align with their purchasing propensities for a company's products.

5 Next Best Action is a customer-centric marketing paradigm that considers the different actions that can be taken for a specific customer and decides on the "best" one. An (usually) predictive model that supports this marketing approach is called a Next Best Action model.

6 For reasons that should be obvious, we called this the "John Smith Problem", which we solved using the approach detailed in: https://eight2late.wordpress.com/2019/10/09/tackling-the-john-smith-problem-deduplicating-data-via-fuzzy-matching-in-r/

7 Data Management Body of Knowledge: www.dama.org/cpages/body-of-knowledge

---

References

Birkinshaw, J. and Ridderstråle, J. (1999), "Fighting the corporate immune system: A process study of subsidiary initiatives in multinational corporations", *International Business Review, 8*(2), pp. 149–180.

Culmsee, P. and Awati, K. (2014), "The map and the territory: A practitioner perspective on knowledge cartography", in Okada, A., Buckingham Shum, S. and Sherborne, T. (Eds), *Knowledge Cartography: Advanced Information and Knowledge Processing*, Springer, London, pp. 261–292. doi: 10.1007/978-1-4471-6470-8_12

Culmsee, P. and Awati, K. (2016), *The Heretic's Guide to Management: The Art of Harnessing Ambiguity*, Heretics Guide Press, Marsfield, Australia.

Nadler, G. and Hibino, S. (1990), *Breakthrough Thinking*, Prima Publications and Communications, Indianapolis, IN.

5

Capability and Culture

Introduction

At this stage in your journey, you likely have an idea of *what* you are going to do. That is, you have defined a direction which includes use cases and problems from various business units gleaned through explorations of your organisation's problem space. It is now time to put in place the capabilities required to forge a path in the desired direction. Related to this is the more elusive notion of establishing a *data culture* – i.e., creating an environment in which data-supported decision-making will take root and thrive. We will cover both these topics in this chapter.

When it comes to capability building, the first thing that comes to mind is the technical talent shortage, exacerbated by side effects of the pandemic and global economic changes. You may therefore be worried about how exactly you are going to find or develop the technical skills required for a data science capability. The first question is: given that good tech skills are hard to find, should you (*can* you?) attempt to hire the people you need to execute your POCs? As always with such questions, there is no definitive, one-size-fits all answer. However, what we have found from our own experience, confirmed by discussions with data leaders, is that there is quite a bit that you can do by harnessing the skills and enthusiasm of existing staff. If done right, this can greatly alleviate the need for significant budget to hire and pay top-market rates for data talent. Indeed, a certain magic happens when an organisation is able to develop a data capability internally. Among other things, it engenders a sense of confidence that simply cannot be created by hiring expensive talent.

In this chapter, we discuss how to build internal capability, develop a data culture, and enhance organisational data literacy. Additionally, we also provide some advice that can help with the "buy" side of the equation, including tips and tricks for hiring and working with vendors, as well as some potentials traps we have gleaned from our experience and research.

DOI: 10.1201/9781003260158-5

Data Talent Archetypes

The first question to consider when aligning your projects with talent required is: what are the different roles out there in the data space and what do they generally do. The second, more pertinent question is – what can they do for you? As we go through the roles, you will notice there is a natural alignment of the roles to the analytics stack and maturity model presented in Chapter 2. It is therefore worth referencing the model (Figure 2.1) as you go along.

Just as putting huge investment in the latest vendor-promoted tool before developing an understanding of people and problems is an exercise in futility, so is hiring the wrong people at the wrong time. Below we outline some of the key roles that exist in the market today. Some of these may be familiar as they have been around for quite some time, others are newer ones that have come into their own in recent years. Understanding what these roles do and, just as importantly, *how people with these role titles see themselves*, can assist in aligning talent with your envisioned projects.

An important reminder before we proceed: the smaller the organisation, the greater the overlap between roles. Accordingly, we will point out overlaps between roles to indicate areas where it may be possible to cross-skill staff.

Database Administrators, Data Engineers, and Data Warehouse Architects

We begin with a classic archetype that has been around since data and data systems have existed: the *Database Administrator (DBA)*. This role dates back to the late 1980s when relational database systems such as Oracle and Sybase (later Microsoft SQL Server) became mainstays of the enterprise data landscape. In the following two decades, DBAs have been responsible for the smooth running and security of enterprise databases, hosted either in-house or in dedicated data centres. Since organisations typically owned the infrastructure back then, the DBA would also be responsible for implementing backup and recovery plans. In those days, it was also common for DBAs to be called on to assist with ad-hoc data extracts as well as for advice on approaches to building, tuning, and automating data pipelines between different systems – things that would, in today's parlance, be termed *data engineering*.

Data Engineers are primarily responsible for building data pipelines to transfer data between different, usually heterogeneous, systems. We referred to these pipelines as ETL (extract-transform-load) processes in Chapter 2. A typical data engineering task might be to build a pipeline to extract data from a cloud-based CRM system (such as SalesForce) to a local (or cloud-based) data warehouse. A data engineer would be responsible for designing, coding, and automating the transfer, as well as ensuring that the transferred data is consistent with that in the source system. As part of the transfer, the data engineer may also transform the data – for example, split names into first name and last name. As more organisations move to the cloud, the data engineer role has morphed somewhat into that of a *cloud data engineer*, an individual with skills in a particular cloud environment such as Microsoft Azure or Amazon Web Services[1] in addition to traditional data engineering competencies.

Continuing with this thread, there are professionals who are responsible for designing the analytical data storage system.[2] These folks are called *data warehouse architects*. This role is largely about designing systems that integrate different data sources into commonly recognised architectures (typically, star schemas and fact/dimension tables which we discussed in Chapter 2). We should mention that the distinction between data engineers and architects is often quite fuzzy; in small organisations, a single person may assume both roles. Even in large organisations, the design and implementation of ETL components are usually shared between both, although in some cases – particularly where there are many data sources – there may be a partitioning of roles with design decisions resting with the architect and implementation with the engineer.

Key Skills

- A common element between these roles is strong skills in SQL to query, create, and maintain database systems.
- Knowledge of different data systems, particularly around how to get data out, the different data formats, how different pieces of data are related, and who (which business unit) owns the different pieces of data.
- A general-purpose programming language (such as Python) and some scripting skills (Bash/Unix/Powershell).

What They Do

- **Data warehouse architect**: Brings together disparate data sources to a single place. Designs and implements data warehouse table structures; provides advice on design of pipelines based on specifics of the infrastructure; builds data pipelines (unless there is a dedicated data engineer). Additionally, architects may also be responsible for stakeholder management and project management.
- **Data engineer**: Builds, monitors, and enhances the pipelines that feed data into the analytical storage system. Performs ad-hoc data extracts.

What They Don't Do

- Architects and engineers are typically not responsible for analysing data, building dashboards, or writing reports. However, most can do this task if needed but many would prefer not to.
- They will usually not undertake statistical analysis or build machine learning models.

Business Intelligence (BI) Developers and Analysts

Up the next level of the data analytics stack are those who build reporting and visualisation systems including dashboards. The main distinction between the developer and analyst role is that developers traditionally build, monitor, and enhance dashboards, while analysts, though they may assist in report building, also respond to ad-hoc business questions pertaining to the reports and are usually responsible for preparing custom reports and SQL-based analyses for end-users.

Since they are responsible for building artefacts that stakeholders see and work with, BI developers will usually work with stakeholders to identify their reporting needs prior to building dashboards. Some dashboards enable business stakeholders to see the data they need regularly to report on; others enable them to explore the data themselves (via filters, dropdowns, etc.).

An important factor to keep in mind is that a BI analyst – as opposed to a more general programmer/analyst or machine learning analyst – is focused on dashboarding tools and SQL rather than languages such as R or Python that are used to perform more advanced statistical analysis and machine learning. That said, there are BI analysts (and developers!) who do much more than dashboard and report building. Safe to say that if someone in either of these roles is regularly coding up machine learning products, it is time for a job title upgrade! We'll say more about this in the next subsection.

Key Skills

- Requirements gathering to identify and document reporting and analytical needs.
- Dashboarding and report building using tools like Power BI and Tableau.
- SQL.

What They Do

- Make data accessible to end users.
- Build, maintain, and enhance reports and dashboards.

- Perform ad-hoc data analyses, mainly using dashboarding tools.
- Work closely with data engineers/data warehouse architects to optimise complex queries or source new data.

What They Don't Do

- They *generally* won't be involved in statistical analysis, advanced modelling of data or machine learning.

From Analyst to Data Scientist

BI analysts not only build dashboards but also *explore* data to find patterns and/or answer specific questions that have not been catered for in reports. This is where the distinction between roles becomes quite fuzzy: what would you call an analyst who can query data (SQL) and analyse data (dashboards, coding languages like R and Python), and even potentially model data (statistics, machine learning) in order to answer a question posed by a business stakeholder?

Answer: a budding data scientist.

A typical data scientist should know SQL, be able to build a dashboard, and be comfortable exploring data to answer questions using programming languages such as R and Python. Generally, the key criterion that distinguishes a full-fledged data scientist from other roles is a knowledge of machine learning and more advanced analytical techniques. However, there are analysts who can and have deployed these techniques to provide great value in business contexts, even if they are not deemed data scientists by their titles.

Key Skills

- Analysts generally have the ability to craft complex queries to explore and analyse data and therefore must have advanced SQL skills. Often, they will also be able to create a dashboard using BI tools. In addition, a good number of analysts today are dabbling in Python or R to manipulate, visualise, explore, and model data.
- Data scientists are generally expected to have all of the above skills plus stronger skills in statistics and machine learning. These days they are increasingly expected to have experience in working with common cloud platforms (see Chapter 6), not just to store and access data, but also to build models and operationalise them. We will say more about cloud platforms in Chapter 6 and building/operationalising models in Chapter 7.

What They Can Do for You

- Analysts and data scientists *should be* storytellers. Many aren't!
- Both analysts and data scientists should be able to take business questions, translate that into technical work, bring together data and domain knowledge in undertaking the work, and develop actionable insights that inform decisions.

How they differ lies in the kinds of questions they answer. For example, an analyst can answer questions such as:

- *Who are our top customers? Where are they located?*
- *What are our top products? Which customers are purchasing specific items or categories of items?*
- *How are our metrics tracking year-on-year? Are there any exceptional regions (under or over performing)?*

Given appropriate data, a data scientist should be able to answer questions like:

- *Can you predict which product any given customer is most likely to buy? (What should we recommend to whom?)*
- *What will our sales be in the next few quarters?*
- *Can we recommend articles, based on what a user has typed in their support ticket?*
- *Can we count the number of shoppers in our store at any given point in time (given video footage from in-store cameras)?*[3]

What They Don't Do

- As noted, while these individuals probably *could*, under pressure, build data pipelines and stores, this isn't the most valuable use of their time, nor is it aligned with positive outcomes for job satisfaction.

The above examples should help clarify the distinction between these roles. Analyses that involve dashboarding or SQL lie in the domain of analysts whereas those that entail the use of advanced algorithms or involve the construction of predictive models are squarely in the realm of data scientists. That said, analysts who are curious and willing to learn can, with some effort on their part, become competent data scientists. Indeed, given the current shortage of talent in the area of data science, it is well worth considering hiring for potential to become a data scientist rather than hiring an experienced one. We'll say more about this later in this chapter.

Newer Data Roles

It is worth mentioning a few of the newer roles that are beginning to appear in the analytics world. These are: *analytics engineer, machine learning scientist,* and *machine learning engineer.* The first two of these are not as yet typical of a modern analytics team. However, as they are gaining more traction in the market, it is worth briefly noting what they do so that you can determine whether your organisation requires them.

Analytics engineer is a curious title that has been around for a while but has taken off only recently.[4] Found most often in tech companies, especially newer software and product-led organisations, one can think of them sitting on the edge of the data lake, taking requests from the "surface dwellers" (the world of analytics and data science), then diving into the lake to bring back what is desired. Concretely, their role is to build data assets from the data lake for analytics teams or projects. As the mantra of a data lake is "pour data in first, figure out structure later", this role has emerged to facilitate the most obvious issue that arises as a consequence: identifying and extracting data from a heterogeneous and (often) messy data lake.

Machine learning scientists are most commonly seen in larger, more mature analytics functions, particularly those that support research and development work. Most data scientists in modern teams are *users* of existing algorithms rather than builders of new ones. Machine learning scientists, on the other hand, research new algorithms and develop new techniques. They typically build their own systems and tools. That said, there is a bit of "role title creep", so you may find folks who call themselves machine learning scientists but don't create new algorithms or techniques. Rather, they use established algorithms and approaches to explore new domains.

Much like analytics engineers, *machine learning engineers* have become more visible in recent times. This role is a hybrid between a data engineer, data scientist, and practitioners from the modern technical sub-field of DevOps,[5] which melds traditionally distinct functions of software *dev*elopment and IT *op*erations into a single function. DevOps really came into its own as organisations began to migrate their on-premise IT infrastructures to the cloud. In a cloud environment, the distinction between development and operations work is blurred because the environment enables rapid development and testing, thus reducing the time it takes to productionise or enhance software products.

Most data science teams tend to be heavy users of cloud platforms and therefore tend to operate in this mode, so much so that there is a new subfield of MLOps. We'll say much more about MLOps in Chapter 7. For now, we'll make the point that a machine learning engineer does for data science what a DevOps engineer does for software development. In other words, the role is critical for productionising and maintaining models built by the data science team. Machine learning engineers understand enough data science to know the different data and technical requirements for the different inputs and outputs of the system, but they may not be model builders per se. This role may not be needed at the start, but it is important to have someone on your team who can do this work as you move from proofs-of-concept to productionising and deploying your data analytics and data science outputs.

Other Roles

In addition to the above, you may need *project managers, designers,* and *software engineers* to scope, manage, and ultimately productionise analytical work. As an example, in a product-led software company, a data scientist may be engaged early to run experiments that can help scope and make decisions on potential product opportunities (i.e., choose between a range of options). They may also be involved in building the analytical engine (model) that does something useful (say, personalisation for a customer facing website). However, the design of the front end would be facilitated by a *designer*; the implementation would be the work of *software engineers* and there would likely be a *project/product management* role involved to coordinate the work done by all these parties. Whilst this may seem to call for a lot of additional staff, it is important to keep in mind that a number of these roles probably exist within your organisation already. As in the example above, a web-driven software company will certainly already have software engineering, design, and product management functions which can be readily engaged for an analytics project. They may need to develop an understanding of the unique aspects of analytics projects but, in our experience, this can be learnt on the job.

The Right Timing

It is important to emphasise that building an analytics team is not a linear process. At first sight, it may appear that one needs data engineers first, and only once the data warehouse is built should one bring in a BI specialist (analyst or developer) to build reports, following which it is permissible to bring in an analyst to begin answering questions … and so on. However, this approach is fraught with peril as it overlooks the essential interactions between different elements of the stack. It is better to involve roles from across the stack early as this can inform technical choices and architectural decisions that can be hard to undo later.

In addition, it is important to note that business value is not solely gleaned from productionised projects. So, for example, it is perfectly permissible to bring in a BI developer or analyst while the data infrastructure is being built, even if their work isn't going to be deployed immediately into enterprise production environments. Indeed, a lot of analytics work never needs to be productionised because it answers one-off questions that inform business decisions or plans. As long as the analyst can get data (even as direct extracts from the source systems) and has access to the necessary tools, they can answer questions and provide business stakeholders with insights to support decision-making processes. In fact, this should be encouraged as it is precisely such work that shapes the direction of your nascent data science function. Here is what Zanne van Wyk (Worldwide Education Industry Architect at Microsoft) had to say about this process:

> "… I had to appoint a team because there was no team, I was given a blank slate. Since the future state had a strong emphasis on data science, the first hire was a data scientist. I wanted their input into everything from the start (remembering, people first before process and technology) and knew they could begin work using the data systems we had. However, I also knew that we will require data transformation, integration and pipelines to productionise the work and so next was a data engineer and it grew from there. The team began immediately targeting low-hanging fruit and showing value so we could pitch for more funding to expand our projects and take on larger pieces of work."

This was echoed by Josh McNeil from Cancer Council:

> "The team originally had good builders. People proficient in SQL who were reliable and skilled, who would always just deliver what they've been instructed to. However, to deliver on the future state; they needed data science skills to provide the extra value and models which would inform our marketing efforts – who we should talk to, what time and what to tell them … ."

The point being that your hiring should be dictated not by an abstract roadmap, but by what will deliver value in the immediate short- to mid-term. Here we see an important link between development of talent and our main message of Chapter 4 about the power of incremental, POC projects as you build out your analytics capability in an emergent way. To be sure, productionising analytics work requires a robust data stack. But to *begin* this process, we would recommend focusing on the skills required to deliver immediate value.

A word of warning with this approach though: it is vital to be open and honest with new staff regarding the current state of your analytics capability. One of the main complaints of data scientists who quit jobs they have taken up recently is a mismatch between expectations and reality. Any manager will know that (and perhaps you have your own experiences here as well!) churn is difficult enough to manage when people are leaving on good terms for good reasons. Churn for negative reasons such as dissatisfaction due to mismatches between job descriptions and reality is even more challenging to manage and can derail your efforts to build an organisational data capability.

Building Capability

When looking out into the market to fill in some of the roles discussed above, it may feel like an impossible mission. The ongoing talent shortage and high salary expectations will appear to conspire against the limited budget you have been allocated to build the new function. A short digression about a research project carried out in suburban Los Angeles about a decade ago may provide some insight into how you can work around this problem.

In 2012, Brian Brown and Emily Hartop,[6] entomologists at Los Angeles's Natural History Museum were working in suburban LA as part of the Museum's BioScan project. The project involved setting up traps and capturing devices for flies around backyards in suburban LA with the aim of finding new species of insects. The project was a huge success, with the first search revealing over 30 new insect species (and many more[7] in the subsequent years).

In analogy, it is quite likely there is data talent lurking within your own "organisational backyard". There are almost certainly groups of dispersed people who are exploring data, building reports and visualisations, and, dare we say, making small forays into data science. Although these adventurous individuals might lack the time or confidence to jump back into formal education outside of work, they are likely to grab the opportunity to learn on the job by working on analytics or data science projects. There may be others who are less keen on becoming data scientists or analytics specialists but want to be able to use data tools to understand what data science can do for the organisation. All these people are your allies in building a capability inexpensively yet effectively.

Sandra Hogan, who we heard from in Chapter 4, used an innovative approach to identify talent in her organisation. Here, in her own words, is the approach she used:

> "... we identified about 150 people across the company who self-selected themselves as working in data analytics. We ran them through a voluntary technical assessment, with questions around data management, statistics, and presentation skills. About half the people did the assessment. The results were helpful in two ways, First, it helped us identify the gaps in skills. Second, we also identified the really highly technical people who were ready for more technical training [towards data science] ... ."

This approach can be very fruitful and is worth discussing in a bit more detail.

Identifying and Growing Talent

When running internal assessments or courses to identify talent or upskill staff, it is important to cast your net wide. For example, running an *"introduction to machine learning in python"* course will only attract those who are considering moving into data science and are confident enough to make the move. In contrast, an *introduction to programming course using Python* would cast a wider net, and a course on *building dashboards* a wider net still. To be sure, the courses you offer will depend on what you need, but the point is to pitch them at the widest possible audience of people who might end up being your future data scientists.

How do you draw attention to your course offerings and the work you are doing? Some of the specific techniques we have seen at work include:

- Self-selection into levelled programmes (beginner, intermediate, advanced, etc.).
- Voluntary tests to place people into levelled programs.
- Tapping into middle management to volunteer people for the programme (as part of regular career planning procedures).
- Organisation-wide broadcasts such as introduction sessions to answer questions about internal career development opportunities relating to data.
- Open invitations to some of the ongoing development opportunities, even if only to view or audit rather than participate actively.
- Putting out a call to join a data champions or data interest group. Some who join such groups are also keen to learn new data skills.

The important thing to remember is that people will typically underestimate their abilities when self-selecting, thinking that a lack of formal training disqualifies them from joining up. It is therefore important to frame your approach in a way that appeals to a wide audience. You may even want to do an initial seminar outlining your plans to identify talent. This should be done on a periodic basis so that someone who missed out on an earlier session, or didn't quite feel ready then, can hop on board with a future cohort.

Another quite immediately accessible potential pool of talent often lies within your IT or – if you are a technical product organisation – software development teams. Here's what Duhita Khadepau (Director of Analytics and Data Science at a construction tech startup), who we met in the last chapter, had to say about this:

> *"Get your (software/data) engineers to do more; there is stuff they can do in the analytics, MLOps space given they already have the technical skills and there are tools which can assist to get them a long way in terms of analytical tasks … .*

Building on a single stack enables incremental learning to be easier (for example, AWS and the continual stream of new services they release)."

The advantage of such people is that they generally have the technical nous to pick up data science skills on their own.

Designing Training Programmes

In order for the courses to have the greatest chance of success, there are some considerations around how they should be designed and run.

Firstly, they should be run as cohort-based training programmes rather than just offering people access to online training programmes such as LinkedIn Learning. Our experience is that people never find the time to do online courses and, more importantly, learning alone is much less effective than doing so in a group. Cohort-based training programmes have the advantage of getting people to network informally, support each other, and even become collaborators down the line. Any data analytics professional will attest to the importance of having a professional network. Unfortunately, it is often the case that they actually work in isolation. Giving them peers to engage with and learn from can enhance staff morale and satisfaction. Cohorts facilitate this collegiate feeling where bonds of peers and "classmates" can be formed.

A second consideration relates to the practical utility of the courses that are offered. Both of us have taught a variety of courses in business and analytics to many diverse groups of students. In all cases, it is the *practical* and *real* nature of the courses we put together that resulted in student satisfaction and was reflected in the excellent feedback we received. For example, many courses on machine learning teach students the theory and assess understanding via exams in which students are tested on how algorithms work or the technical considerations when implementing them. This is *not* the approach we use. Instead, we teach the theory in an intuitive and example-driven approach (though there is necessarily some math involved!). When it comes to assessments, we draw them from real business situations. As a specific example from our classes, students are given past sales data for a car retailer and are required to predict which customers are likely to be repeat purchasers. In addition, they are asked to deliver a business-oriented report for the marketing manager. The latter requires them to focus on the story hidden in the data rather than demonstrate technical virtuosity via good performance metrics. Adapting this principle to corporate training, teaching the theory and code is one thing but the best learnings come from tackling a real corporate problem from your own data (ideally in groups) with the instructor playing an advisory/mentoring role. As we will discuss further when covering ethics in Chapter 8, data training is an excellent opportunity to embed your ethical practices. This is very much in line with what some of the data leaders we spoke with said. Here, for example, is Sandra Hogan's take on this matter:

> *"Whilst courses to develop skills are useful there is always the question of how it is applied. So, any courses that are undertaken ideally should be paired with practical tasks, projects or exercises to make them real."*

We'd go so far as to say that one can even afford to cut back on teaching more advanced algorithms techniques and spend more time facilitating this approach instead. We have found that once students gain confidence in tackling real-world problems, including presentations to business stakeholders, they will go off and pick up advanced techniques on their own on an as-needed basis. When people are motivated, learning comes for free.

Immersion and Other Approaches

The principle behind immersion-based approaches is to put people in situations where they do the job of data scientists or analysts. One way to do this is through secondments or embeddings. This is where analytics professionals are embedded within a business unit for a specified period during which they work on projects relevant to the unit while also mentoring and upskilling analysts within the unit. The projects need not be mission-critical as success here comes from allowing for *learning time* to be built into the project. Although striking the balance between delivering a useful project and upskilling others can be challenging, we have seen that such embeddings result in a rapid upskilling of analysts because they are able to work closely with more experienced analytics professionals. An added benefit is that knowledge flows both ways as the analytics professionals pick up domain knowledge. Moreover, those who are looking to move into analytics leadership roles may find such secondments useful for their own development.

Immersion is a powerful catalyst for accelerating learning. Those who have resided in a country whose language they were unfamiliar with would know this from lived experience – one has to learn the language to do even the simplest tasks such as buying groceries! However, part-time secondments are also something we have seen succeed. In one of the analytics teams that Alex ran, he had team members who would spend two days each week with the central data warehouse team to learn the ins and outs of the data pipelines and architecture. The knowledge gained greatly enhanced the team's capability to build better dashboards and analytics solutions.

Hackathons are an extreme version of immersion. We have participated, mentored, and assisted in a variety of these over the last few years, both internally and externally as public events, and have gained a great deal each time, both in terms of enjoyment and learning. To maximise participation, hackathons typically run over weekends with a run-sheet looking something like this:

1. **Prior to the event**

   Challenges are posted; teams are formed and registered.

2. **Friday night**

   People arrive and mingle. There is an opening address from the companies or departments that put up the data and challenges as well as the sponsors (the folks who pay for the pizza and beer throughout the weekend!). The starting gun sounds and the click-clack of keyboards start.

3. **Saturday**

   Teams beaver away at the challenge, pausing for brainstorming sessions, coffee/food breaks, and visits from mentors who walk around the venue offering advice to those who need it.

   Typically, hackathon challenges may involve some sort of predictive task or may be more open-ended in that teams are asked to find insights from a dataset and tell a story. The mentors play an important part here, standing at arms-length and advising teams on technical hurdles. Representatives from the sponsors or companies who provided the data may also be floating around so the teams can confirm their understanding of the data, sense-check their initial findings, and get some advice that might help in charting out next steps.

   Additionally, it is common to bring all teams together, at least once, to do a quick stand-up around the room in which people discuss what they are working on, their most immediate challenges, and potentially seek advice from other teams. Examples could be "we are trying to visualise this network data but are getting errors with this package". Collegiate acts where members from teams share knowledge and time to help each other get past their blockers are encouraged.

   A hearty meal of pizza and beer (and more coffee) fuel the participants to hack away into the evening.

4. **Sunday**

   It is nearly over. After several more coffee runs, attention turns from the technical work to the presentations. Through the hackathons we have been involved in, we can confidently say that the efforts put into translating the technical work into a visually pleasing presentation and story is by far the most important differentiator between teams. This makes sense: the judging panel is mostly composed of folks from managerial ranks and one has to be able to communicate the significance of one's work to them. Alex vividly remembers a particular hackathon in which a team of PhD-in-Mathematics data scientists were presenting slides full of math and code which were received with total incomprehension. When asked to explain the significance of the results in plain English, the exasperated presenter said, *"Can't you see, this algorithm is beautiful. It is beautiful!"* The team did not place very highly in the final scores.

Final presentations usually take place in the early afternoon with winners being announced soon after. The remainder of the afternoon then eases into drinks and networking opportunities.

In describing hackathons in some detail, our intent is to highlight the benefits to all parties involved. For the more junior participants, the immersion and time pressure dramatically accelerate learning: more can be learned in those 48 hours than in an entire semester of university coursework. Senior participants are able to show off to potential employers by enhancing their analytics profile via a placing. All participants are able to build connections with peers across industries and with the sponsoring organisations. Plus, of course, it is great fun.

There are a number of benefits for participating organisations too. Hackathons are a great way to harness the brain power of multiple teams of data scientists to address problems that are in the organisations' "too hard" basket. For the cost of some prize money, pizza and beer, they can get several teams of data scientists working on their problem and produce a minimally viable product. Where else can you get a handful of prototypes built by experts in such a short turn-around time? Additionally, there have been organisations we have spoken to at these events who make no secret whatsoever about using these hackathons as talent-finding exercises. Organisations could pay recruiters tens of thousands of dollars for the contacts and first-hand interactions with data analytics professionals. You can do that for a lot less money and gain a lot more learning by hosting a hackathon over a weekend.

Seeing the benefits of hackathons, many organisations host internal events. Atlassian famously runs their "Shipit" hackathon multiple times a year across the world with hundreds of participants building thousands of projects each year and having a great time learning new skills and building connections along the way.[8] Other organisations have innovation days, innovation weeks, or the famous "20% time" of Google that produced Google Maps and other great innovations.[9] Some have miniature versions of this with one Friday a month as their own study or innovation day. Of course, giving staff such a large chunk of time to work on innovative analytics projects may not be the easiest sell so early in developing and executing your data science strategy. Yet, giving staff dedicated work time on a hackathon over a few work days that rolls into a Friday evening with social drinks perhaps, can act as a miniature, compressed and accelerated secondment of sorts. Involving people from other business units as roving subject matter, experts can be an excellent way to spark wider interest in the new data science function and develop a data culture within the broader organisation.

Another technique that bridges the chasm between building and buying talent is to make use of the learning opportunities that come with engaging vendors. If you are in the position to use vendors as part of building your strategy then there is the oft overlooked opportunity to get them to help with the development of your internal data talent. Normally, vendors are brought in for their specialist data skills your organisation lacks. With this in mind, you could have some of your staff "shadow" the consultant with the aim of learning. Whilst not a core component of a staff development strategy, being aware of this possibility presents yet another way to supplement your talent development efforts. Moreover, it makes business sense because it can reduce dependence on external staff. As Ian Jackman (General Manager Data and Analytics at Bendigo and Adelaide bank) mentioned to us,

> "We use partners a lot, both for professional services and team augmentation, especially in specific project delivery. We have used these engagements strategically as a way of transferring knowledge and building skills in our people. Generally, having that knowledge transfer and training is a fundamental principle for an effective partnership arrangement. Otherwise, you get an ongoing dependency on that partner or you can't effectively maintain and evolve the solution after the partner finishes. So, ensuring there is a focus on that transition phase up front when working with partners is vital."

We also got a similar vibe from Kumar Parekh (an experienced AI leader in a consulting organisation), who described a typical engagement thus:

> "In my experience across roles I have found that clients want us to collaborate with them. They might have, for example, a couple of data engineers who know data engineering and who can write SQL code to get data from here to there and transform it a bit, but lack the skills required for deployment, containerizing and best practice Devops with CI-CD pipelines, ModelOps or MLOps. So that is where people like us can come in: we bring the credibility, the broad industry view and technical skills which we can teach them as we go. We get these kinds of engagements a lot in medium sized organisations who try to do it themselves with what they have, but then stumble and then we come in to help."

Ongoing Development; "Building a Culture"

Harnessing combinations of the above approaches consistently and in an ongoing manner will enable you to build a pipeline of talent. However, talent by itself is not enough, one must also have the right environment, i.e., an organisational mindset that appreciates how data can support decision-making. This is sometimes referred to as a "data culture". The problem is that culture is intangible; it is not a list of people who are identified as data talent, nor is it a series of courses to train people in dashboards. The culture of an organisation determines how people within it view and act on matters relating to their work. A data culture refers to an organisation-wide mindset about how data is used to inform decision-making. Specifically, it is about encouraging the use of data or evidence consistently when making decisions or, more generally, solving problems.

Working effectively with data is a team sport rather than a solitary activity. So, building and driving a data culture has more to do with (a) hiring analysts who can work with others and (b) putting in place the conditions that encourage a collaborative mindset, rather than building technical skills. The following quote from Sonya Zecchin (an Analytics Leader with experience in diverse domains) is apposite:

> *"… you need to be able to understand problems and, more importantly., you need to be able to work with the business [collaboratively frame problems]. I prioritise that ahead of the traditional data science skills. To teach someone basic skills in analytics, and the ability to use data science tools is easier, I think, than it is to teach someone how to work effectively with business stakeholders to find and frame good problems. I would always err on the side of recruiting people who talk about wanting to help others solve problems … ."*

The importance of this point cannot be overemphasised: decision makers couldn't care less about techniques or technology, but they care very much about being meaningfully involved in solving problems that matter to them.

Communities of Practice

In our experience, an approach that works well is to establish communities of practice around various aspects of data and decision-making. These communities generally form around specific interests such as reporting, evaluation, forecasting or more technical matters such as predictive modelling. They may also be more generally themed discussion groups that get together to share projects, learnings and network with each other. Duhita Khadepau advocates this concept:

> *"Having a community of practice has been one of the important, ongoing anchors for the analytics community as we have grown over time. Juniors can practice presentation, get feedback and everyone enjoys the networking. Every now and then someone very senior pops in which is awesome branding for what we are trying to achieve."*

To engage business users in exploring data-supported approaches to decision-making, Kailash established a "data champions network" in his workplace. Initially he asked department and branch heads to identify those who might be interested in joining and then sent out an invitation to all those who were identified as potentials. Some of those who joined the network have taken the "data message" back to their branches and business units and are now amongst the most enthusiastic and vocal advocates of evidence-supported decision-making.

Matt Minor (Head of Group Data and Analytics at the Blackmores Group) has implemented a similar concept in his organisation:

> *"We set out to identify what we called 'data champions' as we started to embed the Group's first data platform. We started off with around 50, which was pretty good. We've probably watered that down to about 25 to 30 that will grow as our data culture grows. We have a Monthly CoP meeting run by myself and the team. It not an overly formal and intense affair but it gives like-minded people a chance to give and discuss updates in their areas, answer questions, hear from guest speakers and have their input listened to. The aim was to give a space to cultivate this subgroup of people that have got different passions that their particular line manager may not know about or formally recognize in their role. The forum allows us to recognize efforts and examples and the business is now seeing the benefits of allowing people time to pursue this passion. The value of data is being built from the bottom up whereas strategy focuses on top down."*

The community of practice can also serve as an important bridge between business units and the analytics functions. For example, if a marketing analyst is doing a presentation about a project they are doing on advertisement spend optimisation, you may want to invite people from the entire marketing team so that they can see what is possible with analytics. The added benefit is that these people may also help inject a dose of business reality into the discussion by pointing out nuances that the analyst may have missed. A session may also include several different presentations with business representatives from across the organisation (in addition to those proximal to the projects). Such events can be excellent opportunities to build connections between business and data teams. As Hema Prasad (a Data and Analytics Executive Leader) notes:

> *"There's so much to share and learn in data and analytics. A community of practice is a great construct to bring data practitioners together and foster a culture of innovation and collaboration which are key to success in data initiatives. These communities are also a great means of sharing and learning business context and knowledge which are crucial to problem-solving."*

Communities of practice provide a nice focal point to bring together the data and business teams around the craft of analytics. However, to raise general awareness one needs to go beyond such communities into the wider business. As Zanne van Wyk notes from her experience.

> *"Developing analytical skills is very important, however one thing often missed is ensuring that everyone knows what the different roles do. Within the analytics team it is likely everyone knows what each person does. However, outside of this – often the business doesn't know what each person does and therefore where to even begin with their questions and problems. Ensuring that you regularly road-show what they are working on, as well as train the wider business in what each person does and how they can help you can greatly increase the dispersion of analytics uptake around the organisation."*

This brings us to the important issue of organisational awareness about data and analytics.

Data Literacy

As the data capability is growing and the culture is taking shape, you may want to consider an education programme for the broader organisation. Organisation-wide data literacy is a key element of a strong data culture. Here is what Ian Jackman shared with us about their approach to this important consideration:

> *"Data literacy is a core part of our data strategy. That's about building an understanding of data, and how to use it and manage it effectively across the whole bank from the board all the way through the organisation to frontline staff. This is necessary to achieve our aim of building organizational capability. You can't build [an analytics capability] without this part. Importantly, the programs we are building are different depending on the audience to ensure that the content and delivery mechanism is relevant, effective, and resonates. We've got some work ahead of us to do that but it is a core part of our strategic agenda."*

In a data-focused startup, basic data literacy is core to all roles. Here is Duhita Khadepau's take:

> *"Data is part of onboarding for everyone. What are the main metrics being tracked at the organisational level, what are the corporate priorities, what are the main open dashboards, what are the data elements available."*

Hema Prasad notes something similar from her experiences:

> *"Data is not anything new. Either in physical or in electronic format, data has long existed and been a core asset for every organisation. With the explosion of*

digitisation, data literacy becomes a non-negotiable. Data awareness for every employee across all organisational functions is the first step towards data literacy and maturity."

The above is largely about understanding the available data. But there is a more general element to data literacy which relates to understanding how data can be used to support decision-making as well as the right and wrong ways to use data. That is, it is about *critical thinking* – the ability to develop logical, fact-based assessments of situations. Here is what Sandra Hogan said to us about data literacy for the business community:

"Now that they have built this [analytics] community and it is going strong; they are working towards building the data literacy of business roles and these decentralized analysts are crucial for this in terms of support and assistance. For the data literacy; we worked with a provider to customise a data literacy course that wasn't as technical. We focused on critical thinking, how do you develop a hypothesis? How do you frame [good] questions?"

There are a couple of important points made here that are worth noting: *critical thinking* and *hypothesis formulation*. We'll say more about these in the following two subsections. However, before doing that, here is a word of caution about courses from Sonya Zecchin, who we met earlier:

"Going too broad with these courses can be detrimental. Most corporates have mandatory bullying, consent, harassment etc kind of courses. Whilst we absolutely maintain these topics are very important for workers to be trained in and aware of, if they are not managed well and treated as a tick-the-box exercise; they can be a certain derision and lethargy towards them. If data literacy courses are treated this way; broad, boring, abstract and mandatory, they can be put into the same 'mental box' as other poorly executed training modules and it sets back the whole vision of developing a data culture in the organisation."

You have been warned!

Critical Thinking

When talking about data literacy, it is important to keep in mind that *data doesn't make decisions, people do*. That being the case, it matters *what* data is used to make decisions and *how* it is used. Examples abound of people basing decisions on inappropriate data or using data to make incorrect inferences. We'll mention two examples to make our point:

1. When making decisions, people will sometimes selectively seek data that fits in with their views or favours their preferred option. For

example, when managers are pressured to reduce costs, they might decide to restructure their departments by making some roles redundant and outsource the work done by those roles to vendors in low-cost destinations. Such outsourcing decisions are often based on upfront costs quoted by vendors, overlooking hidden costs.[10] In reality, however, the hidden costs can end up increasing the total cost to the point where it would have been cheaper to do the work internally (we discussed an example of this in Chapter 3).

2. Consider a situation where a call centre puts in place a KPI of *calls responded to per day* to measure rep performance. Basing performance-related decisions such as bonus payouts and promotions on this metric is likely to lead to undesirable consequences as reps will try to respond to as many calls as they can at the cost of quality of customer service. As Eliyahu Goldratt famously noted, *"tell me how you will measure me and I'll tell you how I'll behave"* (see Goldratt 1990, p.26). This example holds a general lesson which is that *all KPIs have unintended side effects which need to be balanced by measures that counterbalance them*. So, for examples, *calls responded to per day* could be counterbalanced by *customer feedback* measures. Keep this in mind as you read the section on *measuring culture* later in this chapter.

Apart from gathering data that covers all relevant aspects of the situation, one should also:

1. Distinguish clearly between facts (as supported by data) and assumptions.

2. Account for biases. The best way to do this is to actively *look for evidence that weakens the case for your preferred option*.

3. Arrive at a decision via logical arguments based on data and assumptions.

The above points relate to an important skill that is rarely taught in schools and universities: *critical thinking*, which Tim van Gelder, an applied epistemologist at the University of Melbourne, defines succinctly as, *"the art of being right"*. Paradoxically, the best way to do this is to always keep in mind the possibility that you may be wrong!

It is possible for people to improve their critical thinking skills through training (see van Gelder 2005, for example). You may therefore want to encourage people across the organisation to take courses on critical thinking; many are now available online.[11]

Problems, Hypotheses, and the Scientific Method

Data science, at its heart, is about taking a scientific approach to problem-solving. There are many different representations of the scientific method

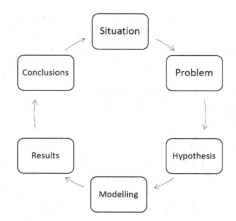

FIGURE 5.1
The scientific method.

(Do an image search on Google using the phrase "scientific method" to see a few). However, all of these depictions are similar in that they are about taking a systematic approach to frame and solve problems.

Our representation of the method is shown in Figure 5.1. Note that this is not the conventional way the scientific method is depicted in data science books. Conventionally, one talks about the process of model building, testing, and refining as being scientific. Here we take a step back and see the entire process – starting from a problematic business situation to framing, modelling, testing results against (business) reality, and then (perhaps) reframing the problem based on what one has learnt – as being illustrative of the scientific method.

One of the things we have emphasised at various points in this book is that in real life you are never given a readymade problem, you are given a *situation* from which a *problem* must be framed. Oddly enough, the scientific method is silent about how to frame problems from situations, which is why we have spent a fair bit of time discussing it in this book. The *hypothesis* bit is about translating the framed problem into something that a data scientist can work with. An example might help to clarify the distinction between the three terms – *situation*, *problem* and *hypothesis*. The *situation* is that a business unit has just been handed an ambitious profit target for the next year. This situation can be framed in different ways that lead to very different actions. Consider the following:

- It is an impossible target; negotiate with management to reduce it.
- Develop new revenue streams.
- Grow the customer based for existing products and services.
- Reduce costs.

Each of these framings presents radically different perspectives on the same situation. When seen individually, each of the framings lead to very different problems. This is why we emphasise the need to frame problems collaboratively. A collective framing process that synthesises diverse perspectives is more likely to result in a problem that takes into account all the important aspects of the situation.

A collaborative problem framing process applied to the above might result in a problem statement whose solution is a combination of "develop new revenue streams" and "grow customer base for existing products". The data team might be able to help with the second part of the solution – for example, by identifying potential new customers. In collaboration with the business team, they come up with a *hypothesis* that individuals who share certain demographic features and interests of existing customers are good targets. They will do some *modelling* to find such customers and present the *results* to the business. The model results will be tested against reality and the business will come to some conclusions – perhaps targeting the predicted customer was a partial success but needs refinement ... or it is a complete failure. The cycle then starts over again, going through the same steps as before. To be sure, some of the steps may be truncated the second time around, but sometimes one might choose to reframe the situation in a different way because of what one has learnt from the first round.

The above example – which is not an uncommon one in its broad strokes – illustrates how data science is "scientific".

Measuring Culture

The notions of culture, talent, and community are admittedly somewhat abstract in nature. However, this doesn't excuse them from being measured and tracked (keeping in mind the caveats about unintended consequences noted in the previous section!). Just as your strategy and projects involve numbers related to business savings or revenue, timelines and budgets, so too can an analytics culture be tracked. Indeed, measuring culture can and should be part of your overall data strategy. The simplest metrics likely already exist in HR data: the number, location, type of existing formal analytics roles. This can be extended to those enrolled in formal development programmes and tracked as they move through different levels of training, attend events, and build their analytics profile. Some other metrics that can be tracked to form a picture of the growing data culture include:

- Enrolments in the different education pathways and programmes.
- Participants in secondment programmes.
- Attendees at the events (community of practice, hackathons, etc.).
- Number of dashboards being produced and who is using them.
- The number of organisation-wide projects and programmes using data to track performance.

Here's what Craig Napier (CDO of The University of Technology, Sydney) had to say about dashboard monitoring:

> *"We are actively monitoring not only how many dashboards are being created and viewed, but who is viewing them, who is coming back, and from what parts of the organisation adoption and engagement is growing?"*

For many of the metrics above, it is not only the raw figures that indicate progress. In addition, it is important to measure the breadth of the metrics in order to understand the dispersion of an analytics culture within the organisation. For example, if the community of practice is attended by 10, 15, then 20 people over a few months, this is noteworthy progress. However, the same community of practice with 20 participants from only 2 business units is not doing as well as one that has 20 participants from 3 or 4 business units across the organisation. As another example, if an organisation moves from 20 to 30 to 40 dashboards, this is progression, but if those are still only made by 2 people and viewed by a single unit, the analytical culture and work is densely concentrated rather than spreading across the enterprise.

In addition to breadth, it is useful to take a cohort-based perspective. For example, consider the cohorts that enrol in each offering of "Introduction to Power BI". One can ask: where do they end up six months, a year or two years down the track? Are they taking more courses, in different positions, are they taking up further courses? In particular, you can compare cohorts to see how different cohorts are progressing. If, over time, each cohort is (as a proportion) taking on more courses and participating in more events then this is a great measure of success for building the organisational data culture. Another way to consider cohort analysis is the broader idea of *repeat customers*. Are people coming back to events, dashboards created, and attending more events? Or are the numbers built off a successful "top-of-funnel" but people are not continuing their interest? An ideal situation is where there is a nice mix of first-timers and familiar faces at events and programmes and as such, tracking this metric can be useful and insightful.

Finally, as discussed through an example in the previous section, it is important to be aware of the potential of metrics to distort behaviours. When proposing any metric, it is helpful to think through the potential negative effects it could have, and put in place mitigations for those via counterbalancing KPIs.[12]

Some Principles for Developing a Data Culture

Overall, we could summarise some key principles when developing and enhancing the data culture within your organisation as follows:

1. **Understand what a "data culture" means for your organisation**

   One way to do this is to "deconstruct the platitude" (see Chapter 3) by asking the question, "what would change if we had a good data culture?" A response might be "better decision making". As this is too vague, you might want to ask, "how would you know decision making has improved?" This should to lead to a discussion about things that can be measured – such as programmes/projects, KPIs, or evaluations. You eventually want to get to concrete things that you can influence.

2. **Cast a wide net**

   Run open events when showcasing projects and ensure that the presentations are pitched at a general audience. When it comes to training, offer courses at a basic level in addition to those that cater to techies.

3. **Give people time**

   Time to learn, time to take on new projects, do secondments, and participate in hackathons.

4. **Give people support**

   This comes from communities, connections, and mentors from a technical support angle. Additionally, it may be non-technical support. Conversation, checking in, general human support is oft underappreciated by managers. The combination of time and support imbues people with the belief that they can have a go and succeed in this new area despite perhaps not having a formal education in it.

5. **Do not overlook the importance of critical thinking**

   As noted above, getting people to understand how to work with data is one thing, getting them to do so effectively is another. High quality data must be accompanied by high-quality reasoning as discussed in the previous section.

When all is considered holistically, a question that often comes up is: how do you know your efforts have been successful? Here's what Sonya Zecchin has to say about that:

> *"You can tell that a culture is developing partly by the phrases that begin to be used; that people are saying 'data driven' and asking 'what is the data telling us?'. Those are good signs and a big development from an environment where this hasn't been said as much. Whilst this is a great start, the next step is to develop some of those fundamental analytical skills that will allow more people to begin not just* **asking** *what the data is but* **questioning** *what the data is saying."*

As an example, you might ask for some data about sales for the last month and receive some *average* measure in return (say, average sales). An important question to ask is: what is the representation of each group in the average? It is easy to see that averages can be misleading. Consider when one reheats a frozen or refrigerated macaroni cheese: on *average* the food may be at a perfect temperature, but that could be made up of a molten outer-rim and frozen core of rock-hard pasta! Similarly, in a business context, one group of users may have a much higher average than another but are much smaller in the overall population so get washed out. Any action taken based on the average alone would be misinformed.

Buying Talent

Earlier in this chapter, we discussed some of the key roles within the data space that may play a part in your growing data function and how these may be filled by identifying and growing talent from within. However, upskilling internal talent may only take you so far, and there may well be a need to go to market. Indeed, it is unrealistic to expect that you will be able to staff your entire data function in perpetuity through upskilling alone. Accordingly, we now provide some guidance on hiring the right kind of people, especially at the early stages of your organisation's data science journey.

It is noteworthy that in the above descriptions of roles, most of them – to some degree – have interactions with business stakeholders as a core aspect of their work. However, as your function grows (and depending on the size of your organisation), there may be the need for specific roles that are completely technical.

Find the Right Mix of Skills

The key skills associated with these roles, which we highlighted earlier in this chapter, are critical for delivering on work. Analysts who cannot build dashboards or write code independently are not going to be of much use in an environment where they are expected to build POCs. In addition, you've also got to keep in mind the inevitability of change: technical infrastructures will evolve, new and better tools will appear on the market and your staff must be able to adapt. Here's what Matt Minor had to say about this:

> *"When you recruit staff, you are looking for strong technology backgrounds who are open to change and moving as you do. The best team is able to not only build for the 'now' but wants to move to the next level. I'm lucky in that I've got a very good team that has at times been six people that service 1200 people around 13 different markets."*

That said, your technical people also need to be able to translate business requirements into technical terms. We have never heard of a marketing or sales manager requesting a data science team to

Please build me an XGBoost model using 5-fold cross validation, and deploy it using Kubernetes.

Instead, they will describe a problematic situation, and the analyst needs to work collaboratively with them to explore the problem space, understand the business success measures and craft an appropriate technical plan aimed at solving the problem. Additionally, analytics projects are inherently iterative and will change over time as more information comes to light. This information should come to light through regular, open communication between analytics and business stakeholders (recall our modified CRISP-DM model in Chapter 2 – see Figure 2.6). As the project moves to completion and it is time to tell the story, it is important to focus on key insights and surface only the absolutely essential technical information, keeping the gory details out of sight. We'll say more about this when we describe an exemplar data science project blueprint in Chapter 7.

In the following subsections, we discuss some ways to test for key technical skills. However, even when doing this, we would strongly advise you to consider candidates' broader knowledge, experience, and curiosity as well as looking for signs of their ability to pick up new technical skills on their own. Analytics professionals who thrive in fledgling analytics functions have comb-shaped skills (broad base, with several areas of deeper knowledge). The best of them also tend to have a knowledge of a variety of algorithms and techniques and, more importantly, a broad base of skills. Data scientists who are only experienced in one particular technical hammer such as deep learning (discussed briefly in Chapter 2) are likely to view all business problems as nails that can be beaten into submission with that hammer.

Value Problem-Solving

Having a broad base of technical skills is good. However, in the early stages of a data strategy execution, looking for analytics professionals who enjoy *solving problems* rather than implementing technology X (e.g., machine learning) will greatly aid your progress. Here's what Sonya Zecchin had to say:

"For data science to succeed, especially in the early days, you need someone to be able to work with the business to understand problems, communicate and iterate together. I prioritise those skills ahead of what we would traditionally think of as data science skills as I have found it is easier to teach someone basic skills in analytics and using data science tools than it is to teach someone who doesn't have that the ability to speak with business and build relationships with the business. So, I always recruit people who are passionate about solving problems, helping people generate business value, who can speak to stakeholders in their language ... and just happen to be in the stream where they use data or coding to do this."

You can sometimes see this in the "passion projects" that applicants put on their resume or talk about in interviews. It is also common for data scientists to have a public Github[13] profile with different projects. Just having this is great as it demonstrates that they engage with their professional interest in a personal capacity (here's[14] a particularly good one). However, it is also easy to game this: beware of profiles where there is a single (or few) project, pushed up in only a few commits over a short period of time … perhaps right after your job ad appeared!

The content of candidates' publicly posted material matters as well. The ones we particularly like are those that take an interesting dataset (ideally from a passion area of theirs) and do some work on it, then publish their work with some commentary. However, candidates who include projects that take, say, the Titanic dataset[15] (or any other overused[16] one) and do a basic classification model on it may not have the skills and dispositions you are looking for. Just to be clear, we applaud anyone who develops something in their own time, but there is a notable difference between trivial projects using well-known datasets and those that are genuinely interesting and insightful. Indeed, you want to be able to distinguish between bandwagon jumpers from the genuine tickets. Here's what Hema Prasad had to say about this:

> *"I believe that the field of Data is very much like any other art or science but more profound. If one wants to become, say, a surgeon, one needs to be really passionate about surgery, right? One cannot become a surgeon just because the profession is in vogue, you know, at that point in time. "Data and analytics" has been a buzzword in this decade and everybody is gravitating towards one role or another within the data space. But it is important to look at whether they have a core set of real skills complemented by a data-centric thinking and the ability to put them into practice, all of which are crucial to business problem-solving."*

Another important point is – does the candidate develop fit-for-purpose solutions? Some problems can be addressed using SQL or dashboard, others may require a rules-engine (yes, even simple *if…then* rule-based algorithms with the right domain knowledge behind them can be quite powerful). It could also be as "boring" as a script that automates something. In a previous role, Alex was asked to write an "algorithm" to help a particular business unit that had one staff member spend two whole days per month copying and pasting data from the front end of a corporate system to Excel as part of the month-end reporting process. A short conversation with the database team and a simple PowerQuery later, that task was reduced to 30 seconds! All it took was a smidgen of SQL and Excel. Perhaps we can sum up this consideration in a wonderful tongue-in-cheek quote that appeared in the twitter-verse recently:

> *A junior data scientist is learning how to make more complex models.*
> *A senior data scientist is learning how to make simpler models.*[17]

The trick is to tell one from the other.

Assessing Broader Skills

There are many ways in which organisations undertake recruitment processes. Typically, larger and more established tech companies (such as FAANG, or now MAAMA[18]) have multiple, multi-hour technical tests and interviews. Established organisations can afford rigorous recruitment processes and indeed require them in order to find the right people to fit very specific roles. For organisations that are in the process of building data science or analytics capabilities, there are a host of other assessment techniques that we have seen and used when hiring dozens of analytics professionals ourselves. These test for the key skills – both technical and non-technical – that we noted above. Here we outline them in brief, with some notes on their use.

Get the Candidate to Work on a Real Data Problem

As we have noted earlier, when we teach courses on data science our assessments often consist of real-life problems that students have to frame and solve. In general, this is a great way to assess candidates' problem framing and solving abilities and should be used as part of your recruitment process. Ideally, you should give them anonymised data from your organisation. If that is not possible, you can pick a dataset from one of the many open data repositories; it shouldn't be too hard to find a dataset relevant to your domain. If you do the latter, be sure to stay away from extremely popular datasets (we have given you some examples of these earlier). In any case you should, get your technical people to modify[19] the dataset because most open datasets have been analysed to death, and there will be many published blogs and repositories detailing various analyses that others have done.

In terms of the actual task, you could (a) ask them to explore the dataset and provide some key insights or (b) give them a brief describing what you want them to do. We tend to prefer a mix of the two: the most interesting responses come from giving applicants a free rein to show what they can do and also testing for specific technical skills. Applicants who do well at both are likely to seek problems and solve them in interesting ways rather than wait for someone to hand them a readymade problem.

Crucially, the brief should require candidates to create a report or presentation for non-technical stakeholders – say, marketing managers or sales managers who know their way around a dashboard but are not data scientists or analysts. Therefore, whilst candidates need to explain what they did and why, they must translate that into intuitive explanations using plain English … with some relevant visuals to boot (text-only PowerPoints are still all too common in technical presentations).

Some people we know deliberately release the data only a day or two before the interview to assess the capabilities of applicants to work to tight deadlines. If you choose to do this, we would suggest including a weekend in the time period; it is unreasonable to expect busy professionals to work on your task on weeknights.

Get Them to Do a Presentation

Presentations are an important way to assess a candidate's ability to communicate technical matters and/or tell stories. Some organisations, like Atlassian, have a dedicated interview in the application process where they go deep into candidates' experiences and projects from a stakeholder management perspective. These interviews are most often led by non-analytics professionals. However, there are other ways to incorporate business stakeholders in the process. Having them sit in on presentations and ask non-technical questions is one. Indeed, this is something to consider when candidates present their findings on the data task described above. The ability to bridge the gap between technical and business perspectives is vital. We have both seen relatively junior applicants move ahead of highly qualified applicants (including extremely well-regarded professors moving back into industry) because the latter couldn't engage with the business stakeholders involved in the process.

Here are some general questions that you can ask:

- What assumptions did they make? How would they relax these?
- Why did they choose a particular technique? What others did they consider and why didn't they use them?
- What are the top X insights (if they didn't highlight these already)?
- What was the most surprising thing they found?
- What was the biggest challenge(s) and how did they (or would they) overcome them?
- What would they do if they had more time? What resources would they need to do those things?

Another critical element worth mentioning is that the presentation must be time capped (10 minutes is plenty!). This tests the applicant's ability to tell an engaging, yet tight, story that includes all the relevant details, keeping in mind the audience at hand.

Finally, we should address the elephant in the room: any take-home test runs the risk of plagiarism. The best way to assure yourself that the work is genuinely the candidate's own is to ask questions that probe their understanding of the problem. One way to do this is to ask them questions about what they would do if they were given related but different datasets or situations. Such questions probe knowledge and skills that go beyond the project so it is difficult to fake good answers to them.If candidates are able to answer these questions satisfactorily, one can be reasonably confident that it is indeed their own work.

Match Expectations

Some data scientists wish to do machine learning all day. Often such data scientists are also not very interested in allied areas such as data engineering, building dashboards, or broader data-related work (such as programme evaluation). These may not be the right kind of data scientist to hire early in your analytics journey. A number of colleagues who Alex studied with when he was completing his postgraduate studies in data science were told at job interviews that they would be applying advanced data science skills at work. When they started, however, they found that they had to build the data infrastructure, data warehouse and reports before doing any of what they wanted to do. Such misaligned expectations can cause unnecessary dissatisfaction and unhappiness all around.

On the other hand, there are a host of others who are interested in getting in at the ground level because of the broad scope of work that comes with such positions. In Alex's case, he was the first data scientist hired in the New South Wales Police Force (one of the largest law enforcement agencies in the world) and gained huge personal growth and enjoyment from the fact that he could shape the nascent data science capability in that organisation. Such an environment is not without challenges, such as the lack of technical mentorship and the anxiety of being the only "go to person" for all queries pertaining to data science. However, for the right person, it can be an opportunity of a lifetime.

Consider a Broader Talent Pool

In these times of stiff competition for talent, you may want to consider broadening your search to include often overlooked demographics. Some possibilities include:

- **Business analysts and finance professionals**. These people often have quantitative skills and many of them are keen to learn new techniques.
- **Mature age workers with related skills**. At any given time, there are a good number of experienced IT workers in the job market. Many of these people are looking to reskill and may welcome the opportunity to learn data skills on the job.
- **Internships and graduate programmes.** A good way to get graduates interested in working in your organisation is to offer pre-final year internships that offer a pathway to an ongoing role after graduation.

Yes, they may choose to go elsewhere after the internship, but if you offer them interesting work during the internship with a clear learning and development path ahead, there is a good chance they will stay.

Here is what Ian Jackman had to say about these non-traditional recruiting pathways:

"We are also looking at a variety of innovative ways to access talent with a focus on the core underlying traits such as curiosity, analytical thinking and problem solving, as opposed to just demonstrated experience in engineering or analytics. One of these is looking into the mature age market where people are looking to reskill from one industry to another. Another is grad programs and forming those partnerships with universities. So, there is no one solution to the talent shortage and we are looking at it via a number of more conventional and creative angles."

Finally, it is worth mentioning that a number of the more recent software tools on the market have made data science accessible to people who are less technical. The point is that you don't need to hire the most technical person right off the bat. Here's what Sonya Zecchin had to say about this:

"There is a relevant analogy here of a modern car that does a lot and gets you from A to B without you knowing what is under the hood. You practice, sit the test and need to do some work to be able to operate the machinery but you don't need to be a mechanic to use it."

Would you trust a novice driver to find their way through a warren of streets in an unfamiliar city in heavy traffic? Probably not. However, chances are they will be able navigate without any problems in a small town where traffic is light. It is possible that a good chunk of the early work associated with POCs will fall in the latter category so not all your staff need be *au fait* with the latest and greatest algorithms and technology.

Conditions over Causes[20]

Thus, far this chapter has been about actions you can take to build your organisation's data science capability and create a data-supported decision-making culture. By their very nature, these actions are explicit – i.e., people, artefacts, or events that one can point to, such as employees or consultants, training programmes, interviews, tests, hackathons. However, as we have noted at the start of this chapter, culture is somewhat more elusive because it refers to things like "mindset" which is something you do not have direct control over. A mindset cannot be enforced. However, one can put in place the *conditions* that encourage the right mindset.[21] To understand how, we will need to take a detour through some interesting research on teams.

Richard Hackman[22] was a Professor of Social and Organisational Psychology at Harvard University. Early in his career, he spent considerable time examining the factors that make teams work well. He studied many different types of teams, aiming to distil the essential causes of their success or failure. But he found that things were not so simple: try as he did, he could not isolate causal factors that influenced team performance. Indeed, every time he developed a model and tested it via interventions on real teams, he found that there was no meaningful difference in performance. He subsequently reviewed the literature and found other researchers had faced the same problem. Even worse, many interventions intended to improve a group's performance not only failed but often resulted in effects contrary to what was intended.

Humans instinctively think in terms of causes and effects. The problem is that in the social sphere it is often difficult to separate causes and effects cleanly. This is exactly what Hackman found in the case of team behaviour: the assumption that causal factors could be isolated from each-other and their effects unambiguously quantified turned out to be wrong. The reality, in case of group behaviour and performance, is that it cannot be analysed in terms of well-defined cause-effect relationships alone. Hackman realised then that instead of trying to isolate causal factors of team performance, it may be more useful to explore the *enabling conditions* that give rise to great teams.

Accordingly, he re-examined and refocused his work in a way that enabled him to examine conditions. Over time, he found six conditions that, when present, led to better team performance. These conditions, if present from an early stage of group formation, had an overwhelmingly positive effect on the performance of the team (Hackman 2012):

1. **A real team**: Interdependence among members, clear boundaries distinguishing members from non-members and moderate stability of membership over time.

2. **A compelling purpose**: A purpose that is clear, challenging, and consequential. It energises team members and fully engages their talents.

3. **Right people**: People who have task expertise are self-organised and skilled in working collaboratively with others.

4. **Clear norms of conduct**: The team understands clearly what behaviours are, and are not, acceptable.

5. **A supportive organisational context**: The team has the resources it needs and the reward system provides recognition and positive consequences for excellent team performance.

6. **Appropriate coaching**: The right sort of coaching for the team is provided at the right time.

It is important to note that Hackman did not rate any one of these conditions as being more important than the others. He emphasised that all are needed for teams to have a good chance of being high performing.

We have discussed some of these factors above, at least partially – namely, items 2, 3, and 6. The other factors – *a real team, clear norms of conduct* and a *supportive organisational context* – though easy enough to talk about, are much harder to put into practice because you have little control on how people will act and interact. Here's where the guidelines for Emergent Design we discussed in Chapter 3 come into their own: they offer actionable advice on creating a context that *encourages* (rather than enforces!) the right actions and behaviours.

Closing Remarks

We hope this chapter has given you a sense for the different roles you may need to consider for your data science team and, more importantly, that building a team does not always involve hiring expensive talent. Often, initial roles can be filled by motivated people from within your organisation, supported by formal and on-the-job training. The key element here is to find the right mix of internal and external staff, the latter may even be consultants on short-term engagements who serve the dual purpose of working on POCs whilst upskilling internal staff. A broader point, implicit in what we have said in this chapter, is that internal efforts in building capability and culture are not just for the initial stages of setting up a data capability, they should be maintained as the capability matures.

When you do have to hire – as you invariably will – it is important that you hire the right people for the job. To this end, we have provided you with some concrete, road tested advice – beyond mere interviews – to help you identify the right people for your nascent data science capability. Along the way, we also talked about how to establish a "data culture" within your organisation – i.e., an environment in which data or evidence supported decision-making is the norm, and people have a mindset of curiosity and critical thinking. Finally, we also discussed what this means in practical terms and what you can do to encourage such a culture to take root and thrive.

Now that we have covered the social elements of a data capability, we can move on to technical considerations.

Notes

1 We'll say much more about the main cloud vendors in Chapter 6.
2 The storage system could be a data warehouse, data lake, or data lake-house (see Chapter 2 for more on these).
3 This example is fraught with ethical issues. For example: are individuals identifiable? How will the results be used? It is important to ensure that there is an ethics/governance checks are in place to avoid misuse of such personally identifiable data. We discuss this at length in Chapter 8.
4 https://trends.google.com/trends/explore?date=today%205-y&q=%22analytics%20engineer%22
5 https://theagileadmin.com/what-is-devops/
6 www.washingtonpost.com/news/morning-mix/wp/2015/03/26/how-a-scientist-discovered-30-new-species-in-l-a-s-smoggy-backyards/
7 https://nhm.org/community-science-nhm/bioscan
8 www.atlassian.com/company/shipit
9 https://mashable.com/video/google-20-percent-rule
10 https://eight2late.wordpress.com/2016/05/03/the-hidden-costs-of-it-outsourcing/
11 See, for example: www.linkedin.com/learning/critical-thinking/welcome-to-critical-thinking-2 (this is an example, not an endorsement!)
12 These days some teams are adopting OKR (Objectives and Key Results) instead of KPIs, though our discussions stand regardless of the current flavour.
13 https://github.com/
14 https://github.com/ndleah
15 www.kaggle.com/c/titanic
16 https://instructor-support.datacamp.com/en/articles/2360699-datasets-to-avoid
17 https://twitter.com/marktenenholtz/status/1514211841827696644
18 https://fortune.com/2021/10/29/faang-mamaa-jim-cramer-tech-facebook-meta/
19 A good way to modify a dataset is to throw in some noise – e.g., change the data in a few rows to include clearly incorrect data, for example, an incorrect date.
20 This section is based on Chapter 5 of Culmsee and Awati (2016).
21 Also see Chapter 8 for a discussion of creating the conditions that foster an ethical mindset within the team.
22 https://hbswk.hbs.edu/item/j-richard-hackman-1940-2013

References

Culmsee, P. and Awati, K. (2016), *The Heretic's Guide to Management: The Art of Harnessing Ambiguity*, Heretics Guide Press, Marsfield, Australia.

Goldratt, E. (1990), *The Haystack Syndrome: Sifting Information Out of the Data Ocean*, North River Press, Great Barrington, MA.

Hackman, J. (2012), "From causes to conditions in group research", *Journal of Organizational Behavior*, Vol. 33 No. 3, pp. 428–444. https://doi.org/10.1002/job.1774

Van Gelder, T. (2005), "Teaching critical thinking: Some lessons from cognitive science", *College Teaching*, Vol. 53 No. 1, pp. 41–48.

6

Technical Choices

Introduction

Data science, like any sociotechnical capability, is more about people and their problems rather than technology. Talking about technology before people or problems is akin to a tradesperson talking about tools before knowing what needs to be fixed. Hema Prasad articulated this as follows:

> *Tools and technology augment the people capability; not the other way around. Tools are far more replaceable than people. The order in which I look at things is really people and process, then tooling and technology.*

This is exactly in line with the emergent design approach and is why the chapters in this book are in the order they are in.

Over the last few years, most organisations have moved large parts of their IT and data infrastructures to cloud platforms. Accordingly, our focus in this chapter is primarily focused around these platforms. We also discuss some guiding principles that you should keep in mind when choosing platforms and offer some advice on working with vendors.

Cloud and the Future (Is Now)

The title of this section reflects the reality that much of current data science work is carried out in cloud computing environments.[1] Indeed, it is quite likely that your organisation is using one of the three major cloud platforms – Amazon Web Services (AWS), Microsoft Azure, or Google Cloud Platform (GCP). Most of the data leaders we spoke to in the course of writing this book were, to some extent or the other, using one or more of these. It is revealing that they generally framed their use of these platforms as an ongoing journey, tacitly acknowledging that it is one without end. This simply reflects the fact

DOI: 10.1201/9781003260158-6

that cloud offerings evolve rapidly and, with that, so do the options available to organisations.

Interestingly, there was a subset of leaders who did not use the journey metaphor. These were invariably associated with start-ups. That makes sense: as these companies are young, they have been on cloud platforms from day one. They are what one might call *cloud-native organisations*.

With that said, we won't waste a great deal of space here discussing the whys of the cloud movement. Instead, we will start by focusing on the benefits of using these platforms and a discussion of the main players in this space.

Cost Savings

Any data scientist will tell you how exciting it was for them when they discovered the world of on-demand computing. No matter how good your personal laptop or desktop, it is simply impossible to compete with AWS Spot Instance pricing, where one can purchase a large virtual[2] machine with hundreds of gigabytes of memory for a few dollars per hour. In comparison with the pay as you go costs for several virtual machines, the upfront cost of on-premise (i.e., organisation-owned) infrastructure is prohibitive.

However, virtual isn't without downsides. Some of you may have experienced or know someone who has experienced, bill shock when accidentally misconfiguring cloud services. A colleague of ours who was participating in a hackathon was extremely fortunate that AWS took an empathetic stance and wrote off a ~$1400 bill that arose from her accidentally leaving several large virtual instances on for a fortnight after the event. To avoid such mishaps, there are start-ups such as CloudMonitor.ai, Cloudyn (acquired by Microsoft in 2017), and Apptio (to name a few) that can assist in optimising cloud spend across the ever-expanding landscape. Without belabouring the point, whilst the cloud offers the ability to quickly harness immense technical power, it opens one up to the risk of accidental overspend due to mishaps such as the above.

A trickier issue is the unnecessary use of complex services that are not worth the cost. For example, the ability to access a machine translation service (a service that translates from one language to another) via a simple API[3] call may sound impressive and far more cost effective than a data scientist' salary or time. However, ongoing heavy use of such a service can rack up a large bill thus making a home-grown model, built and maintained by a staff data scientist, far more economical, even with the salary costs. When considering this, it is worth keeping in mind that the data science world is quite open-source-driven, so there are plenty of good models that you can use for free. This is largely a consequence of the two main languages of data science – R and Python – being open source. Indeed, when someone releases a commercial product, the open-source community soon releases a free competing product.

Simplicity of Setup

When implemented with due consideration of cost and some of the guiding principles we cover later, cloud can provide a way to rapidly uplift your technology stack. At the simplest level most cloud providers offer simple ways to create new virtual computing instances or augment the power of existing ones. Indeed, cloud data architectures are often set up with automated scaling whereby resources (CPU or RAM) are added or subtracted as needed depending on the computing load at any given time. Safe to say, it is a far cry from – not to mention, a whole lot simpler than – installing or uninstalling physical server racks on premise!

The benefits go beyond cost and convenience. Other benefits include software updates and upgrades being readily available and automatically rolled out by the providers, elastic (flexible) storage, ease of building data pipelines as well as a host of other services.

A newer suite of offerings that the main cloud providers have begun to offer includes data science services accessible via APIs. As an example, image recognition services such as AWS Rekognition[4], Azure Cognitive Services (Computer Vision[5]), or Google Cloud Vision[6] that enable one to beam an image to the specified API endpoint and receive a description of what is in the image. We'll say more about these in the subsection on API services below. The point we wish to make here is that the speed with which new technology is productised by the main cloud vendors is impressive and can supplement your growing data capability, especially when running rapid POCs.

Security and Governance

An area that is the subject of robust (and often misinformed) discussion in regards to cloud vs on-premise infrastructure is that of security. The fact is that from a physical security perspective most cloud providers have extremely secure datacentres protected by multiple layers of security, unlikely to be matched by most corporate datacentres. As far as cybersecurity is concerned, these providers have large security teams with highly experienced computer and network security professionals that individual organisations would not have the budget to match. Another related aspect is the rapidity with which cloud security teams are able to respond to potential threats or rollout security updates. To match this, the size and skills on-premise teams would need to be comparable to some of the largest security teams in the world employed by the main cloud providers.

Considerations of security naturally lead on to *governance* which we'll say more about in Chapter 8. For now, we'll note that cloud platforms offer the ability to leverage the security models, procedures, and practices (both technical and operational) of the providers. This enables organisations to effectively "outsource" a not-inconsequential amount of work in ensuring good practices are followed in this area. On more than one occasion when working with clients on analytics projects, Alex has been able to leverage the whitepapers[7] put out by AWS and other vendors to assist with security and governance-related choices.

Backups

When working with computers, there is the ever-present possibility of things going wrong – e.g., hard disk failures, crashes. This is especially true when one works with data. Every experienced data professional would have (unintentionally) deleted some data that they shouldn't have, dropped a table or even worse. To protect against this, all organisations have some form of regular backup and disaster recovery procedures as part of their practices. With on-premise infrastructures, the responsibility for both normal backup and recovery, as well as disaster recovery, lies with the organisation.

The risk of a disaster is low (though arguably on the increase now). However, if (when?) it does eventuate, it is far more devastating to on-premise infrastructures than those hosted in the cloud. A disaster does not even have to be as catastrophic as The Day After Tomorrow.[8] Even something like an intense storm can wreak havoc on on-premise setups. In contrast, the main cloud providers provide offerings that can instantly cut-over to standby services or restore virtual images from replications that are concurrently stored all over the globe. This massively reduces the risk of catastrophic loss of service or data. A case in point is Netflix's approach to data disaster recovery and fault tolerance (i.e., ability to seamlessly continue service in the face of disasters of varying scales)[9]. As mentioned in the article linked to in the endnote:

> *One way to make sure you can deal with a flat tire on the freeway, in the rain, in the middle of the night is to poke a hole in your tire once a week in your driveway on a Sunday afternoon and go through the drill of replacing it.*

To do this in real life, Netflix implemented a collection of software agents that randomly causes issues in their production (!) systems. This routinely tests their ability to recover from unexpected failures and disasters. You can read more about these tools (dubbed the "simian army") in the article in the aforementioned endnote.

The Main Players

There are three main players, who we have already mentioned earlier: AWS, Azure (Microsoft), and GCP that make up a majority of the cloud services market. Latest estimates[10] put AWS at around 40%, Azure at 20%, and GCP at close to 10% with the rest split across a host of smaller providers. This wasn't always the case though. AWS was the first out of the gate and was the dominant provider for a number of years. Their dominance has been whittled down in recent years, mainly by Microsoft.

From our own experiences and the insights of the data leaders we interacted with, there is some general agreement on how the different providers position themselves and the services they offer. Whilst there is considerable overlap in the kinds of services they offer, there are distinct differences in the positioning of those services, which is reflected in the diverse types of organisations they tend to work with. Below we outline some of these differences which might help inform your decisions on cloud providers.

To be clear, there is no universally applicable right answer for which provider to use. Some larger enterprises engage multiple vendors because they can afford to. It is important to note that the cost is not just the cost of the service; one also has to add the cost of the internal skills you will need to work effectively with multiple platforms. Regardless of your organisation size, opting for a single provider, at least at the early stages, will save you a lot of effort, time, and cost. Whilst multi-cloud environments can provide cost savings in more advanced cloud architectures, this isn't something we have typically seen organisations do in the early stages of developing a data science or analytics capability. Here's Duhita Khadepau's take on this:

> "I have found across many different growing and scaling tech companies that building on a single cloud provider stack makes things easier from a staffing perspective. For AWS, for example, it is relatively easy for an engineer to pick up a new service since they already have so much knowledge about the 'AWS Way'. For them to pick up the same service in GCP, which may actually be very similar in function and cost, would take a huge investment of time to learn all the particulars of GCP cloud. We just don't have the time to waste in a growing startup for this and it is lost opportunity cost for engineer effort."

AWS was the first to offer cloud services and is still the market leader. In the early years of the cloud, AWS was the pacesetter in showing how physical infrastructure could be replaced by code-based provisioning of virtual servers and other IT infrastructure. Although that was – and still remains – their greatest strength, it is ironically where some of their competitors (such as Azure) are able differentiate themselves and we'll say more about that below. AWS brought code-first ways to provision, scale, secure, and utilise a range of cloud infrastructure elements. They started with servers, databases, and data architecture elements and then, more recently, branched out to analytics and data science tools and services. This was revolutionary for developers who now had the ability to build data architectures and scale them up or down as needed, *entirely via code*.

API Services

As hinted at briefly earlier in the chapter, nowadays one can access data science on-demand services via AWS APIs. These services can carry out a range of data science tasks such as:

- NLP (Natural Language Processing) task such as sentiment analysis using Amazon Comprehend
- Forecasting Time Series data with Amazon Forecast
- Detect faces and objects in images with Amazon Rekognition
- Translate text with Amazon Translate
- Transcribe text with Amazon Transcribe

With all of these, for a one-off (and reasonable) cost, you can beam your data to their API, let AWS run their models over the data and transmit the results back to you. Whilst the quality of the results varies and is generally a function of the quality of data, such API services can be a valuable supplementary tool for young and relatively green data science teams.

AWS is not alone in providing such services; many of the other providers have similar offerings. Indeed, both Azure and GCP have Natural Language, Translation, Speech, Video, and Text APIs. In terms of strengths and weaknesses, though, the devil is in the domain-specific details. Consider image recognition APIs, for example. If your use case is highly context-specific, it can well be that vendor offerings would not be able to perform well and you would be better off creating your own model from scratch. Keep in mind, though, that vendor offerings tend to improve rapidly and what was sub-par yesterday may not be so tomorrow.

API services offer an easy way for a growing data science team to trial and adopt advanced technologies. This makes them ideal for POCs. However, if you are planning to use them at scale, keep in mind that the costs can add up quickly. Doing some basic estimates around potential usage and cost at the front end of a POC can save you some headaches down the track. If cost turns out to be an issue, you will want to factor in resources to build, deploy, and maintain your own models should the POC prove successful.

Another important consideration with these services is location. This is generally not a concern for those who are working in industries or domains that are not heavily impacted by data residency considerations. However, many government and large enterprises have legislative or internal company policies that require data to be stored in a particular jurisdiction (country or state, for example). This was the case in one of Alex's previous roles in which there were large volumes of organisational data that had to be stored within the country. Unfortunately, for many of these API services, processing is done at a specific location which may not align with legislative requirements or your corporate mandates. Increasingly, though, cloud providers are bringing these services on-shore to more "shores", and building greater controls that enable users to determine where their data is sent and stored. That said, if data residency is important to your organisation, it is absolutely essential that you check this with your vendor prior to signing up.

Code vs User-Centricity

From the early days, Amazon's code-centric approach has made them the go-to vendor for start-ups whose founders and developers generally have a strong tech/coding background. Indeed, often their products are hosted on AWS, which makes the proposition even more compelling. Here's what Duhita Khadepau had to say about this:

> *"Often with startups, one of the key things of going with AWS is because your product itself is on AWS so that makes things easier. Since data is already in the ecosystem, you can take advantage of AWS internal pipelines, tools and connectedness; limiting code that needs to be created and having excellent speed and cost of data movements and processing. Having to push data into BigQuery (GCP) and back would be a pain and a cost."*

Additionally, AWS has historically offered growing companies generous free computing credits, which has added to their attraction for start-ups.

Microsoft (Azure) joined the cloud vendor bandwagon later but did so by taking a very different approach. Eschewing a solely code-centric approach, Microsoft gives users the option of intuitive, graphical user interfaces (GUIs) to their cloud services. Whilst you certainly can use code to engage with Azure if you are so inclined, Microsoft's approach has enabled them to broaden their market to include not just software developers or engineers, but also those who are more familiar with using UI-driven software tools – people like DBAs, BI developers, and data engineers. Indeed, many in this customer base are already familiar with Microsoft's UI paradigm for other data products (such as SSMS,[11] SSIS,[12] SSAS[13]) and are therefore highly receptive to these offerings in the cloud as it is an easy transition.

Microsoft's strong presence in many organisations via their operating system and business productivity software gives them a large corporate market for their Azure analytics offerings. They have leveraged this well by offering customers trial or base versions of new data products such as Power BI, which gives Microsoft the opportunity to introduce them to more advanced data offerings such as Azure ML.[14] Accordingly, Azure's market share has increased rapidly over the last few years. AWS still maintains a stronger footprint in larger scale data processing, storage, and pipelining. However, any comment in this realm could be dated as soon as it is written given the pace of progress and investment by both vendors in this sphere.

It is worth calling out Power BI here as an example of an offering that is currently (at the time of writing) a differentiator between the main players. Whilst there are a host of dashboarding and BI tools out there (see Chapter 2 for some), Power BI has in recent years come to dominate this space. AWS and GCP both have data visualisation products via Quicksight[15] and Data Studio,[16] respectively, but these products lag significantly behind Power BI in terms of features, updates, and particularly the community that has grown around the product. Whilst we wouldn't blindly recommend placing too much stock in reports such as *Gartner's Magic Quadrant for Analytics and BI Platforms*, in this instance it does tell an interesting story of the rise and rise of Power BI. In 2022,[17] Power BI is significantly ahead of its peers, particularly its main competitor who it had battled toe-to-toe for many years: Tableau. We have both seen this journey as it evolved and have ourselves moved from recommending Tableau as our go-to dashboarding product to endorsing Power BI as the leader in the space. Microsoft achieved this not only by being responsive to customer feedback and offering better features, but also by offering support and community building through their own events and those of their huge network of partners. Of course, Power BI is convenient if you are already on the Microsoft stack, but regardless it is currently a market-leading product that we have seen deployed extensively across many different domains and business contexts. Many of our interviewees spoke highly of Power BI and other Microsoft offerings. Here's what Matt Minor said:

> *"We use Microsoft Office and have an Office 365[18] environment. So naturally, it helps to go with Microsoft. We have found it to be a cheaper skillset to recruit than say GCP and AWS. SQL Server and Microsoft's data stack, despite perhaps being a bit older and clunkier, is tried and tested. This will serve us well at this stage of our journey until we need to build upon our current stack and move incrementally to better tools that fit a modern data stack. Another thing that I would call out is that the education and support that surrounds Power BI is off the charts. The community, forums and support that they have built around it with their partners and vendors is a huge asset."*

In conclusion, whilst Microsoft has many comparable services and offerings to the other two, it is notably differentiated in its enterprise-focused approach and has a particular strength in the BI space. This latter is worth calling out as those who are moving along their data and analytics journey often start with reporting and dashboards as their first step, as was noted in Chapter 2 where we discussed the analytics maturity of organisations.

GCP occupies an interesting position in the cloud and analytics services space. It was also later to the game than AWS and was playing catch up for a number of years. It now offers a number of services in cloud infrastructure, data science APIs, and other products similar to the other two main players. Like AWS and Microsoft, it also offers pathways for start-ups. In particular, their data warehousing solution, BigQuery, is seen as a market leader for web analytics. However, unlike AWS and Microsoft, they do not have as natural an audience that they appeal to. That said, it is worth noting their expertise in research when it comes to advanced models for text, video, and other applications of deep learning (discussed briefly in Chapter 2). Google has played a big role in the commercialisation of deep learning technologies with the creation and development of the open-source TensorFlow[19] library. They have embedded this expertise into their data science APIs to deliver some impressive text, image, and video recognition capabilities. Whilst the smallest of the three big players in the commercial cloud space, Google thus maintains a presence in the market by offering, alongside similar compute, storage and processing solutions, some competitive and technically advanced services in data science and machine learning.

Overall, when considering which provider to use for your cloud strategy, there is more that is similar about the main players than is different. As discussed previously, in the early stages, it makes sense to work with a single provider in order to avoid complex architectures and, more importantly, to save time and effort. That said, if you follow the guiding principles discussed below, you will avoid vendor lock-in, which continues to be the bane of large organisations that are often locked into long-term dependencies on enterprise software vendors.

Whilst single cloud may be the general path in the early days, with enterprise effort, scale, and investment you can be cloud agnostic. This will enable you to choose the best product for the use case at hand. As Craig Napier notes:

"One of our principles in cloud first, and cloud agnostic in relation to the specific services and tools we employ. We want to be able to choose the best in breed and be able to easily lift and shift [from one vendor to another] if required, and take advantage of emerging technologies."

We expand on "lift and shift" in the next section on guiding principles. But before we go there it is worth looking at a story about the whys of moving from one provider to another from our interviewees. Here is a story from Duhita Khadepau about why her organisation decided to move from Redshift (a data warehouse service from AWS) to Snowflake (a cloud data warehouse provider):

"One of the larger limitations of Redshift is around analysing JSON[20] objects. Our engineers capture data as JSON objects and save those objects in database columns. These objects are hard to query and caused issues with scalability and speed. So, whilst one of the products built [using this data] was amazing and customers wanted it, the product took 3-5 minutes to give results. With snowflake it's much easier to query the JSON object ... and has much faster processing abilities. There are a few other features, such as the" 'time travel' feature where

you can more easily recover mistakenly dropped data as compared to redshift and the ease with which you can spin up new instances and clone databases for analysts.

It would have been impossible for me to bring Snowflake in at the beginning; I would not have been able to justify the cost to management. At that time Redshift was perfect because it did what we wanted it to and my infrastructure engineers could actually help me maintain it. I didn't have to hire specialised skills... ."

This anecdote is an excellent segue into a discussion of guiding principles for technology choices.

Guiding Principles

Broadening our discussion of technical choices, we have compiled a few guiding principles from our own experience as well as that of our colleagues and the data leaders we spoke with for this book. These will not cover every possible situation, nor will they deal with details. Indeed, as your experience grows and your data capability expands, you will come up with your own learnings. It is worth making a note of these as your organisation's data capabilities grow. We have seen some teams document and embed these principles in a manner similar to corporate values. These principles then become a de facto checklist for any new technology choice and can be referred to at any stage, ranging from early discussions and vendor selection panels, through to implementation and even ongoing review.

Reducing Complexity

For those who are just starting on their data science journey, the most important question when considering new services or technology is: *how is this going to work with what we already have*? This question is very much in keeping with the core philosophy of Emergent Design: you always start from what you have, not with what is out there. As we have alluded to in Chapter 4, the organisation already has a data landscape into which the new service must fit. Therefore, the first thing you need to think through are the connections required between your existing technology stack and the new service. This may be a wholesale transfer of data from an on-premise database to one in the cloud – literally a "lift and shift". On the other hand, it may be just a data feed from an existing system to a vendor API. The point is, you need to think the details through.

Here are some additional questions to consider when looking at new services:

- Will the new service potentially entail additional work in the future (this is sometimes called "technical debt")?
- Does this choice result in a simplification of our data landscape (does it reduce the number of systems or simplify our data pipelines)?
- How easily can we build on this in the future?
- How easily can we replace this?

Here is what Ian Jackman (General Manager Data and Analytics at Bendigo and Adelaide Bank) had to say about this principle:

> *"Simplicity and reduction in complexity is a key guiding principle of our whole organisation at the moment. We've got a pretty complex tech landscape and business landscape so when we are implementing new initiatives, we are always seeking to simplify our ecosystem whilst also enabling future flexibility and scalability. The sometimes easier and cheaper pathway to a tactical solution may have perceived short term gain, but generally introduces more technical debt and complexity that will need remediation and make changes more difficult in the future."*

Blocking Innovation

As mentioned earlier in regards to data science services via APIs, an important consideration for all pieces of the data stack is *how their cost scales*. It may not be as obvious as the pay-per-image of the main cloud provider's image recognition services. Indeed, in an example shared with us of a large enterprise choosing an enterprise data science platform, it was discovered late in the discussion that creating additional machine learning models beyond a set base number would incur significant extra costs. Thankfully this was discussed and re-negotiated as this could have fundamentally stymied the growing data capability. Imagine an analyst in a marketing department who, while scoping out a potential project, had to justify such costs before a single line of code has been written (or button clicked). It is therefore important that the tools and services purchased aren't under any restrictive conditions that hinder staff from doing their work or trying out new ideas that occur to them.

Interoperability

The last two questions from the first guiding principle – "How easily can we build on this in the future?" and "How easily can we replace this?" can be expanded to another principle, that of *interoperability*, which is the ability of systems to work with those built by other manufacturers. The key to interoperability is to modularise your architecture in much the same way that cloud services do via APIs. What this means in practice is that systems within your landscape communicate with each other using industry standards. Building highly embedded and dependent webs of applications that exchange data in non-standard ways build dependencies that are hard to disentangle. This hinders your ability to *evolve* your technology stack as your data capability matures.

Here's what Ian Jackman had to say about interoperability:

> *"We are also focussing on being modularised and API driven in our tech choices these days. Everything should be API connected, which makes it modularized and componentized. In the cloud this is natively enabled, through containers and microservices. Across our Cloud platforms we build so that we have plug and play architectures that we can choose or implement best of breed componentry and have them interconnected in a very standardised way. We don't want to be locked into long term, black box vendor solutions that are monolithic and are therefore reliant on them and can't extend, integrate, or replace components easily. That's the past we've come from and is consciously avoided as we move forward."*

This was echoed by Craig Napier:

> *"We are very wary of buying huge full-stack solutions as this locks away a significant portion of your capability into that software solution. It is putting all your eggs in one basket. We are always looking to, wherever possible use building blocks ensuring interoperability between our solutions rather than full stack solutions. It provides the flexibility to scale, enhance and leverage emerging technologies and adapt to changing business needs. Then we can look at pulling bits out, upgrade bits, extending etc."*

Usability

An important technical consideration that connects people and technology is that of *usability*. This was hinted at in the previous section: AWS has traditionally had less of a UI-first approach as compared to Azure. Although this has changed over time and isn't as stark as it was before, as one gets deeper into the specifics of any of these technologies, the amount of code, scripts, etc. that need be written increase. Here it is important to keep in mind the preferences of your team in terms of which technologies they are comfortable with. As Hema Prasad (an Executive Data Leader) noted:

> *"There are a multitude of tools and technologies that are more or less capable of delivering what we want. Not to forget that these are going to be used by various communities of users within the organisation. Therefore, usability and user experience are top in my evaluation criteria for tools, technologies and products. How comfortable, how easy is it for users to employ the tools and technologies in order to produce the outputs? For instance, if you pick up an ETL tool, there are many market leaders and their tools provide more or less the same outcome. But if my community of users is more comfortable with using tool A versus tool B, then*

I would really tilt towards choosing the former because adoption would be much higher as tool A is the user's choice. Wherever possible, working with what your staff want helps build good social karma, which can come in handy if there are other areas where there may be more to implement that isn't universally loved."

The Effort to Keep Things Running

A concept that is generally familiar in the technology sphere is that of KTLO; or *"Keeping the lights on"*. This is a term for the effort that is required to just keep a system running. When software engineers create a feature or capability in a system, there is a lot of work that goes into keeping it running: maintenance, checks and tests, monitoring, updates, scaling considerations, etc. This can be anywhere from 5 to 20%[21] of the ongoing engineering effort.

The KTLO effort is often overlooked in the data sphere. Although some roles are purely dedicated to KTLO, such as DBAs and staff that maintain the infrastructure, there areas that are sometimes overlooked. Consider a dashboard that your analyst has built for the HR team. The dashboard shows headcount at different units, has annual leave balance projections, monitors sick leave and has a variety of other useful metrics. The HR team use it regularly to pull out reports they need to do their work. Now think, how likely is it that:

1. The HR team will never request updates or enhancements to the dashboard.
2. The data source for the dashboard never changes.
3. The data format doesn't change.

Clearly, none of the above is likely at all: the HR team will want updates; source systems will evolve; data formats will change – new data elements may be added and others removed. In short, once a data product is created, it grows and evolves as the data landscape and the needs of users evolve. KTLO requires someone to do all this work. This story was for a dashboard, but we hope it is clear that it applies to pretty much any data product including machine learning models and, for that matter, to any component in your evolving technical landscape.

From a KTLO perspective, some key questions to ask as data products, technologies, and systems are added are:

1. What tasks are required to maintain and enhance this product? How frequently must they be carried out? How much time will they take?
2. Who will be responsible for this effort?
3. Can we do this in-house or is it a specialised skill that locks us into a vendor or partner?

Transparency

This guiding principle prompts one to ensure that, as far as possible, the inner workings of the product are clear and understood. This manifests in a few different ways as it relates to the way data is ingested, processed, and returned from the technology. Let's make this concrete with some specific examples.

Transparency includes *where* your data is during the interaction. As discussed above in relation to the data science API services offered by the main cloud providers. When the data is ingested, does it stay on-shore? Does it go overseas at any point? If so, to which countries and through which servers (where)? For products as simple as an ETL tool, it may all be local on a desktop, but with more and more products moving away from local desktop distributions it may be surprising that even the humble ETL tool is ingesting data, pushing it off-shore to undertake the transformations, before sending it back to view in your browser. None of this may be apparent through the GUI you or your team are using.

Another angle to transparency arises when considering more advanced tools such as those that build machine learning models. The key question here is: do we know how the model gets its results? This can be tricky to find out as vendors may consider these particulars to be their proprietary information. Yet, it is important to ask the question, if only to understand whether the tools are proceeding in a way that is compliant with your own regulatory (either external, legislatively, or internal company policies) requirements. As a concrete example, a machine learning model that uses data aggregated from multiple patients to provide an outcome to a particular patient could be in violation of regulations such as HIPAA.[22]

To summarise this section: large, monolithic applications can take months or years to modify, which slows innovation and stymies your organisation's ability to evolve. However, as the cliché goes, change is the only constant. Keeping the aforementioned principles in mind will help you deliver data applications that are responsive to change.

Working with Vendors

As we have noted in Chapter 5, working with vendors can offer benefits beyond solving specific problems. If you choose the right partner, you can also use their expertise to upskill people in your organisation. As Ian Jackman noted:

> "...in project delivery, we get a lot of access to partners with a wide breadth of skills and experience. And we use that as a way of transferring knowledge and building skills in our people."

In this section we provide a set of guiding principles for working with vendors so that you can get the best value for your money and avoid some of the common pitfalls of such engagements.

Initial Discussions

The most important thing to keep in mind in the initial discussion is a point we have made in Chapter 4: *vendor's aims are different from your aims* (regardless of their claims to the contrary!). The vendor is sizing up the opportunity, willingness to pay, and particulars of your organisation and context; you, on the other hand, are trying to figure out whether the vendor can deliver what you need at a price that is reasonable.

Often customers will ask vendors for references and/or case studies. You can and should ask for these, but be sure to ask them for those in which they have solved a *similar* problem. A glowing reference for an unrelated problem tells you absolutely nothing. Of course, vendor references suffer from the same drawback as candidate references in recruiting: the vendor will give you only references that are positive. You should, therefore, do some basic independent checks through your own networks.

Finally, you may want to consider engaging the vendor for a trial POC where they work on a small problem that you give them. This gives both parties time to understand each other and determine whether a longer term relationship will work.

Making the Choice

The process of choosing a vendor depends on a variety of factors, not the least being your organisation's procurement policies. Often, the level of diligence required increases with the cost and complexity of the service. At the simple end, where you are choosing between two vendors who offer a similar off-the-shelf service, your decision may be based mainly on cost. However, if your problem is complex, chances are that it cannot be addressed by a standardised service and competing vendors will have to tailor their services to meet your requirements. In this case, your decision cannot be based on cost alone; you will have to take into account other, possibly more intangible, factors such as quality of solution, support, and even compatibility and trust!

Clearly, before you make your decision, you will need figure out what is important to your organisation. The most important point to note is that these decision criteria should be *framed collectively*, i.e., by seeking input from all those affected by the decision. There are many facilitation techniques that can help you do this – a simple brainstorming[23] session to more complex "industrial-strength" approaches[24] (see Culmsee and Awati (2012, 2013)) for some of these, and Awati and Nikolova (2022) for the rationale behind them). Note that simple brainstorming approaches will work just fine for most vendor decisions you will encounter. In our experience, the more complex approaches are needed only for large projects, i.e., those involving significant (multi-million dollar) investments or impacting diverse groups of stakeholders. Regardless of the approach used, keep in mind that the aim is to seek the *widest possible consensus* about the key factors that should be considered when making the decision. If simple approaches enable you to do this, so much the better.

It is worth mentioning that before formulating decision criteria, you may want to improve your understanding of available solutions to your problem. One way to do this is to describe your problem in general terms to a few vendors and ask them to tell you how they would approach it. If done formally, this is a request for proposal (RFP). The information in the proposals often help in formulating decision criteria. Once you have a set of commonly agreed criteria, you would draft up a request for quote (RFQ), which is essentially aimed at getting a detailed cost breakdown of the service sought.

Not all criteria are equal – sometimes cost is the most important criterion but often other criteria will trump it (for example, quality of work or ease of communication). The question then arises as to how criteria should be weighted. A simple and effective way to determine weights is through pairwise comparison.[25] In brief it works as follows:

1. Criteria are compared, two at a time. The criterion that wins the comparison gets a score of 1, the other gets a 0.
2. The criterion weight (for each criterion) is the total number of wins the criterion gets (across all comparisons) divided by the total number of pairs (i.e., total number of comparisons).

Figure 6.1 shows an example pairwise comparison for a decision that has the following criteria:

1. Cost
2. Ability to track work done by vendor (Oversight)
3. Proximity of the vendor (Proximity)
4. Ease of communication with vendor (Communication)
5. Quality of work done (Quality of work)

There is a subtle issue that can sometimes come up with the weightings. If you have a large number of criteria of varying importance, you can end up with a situation in which a large number of high scores on low weight factors can outweigh a high score on a high weight factor.[26] It is important to be aware of this and take steps to counter it if necessary.[27]

	Cost	Oversight	Proximity	Communication	Quality of work	Number of wins	% Wins overall
Cost		*Cost*	*Cost*	*Communication*	*Quality of work*	2	20
Oversight			*Oversight*	*Proximity*	*Quality of work*	1	10
Proximity				*Communication*	*Quality of work*	1	10
Communication					*Quality of work*	2	20
Quality of work						4	40
						10	100

FIGURE 6.1
An example pairwise comparison.

Note: Choices made are in *italics*.

Before we close this section, there is an important point we would like to reiterate. You should ensure that all impacted stakeholder groups are involved in the decision-making process *from the start*. As Sonya Zecchin noted:

> "*A breadth of backgrounds and experiences will allow you to design a broad selection of questions that wouldn't be possible if only the data science team was there to ask technical questions. Whilst everyone may not understand the technology, everyone there will understand their own business and problem space and therefore that brings important value at an early stage. Reservations can be called out and dealt with or acknowledged as a limitation and everyone can understand how this relates to what they are doing.*"

The important advantage of having the widest possible involvement is that of shared ownership over the decision. Rather than the tech team running off, purchasing something, and then trying to shop it around, everyone is part of the decision from the start, so buy in comes for free. When Alex has sat on panels at different organisations when choosing vendors for enterprise analytics platforms and solutions, he has found that having business stakeholders present and involved throughout the process including the technical components is incredibly valuable. It keeps the discussion focused on business-relevant matters, avoiding irrelevant technical detail.

Of course, diversity of perspectives comes with its own potential problems.[28] Although it can result in a broader (and hence more complete) coverage, it has the potential to hinder consensus. Eventually you do need to zero in on an agreed set of options and criteria, and to do that, you have to come to a shared understanding of the issues even if there isn't complete agreement. The well-known decision diamond (Figure 6.2) captures these complementary aspects of option or criterion formulation rather well.

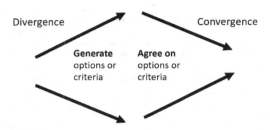

FIGURE 6.2
The decision diamond.

Taking Root…and Growing (the Wrong and Right Way)

We think it is appropriate to end this section and chapter with a cautionary fictional tale about a case management system in an unnamed organisation.

The main functions of the system can be summarised as follows: users log into the system, create cases, manage them, assign tasks and cases to other users, upload files, add statuses of various components, and bring the cases to a resolution.

The implementation starts and the vendor makes some quite reasonable requests. The system has to be integrated into your environment so they need access to your enterprise access management system – Single Sign On/ Active Directory or whatever your organisation uses. In addition, they also require a daily dump of HR data so that cases can be assigned to people based on their employee numbers/branches and workflowed through to manager positions (and also ensure that unauthorised staff do not see cases that they shouldn't). That seems reasonable enough, and although you aren't sure what will happen in the case of a restructure of the organisation, you feel confident that the vendor will work it out.

In the next version of the software, which the vendor insists you have to upgrade to in order to continue support, they offer you a dashboard where you can see how many open cases you have. That sounds useful indeed! "Of course, the dashboard can do so much more", the vendor says, "you can overlay your sales data, your extended HR data (leave, sick days, salaries), and be able to slice and dice your dashboard by all these different attributes to surface relationships. All you need to do is bring your finance, HR, operational data into our system…".

This is an all-too-common story that we have both seen in a number of different contexts. The vendors will attempt to make their product "sticky" by offering more and more features that enable *them* to become more embedded in *your* organisation. What we described above is one of the common paths they take to achieve this. If you're not careful, their product becomes your data warehouse, thus enabling the vendor to spread their tentacles across your data landscape. This often happens imperceptibly, so it is important keep an eye out for this kind of "lock in by stealth". The key to avoiding this is to:

Always partition your operational and analytical systems.

What this means is best illustrated through our story above. Reviewing open cases and being able to click into those is essentially an operational activity. However, once you begin slicing and dicing by dimensions (see Chapter 2) from *other source systems*, you are going beyond what should be facilitated by an operational tool. The correct solution to this problem is to *ingest* data from the case management system into *your* data warehouse or data lake (rather than the vendor's) and build your reports from there. To some readers, this may seem like we are stating the obvious. However, if we had a dollar for every "lock in by stealth" situation we have heard of or even seen first-hand, we'd be able to fund a pretty decent lunch for ourselves.

Concluding Remarks

This chapter has been largely about technical decisions that you will need to make on your journey towards building a data science or analytics capability. In doing so, we have spent a fair bit of verbiage on the decision-making process. The message we have attempted to convey is that although these decisions are ostensibly about technology, you will need to factor in the wider context of your organisation by involving all impacted stakeholder groups in the process. As we noted at the start of this book, data science is a sociotechnical capability. So apart from informing you about how to make good technical choices, we hope this chapter also serves to illustrate how the social and technical aspects of the discipline are intertwined, even in matters that seem largely about the latter.

Notes

1 www.zdnet.com/article/what-is-cloud-computing-everything-you-need-to-know-about-the-cloud/
2 In this book, term "virtual" is synonymous with "hosted in the cloud." Note that this is not necessarily the case. For more on virtualisation see: https://en.wikipedia.org/wiki/Virtual_machine
3 API – an Application Programming Interface is a way for two computer systems to communicate with each other.

4 https://aws.amazon.com/rekognition/
5 https://azure.microsoft.com/en-us/services/cognitive-services/computer-vis ion/#overview
6 https://cloud.google.com/vision
7 https://docs.aws.amazon.com/whitepapers/latest/introduction-aws-security/ introduction-aws-security.pdf
8 https://en.wikipedia.org/wiki/The_Day_After_Tomorrow
9 https://netflixtechblog.com/the-netflix-simian-army-16e57fbab116
10 www.gartner.com/en/newsroom/press-releases/2022-06-02-gartner-says-worldwide-iaas-public-cloud-services-market-grew-41-percent-in-2021
11 https://docs.microsoft.com/en-us/sql/ssms/download-sql-server-managem ent-studio-ssms
12 https://docs.microsoft.com/en-us/sql/integration-services/sql-server-integrat ion-services
13 https://docs.microsoft.com/en-us/analysis-services/ssas-overview
14 https://docs.microsoft.com/en-us/azure/machine-learning/overview-what-is-azure-machine-learning
15 https://aws.amazon.com/quicksight/
16 https://marketingplatform.google.com/about/data-studio/
17 https://powerbi.microsoft.com/en-us/blog/microsoft-named-a-leader-in-the-2022-gartner-magic-quadrant-for-analytics-and-bi-platforms/
18 www.office.com/
19 www.tensorflow.org/
20 www.json.org/json-en.html – JSON is a data interchange format.
21 https://medium.com/iconiq-growth/how-does-your-engineering-organizat ion-stack-up-the-2021-iconiq-engineering-efficiency-report-b9c08c34250d
22 www.dataguidance.com/opinion/usa-harnessing-ai-compliance-hipaa
23 https://gamestorming.com/3-12-3-brainstorm/
24 https://medium.com/@paulculmsee/innovations-in-decision-making-on-a-major-infrastructure-project-35625d590dcd
25 https://en.wikipedia.org/wiki/Pairwise_comparison
26 http://projectthorts.blogspot.com/2016/06/which-one-1.html
27 http://projectthorts.blogspot.com/2016/06/which-one-2_7.html
28 https://hbr.org/2017/06/does-diversity-actually-increase-creativity

---

References

Awati, K. and Nikolova, N. (2022), "From ambiguity to action: integrating collective sensemaking and rational decision making in management pedagogy and practice", *Management Decision*, Vol 60, No. 11, pp. 3127–3146.

Culmsee, P. and Awati, K. (2012), "Towards a holding environment: building shared understanding and commitment in projects", *International Journal of Managing Projects in Business*, Vol. 5 No. 3, pp. 528–548.

Culmsee, P. and Awati, K. (2013), *The Heretic's Guide to Best Practices: The Reality of Managing Complex Problems in Organisations*, iUniverse Star, Indianapolis, IN.

7

Doing Data Science: From Planning to Production

Introduction

This chapter provides you with an overview of the various steps of a machine learning project. These projects are where your efforts in capability and technology building become visible to the business as you frame and solve problems that matter to people across the organisation. We should emphasise that every data science project is unique and unfolds in its own way, so there is no single "best practice" approach to all projects. However, there are a number of good practices that can help you set up and manage projects in a manner that maximises your chance of success. In the following sections, we will give an overview of the key steps that you will want to consider for your projects. Some steps may be more relevant than others in your particular context, so the points we describe should be used as a checklist to think through, rather than a procedure to follow, as you turn to your first data science projects.

This chapter is written with you, the manager/leader of the data team, in mind. You may not be familiar with the intricacies of the ever-changing technologies of data science, and this is precisely why you need to understand the technology-independent commonalities between data science projects. Data science is still a growing field, and there are (as yet) no widely accepted practices. Since data scientists come from a wide variety of professional backgrounds, there is a huge diversity of views on how projects should be done. People tend to assume that data science projects are like any other technology project. As a result of this assumption, important elements are sometimes overlooked. This chapter will give you the knowledge, language, and understanding to manage data science projects from a business perspective. Also, as we have noted in Chapter 5, working with data is a team effort. Accordingly, another core aim of this chapter is to point out how you can involve the business at various stages of the project (summarised in Table 7.1 later in this chapter).

The chapter is structured as follows: we begin with a broad overview of the key stages of the Machine Learning Workflow (henceforth abbreviated MLWF), following which we discuss the sub-tasks in each of the stages.

DOI: 10.1201/9781003260158-7

Although we gloss over technical details, we throw in some references for the curious. Our main intent is to arm you with the key questions that you, as a data leader, should be asking your data scientists as they embark on their projects. It is incumbent on the business to set these expectations else the proverbial cart-before-horse situation will eventuate. Apart from leading to sub-optimal outcomes and loss of goodwill, this can terminally damage the credibility of your fledgling data capability.

The Machine Learning Workflow

One of the earliest and still most popular MLWFs is the CRISP-DM model we introduced in Chapter 2. However, as we noted there, the model is somewhat dated as it was formulated in the 1990s, well before data science became a thing. Alex and his colleagues in the Complex Adaptive Systems Lab at the University of Technology Sydney have developed an MLWF that is more aligned to the high-level steps of data science project work (Scriven et al. 2022). Figure 7.1 is a summarised version of the MLWF. The steps will be familiar to data science practitioners and, indeed, to many readers as we have touched upon some of them in earlier chapters.

The four-stage pathway at the top, labelled "Traditional Workflow", is the typical MLWF that is found summarised in CRISP-DM and in some similar

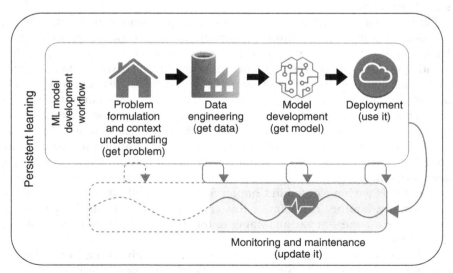

FIGURE 7.1
A modern machine learning workflow.

form in many academic papers. The arrows point from left to right as the project moves from "Problem Formulation & Context Understanding", through "Data Engineering", "Model Development", and "Deployment". Few (if any) existing variations of the CRISP workflow explicitly consider "Monitoring & Maintenance" of the deployed model. However, this is a vital activity in an organisational context where the entire point is to use data science technology to inform and/or improve a business practice or process in an ongoing manner. If one doesn't monitor or maintain a model, chances are that degradation of model performance will not be detected and remediated in time. Another point, which we have noted in Chapter 2, is that data science is an iterative endeavour, so the arrows in the traditional workflow (top part of Figure 7.1) should in principle point both ways. However, to avoid every node linking to every other node and thus cluttering the diagram, we will proceed with the understanding that the arrows depict the general direction of movement, as the aim is to get a working model deployed into production.

The bottom part of Figure 7.1 shows the important bit that the traditional workflow misses: monitoring and maintenance. You will note that the arrows here loop through the elements of the traditional workflow. This makes sense: when models are updated or remediated, the data scientist will often have to get new or fresh data, tweak the model and redeploy it. We will cover this in more detail in the MLOps section of this chapter.

With that said about productionising models, we should acknowledge that some machine learning model building can be purely exploratory in nature. In fact, you are likely to do a lot of this in the earlier stages of growing your data capability. Some of your POCs will be purely "tactical" and may be done in a quick-and-dirty manner to explore feasibility or prove a point rather than to be put into production. However, as your data capability matures, the solutions you build will be expected to be stable and reliable. To do this, you will need to deploy your trained models and monitor and maintain them in a way that delivers ongoing business value. This is not only a matter of performance; the model also needs to be monitored to ensure that it doesn't *drift* and start giving unexpected outcomes[1] (we discuss drift later in this chapter). When this happens, you may need to go back to the very first step of the MLWF and check the formulation of the problem. The faded line in Figure 7.1 is essentially an acknowledgement that the original formulation of a machine learning problem may, in time, need to be revised due to phenomena like drift.

The MLWF in Depth

Figure 7.1 is a high-level view of the MLWF (Scriven et al. 2022). As a data science strategist/leader, you will need to understand some of the details in each of these steps. To this end, we will now give you a brief, non-technical view of the details. Our emphasis is on what you, as the person setting up the capability, should be aware of.

Figure 7.2 summarises the details in each step of the MLWF. You will notice that each section ends with a lighter coloured shape denoting the key outcome of that stage. As noted above, the aim is to move forward (albeit, iteratively) to get a trained model deployed into an organisational decision-making process. Not all tasks detailed in Figure 7.2 are relevant to all problems and domains. However, as your data science capability grows and you start tackling problems across different domains, it is important to keep in mind that you will likely need to incorporate tasks that were not needed earlier. For example, perhaps you begin with some predictive maintenance tasks (such as predicting which sensor is likely to fail) because the data is there and quite structured and (amazingly!) clean. Since the problem deals with elements of infrastructure, you will not need to consider bias or fairness metrics.[2] However, once you start looking at HR or customer data, you will definitely need to incorporate such metrics into your model evaluation process.

Problem Formulation and Context Understanding

The aim of this step is to ensure that the project is set up for success. It is the work done at this stage in framing the problem and drawing up plans that determines how the project will unfold. Indeed, you may well find that a discussion with the business leads to the project being de-prioritised or not given go-ahead due to a realisation that it is not going to deliver the benefits originally envisaged. That is a good thing, particularly when you have several promising projects that have been put forward for consideration. Whilst we have discussed the formulation of POCs in Chapter 4, the practically focused sub-tasks listed here – for example, understanding of prior art, availability of resources and data – can assist in determining the feasibility of candidate POCs.

Firstly, any project – whether it is one relating to data or not – will start with *understanding requirements*. The most important thing to keep in mind, as we have noted ad nauseam, is that these should be business rather than technically focussed. The worst kind of requirements begins with lines like *"This project aims to build a machine learning model that X"* or worse *"...aims to build a Neural Network that X"*. The reason is that you simply do not know at the start what kind of solution you will end up with. It may be (and we have often seen this) that the solution that is eventually implemented is a simple domain-driven rules-based engine[3] as it addresses the business needs with a high enough coverage of scenarios. The famous collaborative filtering algorithm used by Amazon[4] for recommendation engines is still widely used as it can be quite effective but involves no machine learning. The algorithm is based on the notion that if person A and person B have bought similar

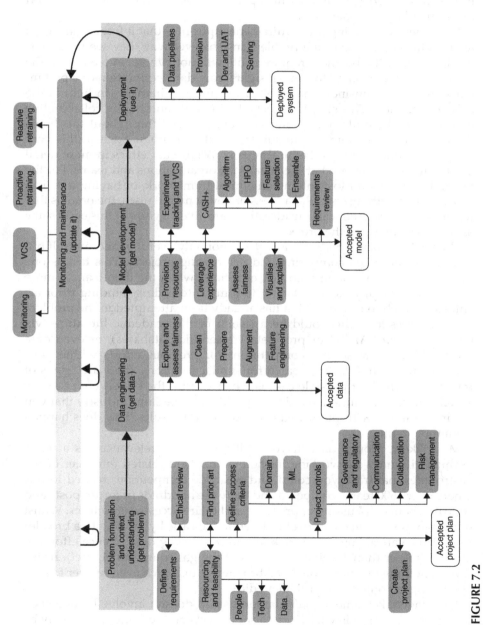

FIGURE 7.2
Detailed machine learning workflow process.

items in the past, then they are likely to continue doing so in the future. So, if person B has bought item X which person A has not, then item X is a good recommendation for person A.

The benefit of defining the requirements upfront is that it frees up the data team to focus on solving the problem in whatever way they see fit. This is not to say that the business requirements will not evolve. Indeed, once the data team comes back with some insights from data exploration or a preliminary model, the business may well tweak the requirements in light of the new information. This simply reflects the iterative and highly collaborative nature of model building, a point we have stressed throughout this book. However, there is an important sub-task and checkpoint exists at this very early stage: undertaking an ethical review. We discuss ethics in more detail in Chapter 8 and cover what this means for organisations and teams. For the team, it may amount to applying an ethical framework, or having a review process or something else.[5] Regardless of how it materialises, the point is that it is imperative that ethical considerations are given a voice at this early stage as well as throughout the project.

The next sub-task – *finding prior art* – is not only useful in and of itself but also has value when comparing and prioritising projects. This task is one that is missed more often than not, especially when the data team is more on the "code-happy" side – itching to jump into coding. Finding prior art entails a search to find out what has already been attempted in the problem space in question. This could be a search of the academic literature (via Google Scholar,[6] ArXiv[7] or proprietary scientific databases), or even data science blogs, data science competitions[8] or previous efforts within your own organisation. Like any search for similar solutions, there are "rings of relevance". The best possible case is when you hit the bullseye – i.e., your search surfaces a solution to a similar problem in the same industry that you are in, complete with published code, data, and results. This does happen from time to time.

More likely, though, is that you will find partial relevance. As a quick example, if you were working in the medical field related to cancer of the gastro-intestinal tract, you could find a Kaggle competition[9] related to this where over 1500 teams competed and there are hundreds of forum posts and code notebooks discussing approaches and their successes or failures. Whilst there may not be such a perfect fit to your use case, by moving to a broader ring of relevance, you could look at *medical imaging* data science efforts in general (rather than specific to cancers of the gastro-intestinal tract). If this reveals nothing of value, you could broaden your search even further to look at imaging in contexts other than medical.

This stage takes time. It isn't glamorous and doesn't involve Python code or big servers, but it is vital work to set projects on the right path. It may be that when considering Project A vs Project B, you find extensive prior art for the former and virtually nothing for the latter. In this case, even if Project B is deemed more important by the business, you may want to undertake Project

A first because you can leverage prior art, resulting in a shorter timeframe for implementation and value generation.

For you, the data leader, there are two important takeaways from finding prior art. Firstly, you should ensure that there is enough *time* baked into projects to undertake the search and review. Secondly, it is worth setting the *expectation* that your data team will dedicate enough effort towards this. Given the broad backgrounds and pathways from which people arrive at data science, this effort can also help individual team members broaden their knowledge of the business domain as well as their own field.

Resourcing & feasibility is up next. Broader considerations of people and technology have been covered in Chapters 5 and 6. Project-specific resourcing is more a matter of your specific context and team size. We will not say much about this as it is a stock standard aspect of all projects. That said, there are some sub-notes here that are worth calling out. Firstly, in addition to technical staff, resourcing is also about making available the technical resources (software, servers) required to run build and run models. Ideally, you already have this in place as you have foreseen the kinds of projects you will be doing. Additionally, you will need to consider the resources required to deploy the model into production if this is required. We will say more about this later in this chapter. The only point we will make is that projects often fail to recognise that the path from development to production can be fraught with unexpected challenges. For example, you may have a situation where you want to embed model predictions into business software, but the latter is a proprietary product that does not allow for integration of external data feeds. In this case you may have to resort to semi-manual workarounds that are an added burden for your users.

In addition to people and technology, resourcing is also about data. It is sometimes tacitly assumed that the data required to undertake a project is available, is at the level of detail required, is labelled (see Chapter 2) and you have permission from the data owner to use it for your project. These assumptions are often implicit and not tested until later in the game. This is why we emphasise the need to do this at the front end of your project. Here are some of the questions you will want to ask:

- Is there enough data available?

  At the risk of a gross generalisation, building predictive models on less than several thousand rows of data can be a challenge because model robustness is generally a function of the size (number of observations) and coverage (are all possible outcomes and outcome paths represented in the data). These are aspects of *data quality*.

- Is it clean enough?

  Another important aspect of data quality, relevant to model building, is the cleanliness of the data. Examples of dirty data abound. Here are some of the common ones we have encountered:

- Illegitimate values – these are data values that are not permissible for the field in question. For example, a day of the week that is greater than 7 or a negative value for revenue.
- Duplicate rows – this often happens in customer databases where the same customer registers more than once (we briefly discussed a case study on data deduplication in Chapter 4).
- Spelling errors – this is very common in address fields in customer databases.

The problem with dirty data is that it can completely destroy the predictive power of a model. Take, for example, the case in which there are two records for a customer in a sales database. The model will treat the two records as two different customers. It is easy to see how this will cause problems for the model.

- Is the data accessible?

  This pertains to whether the data can be extracted from the source system in a timely manner. For example, if you require daily updates to your dataset, then a weekly export from your ERP system will not cut it.

- Are you *allowed* to use this data for modelling?

  This refers to not just organisational rules around data usage, but also government legislation around privacy of personal information (more on this in Chapter 8). As the data leader, it is incumbent on you to set down rules around what data can and cannot be used for modelling.

- Is it labelled?

  As noted in Chapter 2, data is labelled when the target variable (the one you want to predict) is known. An example of a labelled dataset is a loan dataset which contains a column that tells you whether the customer defaulted (Yes or No). This column is the one you want to predict. If the data is not labelled – i.e., the customer default column is not available – the problem becomes impossible to solve using supervised learning as you do not know whether a customer has defaulted and hence you cannot build a predictive model. You might still be able to use unsupervised techniques like clustering (see Chapter 2) but the predictions associated with these are weaker than those that come out of supervised models (also see Chapter 2 for more on supervised/ unsupervised models).

The next element, *success criteria*, should have already been considered in discussions with the business. For example, the business may consider the model successful if it leads to tangible improvement in business outcomes. However, in addition to these, there are technical success criteria that refer to how good a model is. For example, a business objective could be to improve sales. No machine learning model can do this directly. The technical team therefore frames this problem as one of identifying new customers who might respond to a sales campaign based on a knowledge of the response patterns of old customers. As part of the model building process, data scientists will output *performance metrics* such as *Accuracy, Precision, Recall*[10]. An important, but subtle, point is to be made here on technical metric choice. We won't delve too far into the technical details but it should be noted that the classic accuracy[11] score may not always be appropriate, especially in situations where you have *unbalanced* data. This xkcd comic[12] does a great job of representing what we mean here. If one were to create a model that simply predicted "No" every time for the question "Is it Christmas Today", it would be 99.73% accurate. This sounds fantastic but it has missed the single important prediction! Basing a metric on getting the majority class right is fraught with risk in many situations that matter. Consider medicine or spam email detection or predictive machinery maintenance. The majority of the time, your data will be "not X' (Not spam, Not disease, Not broken, etc.) and hence accuracy scores may give a false impression of good model performance. Metrics such as *Precision* and *Recall* may be more appropriate here.

The translation between technical and business metrics can, at times, be simple. For example, *if* the model achieves a certain technical performance output, how many additional sales would be made? However, the devil is in the details, and there are two specific things to watch out for.

Firstly, a performance metric may not be appropriate because it is an overall (summary) measure of *how many errors were made*. A score less than 100% implies that the model has made some errors (incorrect predictions) which should be called out. A more appropriate metric would consider the *cost of being wrong*. In some scenarios, this may halt the project in its tracks. Alex recalls a hackathon hosted by various government agencies in which the fire service sponsored a problem aimed at reducing the number of false callouts (and thereby facilitating a more optimal use of resources). Despite the best modelling efforts of many data science teams, the reality was that nobody would put such a model into autonomous production because the cost of being wrong (failing to send aid to those in need) is too high.

Secondly, consider a lower stakes example: what happens if users on a website receive a bad recommendation? Does it increase churn, or are users lost in terms of loyalty and future value? Unlikely ... and even if this happens occasionally, the company may be willing to take the hit if the recommendations tend to lead to increased sales overall.

Both these examples are situations where the mapping from technical to business metrics is straightforward. There are other situations where the modelling is several steps removed from the direct business impact. In these cases, one should be especially cognisant of the gap between the two and ensure that useful information is not "lost in translation". In formulating this part of the project, it is often asked; "What is a good score?" – 60%, 80%, or 90%? Unfortunately, there is no way to know how your model will perform until it is built. However, if a good prior art search has been carried out, you will likely have a sense of what's possible. Additionally, it is important to frame this in terms of *uplift*. In the recommendation example, there is likely a base (i.e., already existing) rate of users returning to make additional purchases. So, the question here is: do the predictions of your model lead to an uplift (i.e., increase) in that rate?

As a data leader, it is your job to set the success criteria for data science projects. The key takeaway is to ensure that the technical performance metrics that are chosen are aligned with business outcomes. That is, it should be possible to translate the technical measures into metrics that are meaningful to the business sponsors of the project.

Finally, you will need to consider *project controls* that should be put in place before the work commences. Controls around *project governance* (reporting lines, structures, and frequencies), *communication* (status reports, updates, etc.), and *collaboration* (meetings, co-design sessions, co-location, and team-work) are common to all kinds of projects, so you can follow what you already have in your organisation. The only additional point we would make is that data science projects work best in an environment that encourages exploration, trial and error, and continual open dialogue between business and technical stakeholders – indeed, every data science project is an exercise in Emergent Design!

The bit about continual dialogue between business and technical stakeholders is worth elaborating on. A single incorrect assumption can be ruinous. Alex can recall learning this lesson quite painfully on a project he did some years ago with a healthcare organisation. His team had initial discussions with the client, obtained data and scoped up a project to model length of hospital stay of patients. The intent was to understand the reasons for inordinately long stays. The data was clean so the team proceeded with the modelling. However, they made an assumption very early on about how two crucial pieces of data were related. When they were well into the project, they found out that their assumption was incorrect. This meant that all the work they had done from the start of the project including all exploration, modelling, and insights were invalid.

You, the data leader, have the opportunity to set the standards for communication and interaction between business and data teams on projects. It is vital that you emphasise the need for regular conversations with domain experts to avoid situations like the one noted above. These check-ins are an opportunity to share work, share progress, ask questions, and generally minimise the risk of unfounded assumptions. Additionally, regular conversations strengthen the bonds between the data team and the business, giving both a shared sense of ownership over a project, thus creating an environment of trust which increases chances of ongoing engagement with the business unit in question. We summarise specific opportunities for such trust-building through collaboration in Table 7.1.

TABLE 7.1

Opportunities for Collaboration with the Business at Various Stages of the MLWF

MLWF Stage	Opportunities for Collaboration
Problem formulation and context understanding	• Scoping requirements with the business. • Collaboratively translating business objectives to data science objectives and metrics. • Opportunity sizing the impact of potential data science project(s) in business terms, including potential business impact of incorrect model outputs. • Discussing the landscape of prior art and its relevance for projects at hand. • Sourcing and critically evaluating current data assets (including accessibility) for the project(s) at hand. • Setting up regular communication channels, sharing, assumption-unblocking, and discussion sessions for the entire project.
Data engineering	• Discussing and validating insights found from EDA. • Aligning on data quality issues and proposed fixes, including the impact of these choices. • Brainstorming potential features to engineer and additional datasets to add. • Aligning on organisational bias and fairness definitions, then discussing the presence of this in the data and actions to take.
Model development and explainability	• Sharing insights and discussing/sense-checking feature importance scores. • Providing domain insight to assist error analysis efforts. • Aligning on when to discontinue efforts to improve model performance. • Discussing bias and fairness presence in model outputs, and potential actions to take.
Deployment, monitoring, and maintenance	• Aligning business expectations with technical efforts to deploy models and selecting the deployment approach that can meet those expectations. • Testing and providing feedback on test versions of the proposed deployment environment. • Collaborating on a monitoring framework and actions that will be taken for different scenarios.

Data Engineering

The second section in Figure 7.2 is *data engineering*, which involves the initial exploration, processing, and enhancing of data for modelling purposes. We can split this into three distinct subsections. Firstly, exploring for insights and ethical considerations (see Chapter 8). Secondly, cleaning and preparing data. And finally, enhancing the data via augmenting (joining additional data) and arranging it in new ways to provide more information to the model (also called feature engineering).

The acronym "EDA" (exploratory data analysis) is well known to data scientists as a key step in the modelling process. However, exploration for exploration's sake can go in several directions that are tangential to the problem at hand. Also, it can continue ad infinitum if left unchecked, so it is reasonable to set time-boundaries on this component of the MLWF. Continual consultation with and input from the business can be valuable in constraining the kinds of exploration that the data team undertakes. If time permits, there is value in free exploration too, as there could be aspects that the business owners of the data have overlooked. The value of exploratory work lies in the fact that insights surfaced at this stage can sometimes redeem a project (in the eyes of the business) even if the modelling fails. Good exploratory work has value of its own, so it should not be given short shrift.

As someone setting the standards for these projects, there should be an expectation that there are regular working sessions between data and business teams to share insights, discuss questions, and check assumptions. In these sessions, it is not at all uncommon for an "insight" (as considered by the data team) to be dismissed by domain experts to be uninteresting or not insightful at all. Additionally, if you are in a context in which there is an ethical lens to your work, you should put in place measures to ensure that bias and fairness reports of the data are generated prior to model building. You would also want to be looking very carefully at data attributes that hold personal information. We will say much more about these issues in Chapter 8.

As the data team explores, they are also looking for data quality issues that are likely to affect modelling work and drive technical choices around preparation and modelling. We already mentioned duplicates and spelling errors earlier in this chapter. Another example is missing values. Some algorithms cannot handle missing values so work will need to be done to handle these in ways that are appropriate for the algorithm that will be used. This task may appear to be quite technical and therefore not requiring business input. However, that is not so: decisions made during data cleaning have potential to *embed* (often erroneous) assumptions into the data right from the start. We both remember an introductory machine learning class in which we deliberately made one of the columns around 97% null, to test (a) whether students would discover this, and (b) what they would do about it. One particular student made the decision to delete every row with a null value in it. Yes, he deleted 97% of the data in one fell swoop. Whilst this is a valid technique for dealing with missing data in some circumstances (e.g., say 5 rows with missing values in 750,000 rows of data), it was clearly inappropriate in this case. There are a variety of techniques from the simple (as above) to the more complex for dealing with missing data[13] or – for that matter – other common data quality issues. Keep in mind though, that each comes with its own trade-offs.

It is therefore an important requirement for the data team to transparently document and explain:

- What checks were carried out? Did they check for missing values (or invalid values), skew, balance, correlations, outliers/anomalies, duplicates?
- What was found when carrying out those checks?
- What do they *propose* to do about data quality issues (such as duplicates or missing values)? They should also explain why they have chosen to follow this course of action instead of doing something else.
- What other data preparation steps were undertaken and why?

Here it is worth a call out to Chapter 5 where we discussed hiring data science talent. Deliberately putting some dirty data into the take-home data exercise will enable you to test if the candidate understands the importance of data exploration and cleansing. Candidates who do this and write it into their reports/presentations are definitely worth a second look as they are demonstrating the dispositions of a reflective data practitioner rather than a code-happy one.

As an interesting aside, it is often said that data scientists spend 80% of their time cleaning and preparing data. This factoid[14] is oft repeated but if one is curious enough to dig into its origins, it can be traced back to a 2016 report from CrowdFlower[15] which, as it happens, combined "Cleaning and organising data (60%)" with "Collecting data sets (19%)" to arrive at the final figure. The report provides limited details on the number of respondents or methodology, so it is impossible to judge the veracity of the figure. Regardless, it has persisted in data science lore. It is interesting that other surveys find much lower proportions (such as 15% for cleaning and 11% for gathering from Kaggle,[16] or data cleansing at 26% from Anaconda[17]). Whatever the actual figure though, it is fact that data cleaning and preparation is a core activity in the MLWF.

Once the cleaning is done, an important consideration is that of *enhancing* the data. One way this is achieved is through combining the data with other internal or external data sources. For example, using weather data is a common step in new services industries, such as food delivery. Indeed, the old adage "If it's hot, people buy more ice cream" still has a place in the world of machine learning, though machine learning (with enough quality data) would be able to nuance this by surfacing relationships between how hot, where, how much ($), and other factors.

Another way data is enhanced is by casting it into representations that are more informative for the algorithm. This process, which works best when it incorporates business knowledge, is called *"Feature Engineering"*. How it works is best clarified through an example. In the classic housing pricing example (see Chapter 2), the aim is to predict price given the number of bedrooms, bathrooms, and area of a house (and a host of other attributes such as location). One could feed the algorithm the data as-is. However, it may be that estate agents know from experience and their own analysis that people care about the number of bathrooms per square foot area (this is a made-up example!). Based on this knowledge, one would construct an attribute – number of bathrooms per square foot – and add it to the dataset. If the estate agents are right, this should improve the predictive power of the model. To be sure, machine learning models can parse signals from the data without this work, but explicitly representing the data in such a way enables you to pass a "direct message" to the algorithm, telling it explicitly to use this attribute.

In our experience, the activity of brainstorming additional features with business stakeholders and testing those in the model is an excellent opportunity for collaboration and building a joint sense of ownership over a project. If the engineered features turn out to be valuable, business stakeholders will feel that they have made a strong contribution to the modelling process. This is a great motivator for future collaboration.

A word of warning though: just like in many other parts of the MLWF, feature engineering done wrong can derail a project. For example, many feature engineering tools have entered the market – Featuretools[18] is an example. These help with some of the heavy lifting by automatically creating combination features without any consideration of domain relevance. Whilst this work may produce an interesting feature such as "Average sold house price, in the last 3 months for this suburb" (a potentially useful feature), it will also produce "Average sold house price, in the last 2 months for this suburb", "Average sold house price, in the last 4 months for this suburb", and potentially second- and third-order metrics such as "The log *of the* average *of the* median sold house price for the last 4 months for this suburb". One can see how this is just silly. Moreover, if one generates thousands of features, there will be some that *appear* to relate just by statistical chance. So, although these tools have their place, we would caution against using them indiscriminately. A more controlled approach that involves close and deep interaction with business stakeholders is much more likely to yield successful outcomes.

As your data science practice grows, you may want to consider building *feature stores* that serve as a common storage area for features and associated metrics. This can ensure that different teams or projects construct features in a similar way, thereby ensuring that consistent insights are drawn. However, in the early stages, this won't be a primary need.

You may be wondering why we have spent so much time discussing data processing and preparation. This is because of a largely unappreciated truth that the most meaningful progress in modelling is made through proper data preparation. Although this has been mentioned from time to time in various articles and blogs, it is only very recently that this way of practicing data science has been given a name to rally around: Data Centric AI.[19] [20] Whilst picking the right algorithm and tuning yields some incremental uplifts, it is through diligent preparation and cleaning that the most significant progress is made.

Model Development and Explainability

Several of the sub-tasks in this area are largely technical. However, there are a few that are worth noting as areas where setting expectations upfront is important. The task noted as *leverage experience* is a reference not only to the search for prior art, but also a reminder to keep business stakeholders informed and involved as the initial modelling results and insights trickle in. Models don't just return predictions; they can return interesting insights about which variables are driving the prediction. Although algorithm selection and optimisation is the domain of the data scientist, it is important to set the expectation that the data team will be able to explain the reasons for the predictions (which variables drove the predictions) in plain English. This is called *explainability* – and we'll say much more about it later in this chapter and the next. There is a trade-off between the power and explainability of algorithms[21] – the more powerful algorithms tend to be more opaque in that it is often hard to figure out the reasons for their particular predictions. Explainability matters a lot in some highly regulated industries. So much so that regulations in these industries permit only simple algorithms to be used and require that results be explainable.

Let us consider a typical workflow within this section and how business stakeholders can and should be involved. A data science team will try a variety of different models, tune them and score them. Now there are several lines of exploration and understanding that will benefit from business expertise.

The first of these is what is termed *feature importance scores*. Different algorithms will present these in different ways, with varying levels of abstraction. Let's start with a simple example. Consider the following (fictional) model which predicts the price of a house:

$$price = number\ of\ bedrooms * 30,000 + \$400,000$$

Determining feature importance here is straightforward: the number of bedrooms has a positive effect on the price of a house: $30,000 per bedroom. Although more complex algorithms are not amenable to easy interpretation by inspection, there are some tools that can help. The SHAP[22] and LIME[23] libraries are a couple of the more popular ones these days. These libraries determine the importance of the variables by making small changes to individual input variables and seeing what effect the changes have on the predicted variable. If the change in the predicted variable is large, the input variable is important; if not, it isn't important. These models output feature importance scores for each input variable and also show what these scores are per prediction. There are a couple of things worth noting here. Firstly, importance scores are not absolute; they are relative to all other input variables. Secondly, importance is an indication of correlation, not causation.[24] For example, a model predicting volume of international travel from Australia might predict that international travel increases with temperature. However, this does not mean that high temperatures cause people to travel overseas. More likely, it has something to do with the fact that people travel overseas in summer. It is also worth noting that SHAP and LIME are model agnostic as they rely only on inputs and outputs.

Whilst the concept of "feature importance scores" sounds like something squarely within the technical domain, it is important to set the expectation that the data team will work with the business to develop a joint understanding of feature importance. That is, the data team should produce these scores and help the business understand what they mean and, more importantly, discuss the implications of these for the next round of modelling. As an example, a while ago Alex was developing a model to predict final university subject grades based on a student dataset. The objective was to help identify which students were at risk of failing as early as possible in the semester, to help target support mechanisms. An early model found a particular feature that was far more important than any other feature, about 100 times more important than the next one down. It turned out that buried within the construction of that feature was the output variable (the final mark). No surprise that it worked so well! This issue was identified by a subject matter expert from the academic team and the feature was removed in the next iteration of the model.

In addition to looking at the features of the model, business stakeholders can play a useful advisory role in undertaking error analysis. This involves looking more closely at the data from mis-classified cases. For example, let's say the housing price model above generally predicts the price within $20,000. However, this is a general error measure. If you split the error by postcode, it could be that in some postcodes the error drops to $10–15,000 and in other postcodes the error is as high as $200,000! This strongly suggests that you need to dig deeper into what is happening in those high-error postcodes. There could be a huge variety of reasons, from the technical (perhaps there are too few data points from that postcode) to domain-related (perhaps recent rezoning has changed the boundaries of that postcode). Conversations between the business and data teams can help diagnose the reasons for the error and take appropriate action. If the problem is too few data points, then you might decide to get more data on those postcodes (if that effort is worth the potential model uplift). If the issue is rezoning, you may want to include current/past zoning as an additional input variable or even exclude rezoned postcodes from the exercise.

In an earlier section, we mentioned a bias-fairness check in relation to the data that was being used for the model. Once a model is created, however, there is another important step in assessing the bias-fairness of the model itself. This relates to the predictions or outputs of the model, rather than the inputs. We won't delve into this here as we say more about it in the following chapter. The only point we will make is that the process of checking must involve key business stakeholders. There are many ways in which the checks can be implemented, each with their own implications. The data team needs to understand how bias-fairness is interpreted within the wider organisation in order to determine which checks should be implemented.

So now to the actual process of model building – this is the CASH+ section in Figure 7.2, where the acronym stands for the Combined Algorithm Selection and Hyperparameter Optimisation (HPO) problem. This refers to the process of trying out different algorithms on the data, tuning them by tweaking available algorithm settings, and seeing which one works best. The reference to *ensembles* in Figure 7.2 is a nod to the fact that often a combination (or ensemble) of algorithms will work better than any single algorithm. The point to note in modelling is that, if left unchecked, it can turn into an ongoing exercise with a massive and unjustified expenditure of effort. Left to themselves, many (not all!) data scientists will continually "tune" models to try and improve performance metrics. However, it is important to keep in mind that, beyond a point, this effort has diminishing returns. The penchant to "keep modelling" can be partially alleviated by specifying what performance is acceptable in the planning stage. In addition to that, regular check-ins and progress reports can help determine when to call it quits. For example, getting a model from 80 to 88% Accuracy between fortnightly meetings is great progress, but if the next two meetings find this at 88.5 and 88.75%, it is time for the business to determine if the increase is really impactful. It probably isn't. Although there are cases where each 0.1% increase in a metric translates to a downstream gain of millions of dollars, these are rare exceptions.

Finally, once the teams have come together with a model that has passed the ethical checks as well as the metrics set for technical performance, it is important to do a stop-check against the requirements. One can then determine the business implications of the model results, and do back-of-envelope calculations to estimate the impact of the likely volume of errors. It should be noted that these can be both positive and negative. For example, for a loan defaulter prediction model, setting the performance metric threshold requires one to balance the benefits of writing new loans that will make the bank money against the risk of making bad loans. The point here is that the technical steps may have taken twists and turns, so it is important to stand back and ensure that the original business aims have not been lost, and that there is still a clear connection between the technical work produced and the business problem it was commissioned to solve. Once all these are aligned, it is time to move the model into production.

Deployment, Monitoring, and Maintenance

Deployment of a model is inherently a technical consideration, but one that should be surfaced as a consideration when proposing the resourcing for the project. The modelling may result in changes to the original deployment plan, but, overall, it is likely to remain largely unchanged (assuming, of course, that the model is deemed worthy of deployment!). There are a number of technical considerations in deploying a machine learning model, but these are driven by business needs. For example, some key questions may be:

- Do you need real-time predictions, or can you run predictions in batch overnight? As we had noted in Chapter 2, your data refresh frequency should match business requirements.

  The main technical consideration here is that real-time predictions come with technical challenges and are generally more expensive to implement than batch predictions. This cost should be justified by the envisaged business return.

- Will the model be housed on cloud/centralised servers, or does it need to be run on the *edge* (at the point of data collection)?

  For example, in IoT devices on remote machinery that do not have robust internet connections, it may be that models should be deployed directly to devices in a manner that ingests live data, makes predictions, and takes appropriate action without needing to return the data to a centralised server each time.

- What kind of volume and velocity of predictions are needed?

  For example, are we considering a scenario where an internal user is happy to hit a button and wait a few minutes for predictions. Or is this a model that will provide customised article recommendations on your support page and therefore needs to return predictions in a fraction of a second (and your site has thousands of viewers logged on concurrently)?

- How will you log predictions to complete the loop?
  This is a vital consideration for continual learning, as we will discuss below. In some scenarios, loop completion may be logged easily as part of the end-to-end process – for example, a user on a website that has appropriate tracking installed can allow you to see if the user made the purchase after your recommendation just from the tracking logs. However, if you are in B2B sales, and a model recommends prospects for your sales team to call, how can you access the data on which ones ended up converting? Typically, this data will be in a separate CRM system. With what frequency should you access that CRM data and how can it be linked to your model predictions?

As you can see from the above, details of deployment are fundamentally driven by business requirements.

The practices associated with deployment, monitoring, and maintenance have resulted in a relatively new practice area known as "MLOps" (a portmanteau of Machine Learning and DevOps from the world of software).

Whilst still new, this emerging field encompasses the practices of deployment, monitoring, and maintenance of machine learning models into production systems. Deployment is only a part of the story because, unlike a software product that needs occasional bug fixes and updates, a machine learning model requires a larger set of ongoing efforts to maintain performance. There is a perception that machine learning models will "automatically learn over time" as they get more data. Let us be crystal clear: without implementing holistic MLOps practices (most especially around retraining models), a model will not "automatically" learn over time. In fact, a deployed model left on its own will only get *worse*[25] due to *drift*. We'll discuss this in more detail below, but an example might help illustrate the phenomenon. If we were to ask you whether your purchasing patterns are the same today as they were five years ago, you would probably respond in the negative. Indeed, this is probably true on a wider scale too – purchasing patterns drift in time at all levels: individual, group, and population.

So, what exactly does one need to do besides maintaining the technical infrastructure needed to host the model, output predictions, and pipe it fresh data? Firstly, there is the consideration of performance metrics that need to be monitored. The most obvious of which is model performance. A model that you trained and was 92% accurate in your tests will not stay this accurate forever in the real world. It will change – typically decrease in time – and you need to continually monitor model performance to detect this *model drift*. Secondly, if you are required to test for bias and fairness, the metrics associated with these must be monitored in production. Finally, another important element to monitor is the (new) data that is being fed into the model. As noted in our example above, the data you modelled on several months (or years!) ago may have changed qualitatively with societal or other changes. This can result in two distinct kinds of drift: *data drift* and *concept drift*. The first, data drift, is easy to detect by implementing checks on statistical properties of the data and setting alerts that notify you when specific properties change significantly. The latter, *concept drift*, is harder to detect as it refers to scenarios in which the *relationships* between your data and the target change. Using our housing price example, data drift might occur when lots more apartments are built in areas that originally had free-standing houses, resulting in changes to the square footage, amenities, and bedrooms attributes in the data. On the other hand, concept drift might occur when increased migration due to a new working visa being rolled out causes higher demand and hence the houses with the same attributes are now worth more money. Whilst this sounds complex, it is another area in which the open-source community is building useful tools[26] to assist with this area of MLOps work.

The point of setting up these alerts is to warn you about deterioration of performance. What you do about it typically translates to some form of model retraining. There are choices to be made here in relation to whether to retrain the same model on new data or to build another model from scratch using a new algorithm. This can also involve various levels of automation. For example, a performance drop below a certain threshold can be a trigger to retrain the same algorithm on new data and then swap the new model in using an appropriate deployment technique. We begin to see just how divorced from reality the notion of "*it will learn over time*" is. *Learning over time has to be built in to the system; no algorithm learns automatically.* Moreover, we have considered only *reactive* retraining, where the retraining process is triggered by deteriorating performance. *Proactive* retraining is also possible, in principle. Here one continually tries out new and different algorithms and swaps in new models that perform better than the currently deployed ones. This notion of truly autonomous machine learning is not often realised in practice today, and with good reason. There is a need to include humans in the loop, especially domain experts to check and oversee these processes and crucially sign off at key points (more about the importance of this in Chapter 8). In addition, having servers searching for new models 24/7/365 would be an expensive endeavour. Few papers in the space of autonomous learning acknowledge that there is a *cost* to retraining (see Žliobaitė et al. 2015[27] for example). The point is this: the level of sophistication of your retraining processes should be determined by a cost-benefit exercise.

Additionally, there are a number of different modes and techniques[28] to deploy and redeploy models. You will need to determine which ones are applicable to your use case. In particular, you should ensure that the selected method factors in the considerations discussed above: i.e., what to monitor, what thresholds to set, what kind of actions will be taken, the level of automation (e.g., automatic retraining), and the various guardrails put in place to manage the project. Whilst data scientists can build models, it is quite possible that they don't have the necessary DevOps, cloud, and software engineering skills to properly deploy and maintain a production machine learning model. Understanding these requirements upfront and making arrangements for the appropriate resources can help ensure that your projects (and data scientists!) aren't set up for failure.

Throughout the MLWF it is important, as a guiding principle, to ensure that you have *version control* embedded in your technical systems. This is about keeping track of different versions of models as they evolve, but it is more than that these days. Apart from code, one might log different experiments (trials of different models) and even keep track of different versions of data.[29] Lack of reproducibility is a known problem across some scientific disciplines[30] including data science[31] (as one example, a recent large study[32] of over 1.4M data science notebooks found about 24% could be re-run and over 80% of those produced different outputs). As you might imagine, a situation in which you cannot replicate your results can lead to massive loss of credibility.

It is therefore important that you set expectations around implementing appropriate levels of version control.

This section provided only a brief overview of the emerging area of MLOps. For more details, we recommend Chip Huyen's highly practical book, *Designing Machine Learning Systems* (Huyen 2022), as well as (for the more academically inclined) this[33] recent paper by (Kreuzberger et al. 2022).

Dialling It Down

With all this being said about the potential complexities of putting models into production, it is important for us to emphasise that our intention is not to scare our readers off from using machine learning. Our intent is to provide a high-level overview of the different aspects of the MLWF that you will want to consider when delivering machine learning projects. True to the emergent principles we promote in this book, this needn't (and indeed, *shouldn't*) be implemented on your initial projects. You will learn what you need as you go along. Our advice on the importance of incremental, proof-of-concept projects applies just as well to figuring out the appropriate processes required to deploy models. Indeed, in some cases it may be appropriate to "deploy" a model in an ongoing highly manual fashion, without going through any of MLOps complexities discussed in the previous section. An example from Sonya Zecchin illustrates this point rather well:

> *"One of the groups that I worked most closely with was an outbound marketing team and there was a lot of scepticism about how we might use, in this case predictive modelling, to help them better target prospects. A lot of this was around the difficulty in explaining and profiling the targets right; why was it that the model was suggesting this?*
>
> *We knew from the machine learning metrics that these models could give you a far better target than random. However, initial interactions found that marketing wanted to profile the recommendations and then go after that profile. For example, if we found that a number of the top prospects had a certain age grouping and spending combination, they wanted to take that away and then target all of those people. Which isn't how the model works, as it takes into account a whole host of variables that will target different ages and people based on much more than just these features to determine their suitability. So, it was quite a hard sell when the way ML was going to provide targets was quite different to the way of working that the department had so far.*

The way in which we got over that was to construct an experiment in which we partnered with the business and put the model head-to-head with the existing practices. We ran the tests and the ML method greatly out-performed the traditional methods of selecting prospects. We had overwhelming feedback from the outbound telemarketing team who came back and said "no, no we want more of what you sent us in that list from the test!"

In this example, one can see the model moving from a proof-of-concept into "live" setting but without investment of time, effort, and technical resources for a robust MLOps setup. There were no concerns about drift as the data was changing slowly, and model performance was monitored via feedback from the team. Our point is that it is sometimes perfectly fine to manually extract data and have the data scientist manually re-run their data engineering and model prediction code on their own laptop and then email results in Excel (horror!) to the stakeholders. As the data function matures and credibility is built, there will be less of a need to have such a step between prototype and full production ... but, on the other hand, it could very well remain a valid step in every data science project. The time lost from this additional manual step is repaid many times over through enhanced business-data collaboration, and it also provides a great opportunity to iron out issues before moving to a full-fledged production setup.

Concluding Thoughts

In this chapter we have provided an overview of the stages and sub-tasks in a typical end-to-end machine learning project, from planning to production. We would emphasise again that you have a great deal of flexibility in what you implement and how you implement it. That said, the chapter should serve as a useful checklist of stages and tasks that should be considered in each project. Our discussion also serves to reiterate a point we made in Chapter 2 when discussing CRISP-DM, the progenitor of the modern MLWF: that of the need to have business stakeholders embedded, informed, and involved in *every* step of the project. As we noted there, handing over some data and a brief to a data science team and then checking back in 3 months for the "final product" is the worst thing one can do. To this end, we would like to end this chapter by recommending that readers review Table 7.1, which summarises the MLWF stages and the opportunities and ways in which business can be involved in each of them.

Notes

1 www.theverge.com/2016/3/24/11297050/tay-microsoft-chatbot-racist
2 We will discuss bias and fairness in Chapter 8.
3 https://rviews.rstudio.com/2020/05/21/modern-rule-based-models/
4 www.cs.umd.edu/~samir/498/Amazon-Recommendations.pdf
5 One option would be to use Gary Klein's premortem approach discussed in Chapter 3.
6 https://scholar.google.com/
7 https://arxiv.org/search/cs
8 www.kaggle.com/
9 www.kaggle.com/competitions/uw-madison-gi-tract-image-segmentation
10 www.mage.ai/blog/definitive-guide-to-accuracy-precision-recall-for-product-developers
11 Accuracy is the ratio of the number of correct predictions divided by the total number of predictions.
12 https://xkcd.com/2236/
13 https://towardsdatascience.com/7-ways-to-handle-missing-values-in-machine-learning-1a6326adf79e
14 *"an item of unreliable information that is reported and repeated so often that it becomes accepted as fact"*.
15 https://visit.figure-eight.com/rs/416-ZBE-142/images/CrowdFlower_DataScienceReport_2016.pdf
16 www.kaggle.com/datasets/kaggle/kaggle-survey-2018
17 www.anaconda.com/state-of-data-science-2020
18 www.featuretools.com/
19 https://mitsloan.mit.edu/ideas-made-to-matter/why-its-time-data-centric-artificial-intelligence
20 www.youtube.com/watch?v=TU6u_T-s68Y
21 Though less so these days with the variety of explainability techniques and tools (see explainability section).
22 https://shap.readthedocs.io/en/latest/index.html
23 https://lime-ml.readthedocs.io/en/latest/
24 www.theguardian.com/science/blog/2012/jan/06/correlation-causation
25 An interesting parallel can be made here to the second law of thermodynamics. That without work, the universe tends towards disorder.
26 See https://github.com/SeldonIO/alibi-detect for one such tool.
27 Žliobaitė, I., Budka, M. and Stahl, F. (2015), "Towards cost-sensitive adaptation: When is it worth updating your predictive model?", *Neurocomputing*, Vol. 150, pp. 240–249.
28 For example, Blue Green, Canary, Shadow, staged to name a few.
29 https://databricks.com/blog/2019/02/04/introducing-delta-time-travel-for-large-scale-data-lakes.html
30 https://en.wikipedia.org/wiki/Replication_crisis
31 www.science.org/doi/full/10.1126/science.359.6377.725
32 https://ieeexplore.ieee.org/document/8816763
33 https://arxiv.org/abs/2205.02302

References

Huyen, C. (2022), *Designing Machine Learning Systems*. O'Reilly Media, Inc., Sebastopol, CA.

Kreuzberger, D., Kühl, N. and Hirschl, S. (2022), *Machine Learning Operations (MLOps): Overview, Definition, and Architecture*, arXiv preprint arXiv:2205.02302.

Scriven, A., Kedziora, D., Musial, K. and Gabrys, B. (2022), "The technological emergence of AutoML; A survey of performant software and applications in the context of industry," arXiv preprint arXiv:2211.04148.

Žliobaitė, I., Budka, M. and Stahl, F. (2015), "Towards cost-sensitive adaptation: When is it worth updating your predictive model," *Neurocomputing*, Vol. 150, pp. 240–249.

8

Doing the Right Thing

Does Data Speak for Itself?

It is often said that data speaks for itself. This is simply not true: data has to be given a voice. It is the job of your data team, working in collaboration with your business stakeholders, to do that. This may sound completely counter-intuitive, so an example may help explain what we mean by "giving data a voice."

Consider the dataset shown in Table 8.1.

This dataset represents statistics for a Sydney suburb over five years. Assume the numbers are accurate so, yes, they are objective. So far so good. Right?

Now, imagine you represent a property development company who has applied for planning approval for a new apartment building. The council's affordable housing requirements mandate that 10% of the apartments need to be sold at under 20% of the market value and the design needs to meet strict environmental controls. You have agreed to all of this in your plans. You know there is considerable community opposition to the development, and you are briefing a PR firm on developing a communication plan to help overcome negative feelings. What do you let them know about the suburb that demonstrates your development is necessary?

Take a few minutes to jot down some data from the table that will support your case.

Now assume, instead, that you are part of a group from a local social justice centre that represents underprivileged people in your community. Your area is going through many changes and you are asking the council to expand their programmes to assist locals who may be struggling financially, or people who may not be able to afford to live in the area anymore.

Again, take some time to note down data from the table that will support your position.

Look at the data you used in the two cases. What does this tell you about "data speaking for itself"?

> *The point we wish to make is that what you see in the data depends critically on your role and interests. Data does not speak for itself; it has to be given a voice.*

DOI: 10.1201/9781003260158-8

TABLE 8.1

Data on a Fictitious Sydney Suburb

Metric	2019 Figure	2020 Figure	2021 Figure
% Population on unemployment benefits	6	8	14
% Child population in public school	45	48	42
Median weekly rent	430	475	470
Median house price	950,000	1,100,000	1,150,000
Average household income	125,000	138,000	142,000
% Child school completion rate	88	84	80
% Adult with higher education	87	86	88

As a real-world example of this, we recall a story shared from Zanne van Wyk:

> *"I can remember once being approached by a senior leader and were asked why boys left our education system in year 10. It was quite perplexing because in our area, there aren't any boys only schools and we couldn't imagine they were all leaving to go to the big city. The data team just couldn't understand it and provide an answer. So, I sat down with an Assistant Director of the schools and I asked his view. He said 'Oh yes, easy, coal prices.' And that was the answer. When the price of coal went up, the schools near mining areas would lose boys in year 10 to work in the mines; especially those from families with financial difficulty. We were able to build a dashboard and a model out of this that assisted to plan for this in the future."*

This brings us to a key issue in the development of a data strategy, one that has been gaining importance in recent years, which is only going to accelerate in the coming years: *data ethics*. Given the many, recent well-publicised dangers associated with data breaches (in industries as varied as Universities,[1] the Arts[2] and more industries[3] beyond just Social Media[4]), privacy and algorithmic bias, governments are gearing up to legislate what companies can and cannot do with data. Importantly, this trend is reaching beyond just privacy legislation and we'll say much more about this below. This is one reason to factor ethical considerations into your data strategy. Fortunately, you are in luck because an approach based on Emergent Design is inherently ethical since it considers diverse perspectives from the ground up and puts people at the centre.

Being ethical is more than just running through an ethics checklist prior to building a data warehouse, undertaking a project or rolling out a model; it is about adopting an inclusive attitude through the entire process of establishing and running your data capability. This probably sounds a tad over-the-top at this stage, but we hope the ethical aspect of Emergent Design will become clear as you work your way through the remainder of this chapter.

Another aspect of this exercise is that it calls into question the notion of objectivity of data. There are two related aspects to this:

Firstly, when data is presented in a form such as the one above, it is not clear as to how the data was collected and processed. For example, do the unemployment figures include only those actively looking for work? How was income or rent computed? When such questions are asked, the data seems less certain and objective than they appear to be at first sight.

Secondly, if different stakeholders can interpret the same data in different ways, each of which can be justified, then the notion of objectivity goes out of the proverbial window (What is *the* correct interpretation? Ans: there are many!). Of course, this does not imply that data is entirely subjective and can be interpreted in any way one wishes. What it does imply, however, is that the "correct" interpretation of data is an *intersubjective* affair – that is, it ought to be determined by consensus between all parties that have an interest in the data and are affected by it (Mingers 1995). In brief: interpretation of data is, at its heart, an *ethical* matter.

In this chapter, we will explore the issue of privacy and ethics in AI/ML and its organisational ramifications including compliance with legislation, data/AI governance and what ethics means in practical terms. We will begin with a discussion of recent trends in data protection regulations that have implications for your data science capability. Following that we cover data and AI governance, emphasising how the latter can be considered a superset of the former. Finally, we provide practical tips on getting started with governance along with some guidance on what you can do to ensure that ethical practices are baked in from the very beginning.

Might Do Now, Must Do Later?

There is a growing awareness of the interaction between data analytics and regulation, particularly since the European Union introduced the General Data Protection Regulation[5] (GDPR) in 2016. A key difference between GDPR and other regulations that came before it is that it has strong penalties attached to it. There are a number of examples where the fines issued to violators run into several million dollars[6]. Even services that one might think are untouchable, such as those from Google, have been affected. For example, the Italian Data Protection Supervisory Authority determined websites that use Google Analytics without the safeguards set out in the GDPR are in violation of data protection laws.[7]

The GDPR has paved the way for a number of other regulations such as the LGPD in Brazil in 2018, which granted very similar data protection rights as the GDPR did for its member states citizens. The GDPR is a long read. From a data strategy perspective, it is particularly useful to consider the fundamental rights that are enshrined in it.[8] They are:

1. The right to be informed
2. The right of access to data/information
3. The right to correction
4. The right to deletion
5. The right to restrict processing
6. The right to portability (of data)
7. The right to object
8. The right to not be subject to automated decision-making

As you will notice, these have immediate implications for how you use and store any personally identifiable information[9] (PII) that your organisation collects. If you don't put appropriate checks and protections in place now, you will be scrambling to implement them if (when!) these similar regulations become law in your jurisdiction. A subtle point here is that if you have customers who are covered by GDPR, you are required to abide by it in relation to all the personal data you have on those customers, *even though you are located in a country that does not fall under the ambit of GDPR.*

Here are some of the considerations associated with each of the above:

1. The right to be informed

   If people ask about what you do with their data, can you provide them with answers to the following:

   a. Where is the data stored? Where is it processed?
   b. How is it being processed? If at the individual level, why so?

2. The right of access to data/information

   People can request an export of all the data you have about them. Is there a contact to whom they can send a request for their data? Can the contact easily retrieve the requested data and present it to the requester in a timely manner?

3. The right to portability (of data)

   Is the data in a reasonable, commonly used format? For example, instead of csv or json formats (which are standard, commonly used formats), screenshots of their data pasted into a Word or PDF would be unreasonable. Not only is the latter a bad format, it is also highly inappropriate to screenshot personal data. .

4. The right to correction

   Is there a process in place for individuals to request corrections to any errors in the personal data that you hold about them?

5. The right to deletion (a.k.a.: *the right to be forgotten*)

   Is there a process for someone to be able to request deletion of all personal information that you hold about them? Once the data is deleted, is there a process to inform individuals that their request has been fulfilled. If not, is there a way for individuals to request confirmation?

Note that the above (informing the user) applies to data corrections too.

6. The right to (temporarily) restrict processing

   Can individuals request that you temporarily halt using their data? This might happen if:

   a. They contest the accuracy of their personal data and request that you verify its accuracy;
   b. their data has been unlawfully processed but rather than request erasure, they wish to restrict processing;
   c. you no longer need the personal data but they need you to keep it in order to establish, exercise or defend a legal claim; or
   d. they have objected to you processing their data, and you are considering whether your legitimate grounds override theirs.

7. The right to object completely (to processing/usage)

   This follows on from point (6) but is a permanent removal from said processing. Can you do this, demonstrate that you can do this, and ensure that their data continues to be excluded from processing in future?

8. The right to not be subject to automated decision-making

   This point is particularly relevant for your data science capability. As was noted in Chapter 7, having a human-in-the-loop at various points of a machine learning project is critical. Whilst tools that automate machine learning[10] can ease the tedium of model building and tuning, it is vital that the actual decision be made (or at least reviewed) by a human in situations where humans are the subjects of models. An example might help clarify what we mean: you can make automated decisions to stop a conveyer belt in a factory floor machine process because your model says it might break. However, the decisions made by a loan application assessment model are quite different and should have humans in the loop.

In summary, the main takeaways from GDPR are:

- Inform individuals (via opt-in and information packs) about what data you collect about them and why.
- Document how PII relating to individuals is stored and processed. The processing includes analytical process – i.e., what personal data is being used to build models.
- Ensure all teams that have access to PII are aware of their obligations under GDPR.
- Have in place processes to fulfil the obligations noted above.

In addition to GDPR and similar regulations that are already in place, there are AI/data[11] regulations around the responsible development of these technologies on the horizon. Whilst these are still in a nascent stage (at the time of writing), they are gaining attention globally. Early signs of these have shown up in various jurisdictions: for example, in government budget papers (such as Australia's 2021–2022 Budget Fact sheets[12]) and new taskforces (such as the artificial intelligence research resource task force[13] set up in the US). The Office of the Australian Information Commissioner also recently published a guide[14] to help organisations navigate the relation between privacy principles (as articulated in GDPR and the like) and the new world of analytics.

Responsible AI

Although it has been a long time coming, there finally seems to be a growing appreciation of the destructive potential of AI if left unchecked. For example, Standards Australia published an AI standards roadmap[15] aimed at "*[ensuring AI-related standards] are developed in a way that takes into account diversity and inclusion, ensures fairness, and builds social trust*". It has also published a governance standard for AI in line with the ISO standard; *Governance implications of the use of artificial intelligence by organizations.*[16] The New South Wales government has moved to create an AI assurance framework[17] which notes that:

> *From March 2022, the AI Assurance Framework will be required for all projects which contain an AI component.*

In other words, the framework is now a requirement for all AI-related government projects.

The European Union, as a leader in this space, began with a proposal[18] for the regulation of AI among member states in 2021 which could contain powers[19] such as requiring models to be *destroyed* or *retrained*. This adds additional complexity to the considerations we presented in the MLOps section of Chapter 7. No longer is it enough to ensure models are up to date and performant, one must also ensure that they are continually checked for potential violations of regulations, with breaches being acted upon in a timely manner. This is increasingly being seen by regulators as a "must have" rather than an optional extra.

Vendors have seen this coming and have been active in developing the notion of *Responsible AI*. For example, Microsoft (a leader in this emerging space) has developed an internal playbook on Responsible AI[20] based on the following principles:

- Fairness
- Reliability and Safety
- Privacy and Security
- Inclusiveness
- Transparency
- Accountability

We will touch upon some of these later in this chapter.

The inaugural Responsible AI Index report 2021 (https://ethicalai.ai/resp onsible-ai/), which surveyed over 400 Australia-based organisations about their awareness and intentions around the use of Responsible AI practices noted that 51% had an AI strategy, while 32% believed they were capable of implementing responsible AI. A mere 8% had mature responsible AI practices already in place.

The following example may help highlight the importance of the considerations around Responsible AI:

> *Consider a medical device that takes a blood sample and determines if the patient has a particular condition. Such devices must pass all kinds of strict regulations involving testing, certification etc. Additionally, the medical practice or hospital would have policies and procedures to ensure that the devices are functioning correctly. Now, what if instead of a medical device we had a model which takes in the sample, reads in the data and makes a prediction about the patient's condition. Clearly, this should be subject to the same oversight and rigour as the device, right?*

It is clear that an organisation working on AI in medicine would (should!) have internal checks in place. However, there is now an increasing awareness among governments across the world that all AI work needs external oversight. Make no mistake, AI regulation is coming.[21] It is therefore clear that you will need to ensure that your data practices are compliant with regulations. In addition, you will also need to understand which elements of Responsible AI might apply to your situation and how you might want to implement them. These considerations and many others go under the banner of *governance* which we turn to next.

We will first cover *data governance*, which has been around ever since the early days of relational databases. Data governance, as it is currently framed, does not explicitly cover issues such as Responsible AI. Nevertheless, you will still need to ensure that your capability operates using good data governance practices. We will discuss how you can get started with this. Following that, we will briefly discuss *AI governance* which, though still a nascent field, needs to be considered as it is relevant to operationalising Responsible AI. In the final section, we will draw a connection between governance and ethics, one that is crucially important yet often overlooked in the literature as well as in practice.

Data and AI Governance

Data governance is about the *processes, roles and responsibilities* relating to the *management and use of data*. It includes compliance with regulations and internal policies but is *much* broader than both. As we will see below, it is an umbrella term that covers all aspects of data management. We will first cover data governance in general and then briefly discuss how to get started implementing governance before circling back to AI governance.

Data Governance and Data Management

The Data Management Association (DAMA) defines data governance as *"planning, oversight, and control over management of data and the use of data and data-related sources"*. DAMA publishes the DMBOK (Data Management Body of Knowledge), which is generally considered to be the authoritative resource on data governance. The latest version of the DMBOK identifies the following "knowledge areas" relating to governance:

- **Data Architecture** – a description of how data is organised and structured to support business processes and, more broadly, the work of the organisation.
- **Data Quality** – planning, implementation and control of assurance activities aimed at ensuring that data is fit for purpose and meets the requirements of the business.
- **Metadata** – information *about the data* that you hold. This includes information about what the data element means, where it came from, when it was created / updated, the technical and business processes it impacts, rules and constraints around its use etc.
- **Data Modelling and Design** – processes around eliciting business requirements and developing data models to support them.
- **Data Storage and Operations** – processes and technologies to support data storage across the lifecycle of the data.
- **Data Security** – processes to ensure appropriate access to organisational data assets and prevent unauthorised or improper use.
- **Data Integration and Interoperability** – processes relating to the movement and consolidation of data in and across organisational data stores and applications, and (where appropriate) those outside the organisation.
- **Document and Content Management** – processes around the management of unstructured data (text, images etc.).
- **Reference and Master Data** – management of data that describes the core entities of the business (such as, for example, customers).

- **Data Warehousing and Business Intelligence** – processes around structuring and presenting data relevant to organisational decision-making.

Note that we have paraphrased the DAMA definitions because they are somewhat cryptic. We also want to remind you that *data governance* is an umbrella term that encompasses all of the elements of data management listed above. From a perusal of the elements, it should be clear that most (if not all) of the areas noted above are relevant to AI, but there are some important missing elements. We will look at this in a later section.

Considering the scope all these elements when taken together, it should be clear that one will never be *done* implementing the various data management practices; each of them will evolve as your data science capability evolves. Implementation is a process of continuous improvement that never ends. In that sense, it fits perfectly in the Emergent Design paradigm we advocate. As Firas Hamdan (Data Governance Lead at KPMG Australia) mentioned when we spoke with him:

> *"Governance needs to be considered as an operational function, not a project. It is never finished and done; it needs to be kept alive. This has a very human element, around educating and working closely with business units and the people inside."*

So, with the above in mind, how does one start the process of building data governance into your new data capability?

Getting Started with Data Governance

As we have noted at various points in this book, picking up and plonking a framework into an organisation, without due regard to context, is doomed to fail. Indeed, here is what Firas Hamdan had to say about this:

> *"An organization I worked with had already tried a governance project by taking one of these frameworks out there and just copy-paste into their organisation. It failed massively and they were on the back foot from a trust and culture perspective. So, when I came in to help them, we had to really work hard to bring the people back onboard. People try to jump into the frameworks (industry or literature) because it is the easiest thing to do. In reality, this stuff is hard. Not hard because it is difficult to do, but because it involves continuous work. Standards and frameworks are just a starting point to develop something custom to your organization."*

As noted by Firas, the DAMA (or any other) framework gives you a *starting point* for your governance efforts, but it does not tell you in which direction you should go. That is a decision for you to make.

How Do You Figure Out a Direction?

The etymology of the term "governance" offers a hint; it originates from the Greek word *kybernetes*, meaning *helmsman*. In days of yore, helmsmen were wayfinders who used their lived knowledge of the seas and skies to navigate their way across sometimes treacherous waters. The word "treacherous" is apposite; the term "data governance" often evokes negative reactions from data professionals because of their prior experiences with overly controlling and bureaucratic governance processes. When we asked Firas about how to resolve this, here is what he suggested:

> "When it comes to people who work with the data, they are not as concerned with control and regulation. Instead, you need to address their problems, discuss what is relevant to them. For example, a common entry point I have found with analysts is data quality. Data analysts struggle with dirty data and often feel alone without any help. So, if you present yourself as someone who is keen to help (because you are) then you can build the trust with these people in this area then move to broader governance topics. Another common pain point is data access (particularly for business users) so this can be a launch pad for discussions with them."

He then gave us the following example from his experience:

> "I remember working a big organisation in Australia, doing forecasting for workforce management. It was impossible for their data scientists to build forecasts over 60/70% accuracy because of poor data quality. We solved this by fixing data quality from the source which greatly improved results. My point is, governance doesn't have to be a big top-down policy implementation, it should be built from the ground up. Use the problems that people face as a means to plant and embed the policies."

We hope you agree that this is but Emergent Design! Good data governance is about enablement rather than control. Therefore, your first step in implementing governance is to look for ways in which you can solve problems that matter to people. *Data quality and end user data access are two good starting points as these are near-universal issues.* The following is a (non-exhaustive) list of some good starting points as they are near-universal issues for data teams:

- Data quality
- Data access
- Data conflicts (for example, the same customer having different addresses in databases owned by operations and marketing)
- IT red tape (for example, bureaucratic approval processes for moving a database or model from test to production)

Data Stewards and Councils

Getting started on governance is one thing, keeping it going is another. To ensure that governance efforts do not falter, it can be helpful to institute formal roles or structures aimed at maintaining the initial momentum. A number of the data leaders we interviewed did this by establishing data steward roles and/or data councils within their organisations. The specifics of these in terms of responsibility and remit depend on organisational needs, but we noted the following commonalities:

- Distributed domain experts given responsibility over an area of data

  These *data stewards* serve as subject matter experts and arbiters of data quality for data in a particular domain. Here's what Craig Napier (CDO of the University of Technology, Sydney) had to say about this role:

  "We use a system of decentralised domain experts who know a particular area of data very well. They are key in helping address data quality, helping integrate these data sources to the central data stores and champion usage of data in their areas."

- Bringing people together regularly for open discussions (data council)

  The data council meets monthly or quarterly for strategic discussions about data across the enterprise. This is a forum in which larger issues can be surfaced and discussed. These might include cross-functional meetings with representatives from various areas of the business (associated with key data generation and usage) as well as the data and technical teams. By having such a forum that meets regularly, you can avoid nasty "data surprises", as Duhita Khadepau (Director of Analytics and Data Science at a construction-tech start-up) notes:

  "We need to meet regularly given the growth and exciting projects of our data teams. When someone wants to change a metric or a data source, they can share with the forum and those downstream won't be surprised to learn that their data has changed completely or gone missing."

Regardless of the specific roles or processes you choose to implement, the crucial thing to keep in mind is that this is less about enforcement and more about having open discussions. In fact, you may want to avoid using the word "governance" altogether. As Matt Minor (Head of Group Data and Analytics at the Blackmores group) notes:

"We have data stewards and a data council. We tended to avoid language that may indicate too much authoritarian control such as 'governance'. This group isn't there to 'police', but to provide a platform for experts and technologists to

come together and ensure the business needs are being worked on, that a date culture is being promoted and evangelised and we build performant and robust technology solutions."

Data governance works best when implemented with a light touch.

What about AI Governance?

When going through the knowledge areas listed in the data governance section, some readers may have noticed a glaring gap: the knowledge areas do not explicitly mention ML or AI, let alone the topics listed in the principles of Responsible AI. This is indeed true and is so because the DAMA framework, much like the CRISP-DM framework (see Chapter 2), predates the rise of ML and AI by at least two decades. There have been very recent attempts to redress this, but relatively few that focus on *organisational* AI governance (see Schneider et al. 2022 and Mäntymäki et al. 2022 for example).

Mäntymäki et al. define AI governance as,

> *a system of rules, practices, processes, and technological tools that are employed to ensure an organization's use of AI technologies aligns with the organization's strategies, objectives, and values; fulfills legal requirements; and meets principles of ethical AI followed by the organization.*

We think, this is a good definition because it makes explicit reference to the regulatory **and ethical** aspects of governance that are relevant to Responsible AI (and are missing in the DAMA framework). There are three elements: organisational, legal and ethical. The organisational aspect is implicit in the emergent design approach so we can take that as covered already. The legal aspects have been covered in our discussion of GDPR and the impending regulation of AI that is foreseen to be on the way. We will now cover the ethical aspects by taking a closer look at some of the elements of Responsible AI.

Trust

Trust in AI is a topic of growing interest in academia and business alike. However, what exactly does *trust* mean? Governments, business and academia are all wrestling with this concept. How to categorise it and how to align data practices to it. As a recent example, The United States National Institute of Standards and Technology explored[22] trust in AI, referencing accuracy, reliability and explainability as core tenets.[23] Indeed, technical performance measures such as accuracy and reliability do make sense here: consistently performing and delivering on stated objectives and expectations builds trust. We won't spend much time on these tenets as they are not unique to data science and even go beyond data practice itself and are thus familiar to most people.

A note we will make, however, is that with the rising trend of data sharing and a data economy rising between organisations, that our discussions of responsible data practices take on a much larger scope. As Jan Lambrechts (Data Ethics lead at ANZ) notes:

> *"We've done some of our own research with our own customers trust is not just a singular concept. For example, people might have trust with the banking industry because of regulators like ASIC and APRA. However, people have a spectrum of trust with the organization itself, that comes from how you use the data. Whether you are keeping it safe, using it for stated purposes and not sharing it with anyone you don't want to. Even if they trust your brand, what is this brand you are sharing what data with?"*

In summary, as we work through the concepts of governance, ethics and responsible data practices, keep in mind this important nuance:

> *As soon as you share a user's data with a third party, you are morally responsible (in the consumer's eyes) for that organisation's data practices.*

Explainability and Transparency

Explainability in the realm of data science refers to how well the rules by which a model arrived at its results or predictions can be understood by a human. The objective of explainability is to understand why the model is producing a particular result. We have provided a more technical overview of explainability in Chapter 7, discussing some tools and techniques that can be used in a model-agnostic way, to understand what is happening in the machine learning artefacts being created. This isn't just a growing academic interest though; customers expect explainability. For example, a recent Capgemini report[24] found 71% of consumers want clear explanation of the results produced by models.

Transparency refers to making visible the flow from data (what data was used? how current is it?) to modelling (what modelling processes were used?) and results (what metrics were used?). The objective here is to "open the black box" so to speak and enable consumers to understand exactly what was done, without necessarily understanding the results (the latter would go under the banner of explainability). Indeed, when governments begin to use automated algorithms for things that deeply effect people's lives such as plans and funding allocation to users under the Australian National Disability Insurance Scheme[25]; transparency is not a nice to have – it is a must have.

Bias and Fairness

A core part of building trust that has yet to been covered in this book so far is that of *bias* and *fairness*. This too has gained more attention in media and organisations of late, with IBM's Global AI Adoption Index (2021) finding 87% of respondents rating *Ensuring applications and services minimize bias* as an important aspect of AI trust and explainability. Interestingly, in the Capgemini survey noted above, 35% of surveyed executives were aware of the issue of discriminatory bias with AI systems in 2019, and 65% in 2020; awareness *is* growing. We now discuss further what is meant by these somewhat confusing terms and how to consider them in your work as you grow your data capability and practices.

A good place to start is with academic works in data science that have been grappling with issues relating to bias and fairness for some time. We summarise the key implications of these works for data analytics practice, so that these checks and balances can be woven into your analytics projects, especially at the key junctures mentioned in our presented MLWF blueprint (Chapter 7).

Let us begin with a definition of fairness used in the comprehensive paper by (Mehrabi et al., 2021)

> *the absence of any prejudice or favouritism toward an individual or a group based on their inherent or acquired characteristics*

This seems a nice place to start. So, what then is bias? We can again borrow a straightforward definition from Chomiak and Miktus 2021 to start us on our discussions:

> *inclination or prejudice for or against one person or group, potentially causing a situation that is unfair*

This reveals the crucial link between bias and fairness; the *presence of bias* in analytics practice (from data, from algorithms or other sources) *can lead to outcomes that are unfair*. With that in mind, it would seem logical to begin with the data. There are a host of ways in which bias can be found in data, some of which was alluded to in the allegory that began this chapter about data being given a voice. Borrowing again from Mehrabi et al., 2021, they list a quite comprehensive list of biases that can be found in the data itself, a selection of which is reproduced below:

- Measurement bias
- Omitted variable bias
- Representation bias
- Aggregation bias
- Sampling bias

- Historical bias
- Population bias
- Self-selection bias
- Linking bias

Some of these would be familiar and some would be new. Discussing these in detail would take us too far afield so we'll leave you to read the references. An interesting read in this space is Suresh and Guttag (2021), which aligns potential sources of bias to the stages of the MLWF. However, keep in mind that not all biases will be relevant to your context.

Although these may seem conceptual ideas, just as we can measure (many forms of) bias in our data and analytics practices, so too can we measure Fairness through a variety of metrics. Here are just a few commonly used ones:

- Equalised odds
- Equal opportunity
- Demographic parity
- Fairness through unawareness
- Treatment equality

There are also a number of algorithms that exist which can help to repair or mitigate issues detected in relation to bias and fairness. Each of these have their own method and considerations (see more below around tools that implement these). Some excellent, if somewhat contrived, examples on how these metrics differ can be found on the Google Developer glossary.[26] The crucial point to take away from these examples is that the same model, producing the same results and exact same predictions can be considered both fair and unfair, depending on the particular metrics used.

We are aware that our coverage of these elements from a technical standpoint is brief and necessarily incomplete. The point we wish to make is that bias and fairness considerations are not simple, nor are they but mere concepts that can be written into a policy or values document and considered "addressed" by doing so: implementing them involves work. Most importantly, they can be measured but although there are technical tools to assist, they should not be *automated*.

Given all this, where should you turn to for guidance on what to do to ensure you are doing the right thing? Whilst there is no simple formula, we can provide some advice to get you started:

1. **Determine what matters to your organisation.**
   a. What are the sensitive variables or aspects to the data you have? Label these in the database. As of the time of writing some major vendors are beginning to incorporate sensitivity labels in their

databases. Typical sensitive attributes may include, gender, ethnic origin, income etc.

b. What kind of scenarios are you trying to avoid? For example, discriminating on the basis of some demographic attribute.

As Jan Lambrechts aptly notes;

"An important place to start is with the data stores themselves and what kind of data is there and what kind of sensitive variables you have. Then consider what kind of scenarios that could unfold as you consider your use cases. It is two sides of a coin – data has opportunity but there is a risk if not approached ethically. Considering the platforms and data science and analytics projects is often too late to consider ethical issues that are baked into the data sources themselves."

With a knowledge of the sensitive attributes, you will have a better idea of how to frame bias and fairness. Beware of *proxy* variables though – that is, variables that are indirect indicators of demographic variables. For example, if you exclude ethnicity but include postcode as an attribute then the latter could indirectly contain information about the former (consider the case where a certain postcode has a majority population from a particular community then data from that postcode is likely to be from that demographic). Sensitive variables can sneak in through the backdoor, so to speak.

2. **Become informed.**

There is no easy way out of this. Ethics and ethical data science does require you to think things through; it is a considered activity that cannot be automated (that said, see point 3 below). However, there are a number of resources out there that can help you understand the different biases and fairness metrics. It is important that those who are leading the data capability are well informed on the options that are out there. This, coupled with a knowledge of the sensitive variables in your data, will help you figure out what you need to do.

Finally, it should be clear that this is an inherently iterative process that must involve a wide variety of stakeholders. We made a callout to diversity on interview panels (Chapter 5) and vendor panels in (Chapter 6) and again this is worth mentioning here. Having diversity and inclusion of many voices, when deciding on ethical principles and fairness metrics, can give a greater chance of catching things that would be missed by a homogeneous group of stakeholders.

In addition, here are some resources you might want to look at.

a. https://arxiv.org/abs/1907.09013

    b. https://github.com/tensorflow/fairness-indicators/blob/master/g3doc/guide/guidance.md

    c. https://blog.tensorflow.org/2019/12/fairness-indicators-fair-ML-systems.html

    d. https://theodi.org/service/consultancy/data-ethics/

3. **Leverage tools.**

Whilst we noted that you cannot automate ethical data science practice, you can certainly leverage tools that will assist in generating the metrics needed. There are a number of open source tools available. Here are some notes on the more prominent ones, with the usual caveat that this list is likely to be out of date as soon as this is in print!

AIF360, created by IBM, generates a variety of metrics as related to biases and fairness (including explanations of the metrics) as well as bias mitigation algorithms from other research.

Fairlearn is another leading open source library, developed and released by Microsoft, which is very similar to AIF360 in the level of development, documentation and maintenance. It also contains some overlap in the metrics that are offered in AIF360. The documentation contains more explanatory notes around the concepts of bias and fairness as well as extended further readings of books and papers. Also, like AIF360, it offers mitigation algorithms which can help in particular instances. The maturity of this library is indicative of Microsoft's wider investment and effort towards leading in this space.

What If Tool from Google is primarily for creating scenarios from a trained model. For example, if a certain data point had some particular values for Variable A and Variable B, what would the prediction be? As you toggle up the value of Variable A, how does this affect things (holding Variable B constant)? This tool is more interactive and simpler than the two noted above, with 5 common fairness metrics as applied to their model (Group unaware, Demographic Parity, Equal Opportunity, Equal Accuracy, Group Thresholds).

There are a variety of other tools[27] that are not as well established. Importantly, whilst there are a variety of tools that can assist in creating metrics, these are dangerous in the hands of the uninformed. We highly recommend your staff read about these tools before using them. An excellent reference and critical analysis on some of these tools is Lee and Singh (2021).

Keep in mind, the tool is step 3 of the process, not step 1!

4. **Finally, integrating this knowledge and technology into processes.**

As was discussed in Chapter 7, when undertaking a machine learning project, there are various stages in which there should be checks regarding bias and fairness. To briefly recapitulate those are:

a. When exploring the data during the Data Engineering phase. This is not just technical checks on representativeness and the like, but also ensuring questions are asked about the lineage and sourcing of data (where has it come from? How was it collected? By whom?) to understand the risks of potential biases in data acquisition.
b. When checking model results. This is mostly about checks on the fairness of outputs. Whether Demographic Parity or Equality of Opportunity (which often will conflict) are chosen as the fairness metrics, it is important to factor this in when scoring models that are trained in the experimental phase.
c. Finally, the often-forgotten bit: monitoring in production. As outlined in our MLOPs section (Chapter 7), not only does the data need to be monitored and the model for performance, but also for indication of bias and fairness issues as defined by your own organisational discussions on the matter.

In addition to the above, as we noted on Chapter 7, there is an important ethical checkpoint right at the inception/planning phase of a project to identify potential issues even before you start. There are some nice tools like the Open AI Ethics Canvas[28] to help with these discussions.

Although this section covered the more technical side of bias and fairness in machine learning work, we hope two points are clear. Firstly, that, whilst it is a complex area, there are metrics and tools to assist in actually implementing ethical considerations in your analytics projects. Secondly, that despite the tools, it is something that should not be outsourced entirely to a machine. You will need to embed an ethical culture within the team. Our final section is about how to do this.

Acting Ethically

Even if data governance processes are implemented in the manner suggested above, there is no guarantee that people will actually follow them. It is in this final but crucial section we outline the link between governance and policies and ethics:

> *whilst governance tells people what they must do, ethics drives what they will actually do*

Above we have discussed privacy, data governance and AI governance. These often inherently have an ethical basis to them; whether from corporate principles or from legislation (which *should*, at its heart, be built off an ethical imperative for the government to take care of its citizenry). Given this, some organisations may "bake in" their ethical considerations into these areas, though most (as we have found when discussing with our data leaders) will formulate an ethical framework or set of principles to specifically call out and highlight the ethical lens to be applied to the data work of the organisation.

As Sylvia Jastkowiak (Principal Advisor, Data Ethics and Privacy) notes:

> *"There are lots of assessments and design methodologies (like privacy by design) that help with the privacy compliance objective. These are a nice starting point as they're often grounded in ethical considerations. However, the tricky part is moving beyond the concept application in one project and applying them more broadly into processes that are utilised across an organisation in business operations."*

Indeed, governance (like strategy) needs to be moved off paper into the real world. Operationalising it is a challenge. As Jan Lambrechts notes:

> *"There are many ethical frameworks and some great resources out there to build a set of principles, but it is how you make it **real** that stops it ending up as a piece of a paper in a drawer. It is not over once you create a framework. The crucial bit is how to operationalize it, govern it and make it useful for people."*

Additionally, Dr. Kobi Leins (Associate Director, Data Ethics) highlights how, whilst there is a need for top-down buy in and support from the top, there is a need to embed ethics into everyday operations lest it become some other forgotten policy piece.

> *"This needs to come from the top. Boards need to have a position on their data and how it is used, and that position needs to filter down into policies and procedures within whatever business you have. But top-down is not enough, as you need to operationalize the policies. That is where bottom-up communities and communication is important."*

The problem is ethics are not a list of do-good principles that adorn an office wall or website. Ethics emanate from each and every one of us and are produced through the assumptions we make and the actions we take based on them. Even so, the ability to influence the ethics of an organisation is critical to the success of your work. In this spirit, we offer some tips on how you can do this.

Find What Matters

Embedding ethical practice is not a single-mode activity. There is a need to present and engage with various levels, units and *humans*. To influence the ethics of an organisation one must first understand what matters to people and the nomenclature they use to manage the things that matter. For example, when considering the board and the corporate level, one experienced data ethics practitioner we spoke with learnt that in many of the organisations they worked with they found that using the "language of risk" was the most effective way to discuss at the corporate level. This may not just be from a legislative point of view now, depending on your jurisdiction, but reputationally and brand-based risk is very real in this space.

One doesn't need to Google very far to find examples of companies misusing data; however, even in some of the more recent examples with organisations failing to take a considered approach to using facial recognition and biometrics data, the fall-out from this is considerably more than some extra steps taken up-front to consider the possible implications and adopt an ethical approach to using the technology. Here's what Jan Lambrechts said about such data:

> *"Biometrics is a useful technology, but when consumers don't feel informed, that they have a choice then they won't feel trust towards the organisation and that is very hard to get back."*

Sylvia Jastkowiak similarly echoed these thoughts:

> *"The technology itself has so much potential for good uses (many are, I believe, yet to be uncovered) but the implementation strategy for some of these more public use cases clearly don't have practical ethical guidelines or understanding embedded in the solution implementation. Seemingly simple concepts like businesses getting consent and being transparent about said use cases are being 'lost in translation'. Often it isn't that organisations have an evil hidden agenda concerning the utilisation of personal consumer data, but the public often feels that organisations are being deceptive when their intentions are not clear. Once that trust is broken (or when it is never established in the first place) it puts all related stakeholders under a cloud of suspicion. We need to ensure we are having conversations with end users as well as working on internal privacy and data ethics development, otherwise the distrust will set the industry back in terms of using new technologies for the right purposes"*

Here, it is important to acknowledge that this stuff does take time (and money). As Dr. Leins noted:

> *"We've got to be honest, taking the time to thoughtfully use data costs. It costs time and money."*

The risk-based approach isn't the only way to position ethics. There are studies[29] pointing to ethical practices being a driver for value. The trend of social consumerism as a consumer desire[30] (increasingly, expectation[31]) is something which spills over into the ethical handling of data; people increasingly expect organisations to do the right thing.

Whilst there is the corporate angle, equally important is the pitch to employees who do the day-to-day work of organisation. What matters to one individual may not matter to another. The corporate angle of risk and reward may not resonate with many employees. For some, it will resonate to align the promoted ethical framework with existing company values. For others, it may be tying the ethical framework to something larger. Sylvia Jastkowiak mentioned that their organisation's ethical framework was aligned to UN Sustainable Development Goals (SDG). This connected the work done by employees to a larger cause, as she elaborated:

> *"A piece of paper is one thing, but connecting the framework to a higher purpose is how you can motivate people to resonate with business ethics. For our organisation, aligning to these kind of sustainability and social development goals fits well with the company mission of making a positive difference to communities through technological advancement. It gave the framework 'tangible' relatability."*

The point is that, depending on the kind of organisation, embedding ethics may be better achieved through language of "risk", "company values" or "sustainable development" – things that matter to people in the organisation.

Build in Diversity

If you have the luxury of building a team from scratch, another consideration is being aware of the diversity teams. Having diverse or representative teams from the outset is a way to embed inclusivity in the values of the team. As Dr Leins expands:

> *"It's clear that more diverse communities with more conversations increases the chance of having the conversations that matter in relation to ethical data science practice."*

An important aspect of ethics is *understanding that there are a multiplicity of values*; we each have different values, and being ethical includes the ability to discuss our values openly with a view to reaching a shared understanding. There are two aspects to this consideration to tease out explicitly.

The first is that by bringing together diverse individuals with different values, experiences and stories, there is a larger "pool" of human experience which one can draw from.

The second is creating a "holding environment" in which diverse viewpoints on an activity can be surfaced through dialogue (Culmsee and Awati 2012). Unlocking those multiple viewpoints is crucial, as there is then a greater chance of flagging potentially unethical activity for further review. The day-to-day work in an organisation often has grey areas and blind spots that remain unseen, and it is only by looking at these work routines through an ethical lens that these might become visible.

Establish Meaningful Rituals

It is important to establish meaningful rituals and working relationships with individuals so that they feel inherently valued and bring "their whole person" to work. If a team member leaves their values at the door then where is the moral compass of the team's work? Team and group rituals can include semi-regular check-ins on "are we living our values?". A team where individuals feel valued and bring their whole person to work encourages real engagement with the methods by which the team is achieving its objectives in relation to group and company goals. Where there might be points of friction, it can enable an open dialogue on how to work through them. As noted immediately prior, bringing together diverse individuals brings a pool of varied human experiences. However, there needs to be norms set, where people can express themselves and bring themselves into their work.

This means establishing these regular check-ins and conversations and embedding a culture of sharing and asking questions. It can be particularly daunting for a business stakeholder to ask questions in a technical environment, so it is incumbent on data teams and those leading data teams to work to enable environments where there are "no dumb questions" and everyone can feel comfortable to raise a concern. This requires a degree of humility, and as Dr Leins notes:

> *"Humility is a difficult cultural piece to foster but it pays huge dividends in fostering environments where self-reflection can flourish and help promote ethical data science."*

The aim is that this will become an organic ritual that occurs within teams and projects, but there is also merit in formalising a version of this; to formally acknowledge that this kind of interaction is encouraged and create a safe space for such conversations. This can take the form of weekly "challenge" sessions where work can be played back to other team members and healthily challenged for its assumptions and (potentially unintended/unforeseen) impacts. Atlassian, for example, is a big advocate[32] of this approach, terming it "sparring".

In a leadership style, this can be an openness from a leader to share their experiences of, for example, when their values had been challenged, or their advice had not been heard and the process they went through to overcome and work through those circumstances. This is a "showing by doing approach" to ethical dimensions of the work and can be as simple as a post in a Teams or Slack channel.

Continual Awareness

In order to foster and grow an ethical culture, there needs to be a deliberate effort to build awareness around the ethical practices of the organisation, either through a framework or set of corporate values and principles.

The most obvious way to do this is through regular broadcasts: company-wide newsletters, announcements etc. that include reminders or elements of this ethical work and practice, perhaps as well as updates in the area. However, this must be supplemented with approaches that are "closer" to actual work. Training and actual work are excellent opportunities to meld ethical practice and data practice; in a sense, making them one and the same from the organisational standpoint. For example, analytics training on company metrics, key data sources, dashboards etc. during on-boarding (see Chapter 5) is an opportunity to talk about ethics. Any model building should be accompanied by an ethical analysis which is then subjected to a sparring session as discussed in the previous sub-section. The message needs to be reinforced through multiple channels at multiple levels.

This general awareness should be paired with deeper work for those that require it. As Jan Lambrechts notes in his current practice:

> "Aside from general awareness, you also need to go quite deep with those more mature areas of the business, that are working more advanced data use cases or in more ethically sensitive areas. For those teams, you can work much more closely but crucially as an advisor and enabler rather than controller. I have found open, collaborative workshops are best where you understand the space, potential issues and set in place guardrails and checks to give the best chance of responsible data work."

The overall aim of this awareness piece is twofold. To ensure people are:

- aware of the ethical practices of the organisation, and how to apply them to their work,
- comfortable raising issues they see as being ethically problematic.

The second point is gaining more attention as the notion of building a "Speak Up" culture has become a thing in recent times. Jan Lambrechts articulates this using an analogy with Work, Health and Safety issues:

> "We could consider this parallel to like occupational health and safety. That is everyone's responsibility if you see a cable lying around; and you have a clear line for who to notify and speak up if you see something that isn't right."

Leverage Existing Tools (to a Point!)

There are some tools, frameworks and techniques that can assist in building an ethical framework and operationalising it in your work. The following are just a few examples: resources available:

- The data ethics canvas[33] from the Open Data Institute
- Frameworks and tools from government bodies such as the Office of the Australian Information Commissioner[34]
- The NSW Government AI Assurance Framework[35] (which we noted earlier)

It is important to keep in mind that these are a starting point, and must be carefully customised to your context. There is no magic button or all-encompassing framework-to-rule-them-all that can take care of ethical data practice in your organisation. It takes work to set up and go on; however, we hope the case has been made that it is worth it.

In Closing

In this chapter, we have taken a journey through the difficult and complex topics of privacy, governance and ethics. We hope that the stories, examples and advice provided have made these concepts clearer (and less scary!) than they may have been prior. At this juncture, it is important for us to resurface and emphasise the key point of this section. That point is:

Whilst governance, policies and frameworks can tell you what you must do; ethics is what drives the individual in their everyday actions to do what they actually do.

Of course, you cannot hope to control individual behaviour, but through the discussions in this chapter we have highlighted how you can influence it and build a culture where ethical behaviour can shine through. We leave you with the following points to ponder over and act on:

1. Data does not speak for itself – it is your work that will give it a voice.
2. Be humble – your (or your team's) point of view is highly likely to be incomplete.
3. Value diversity – the greater the number of viewpoints that are considered, the greater the chance of an ethical outcome. Always act to increase options.

4. Strive to create a valid approximation of reality – solutions that are transparent and explainable.

5. Simple and effective – create solutions that are as simple as possible, but no simpler.

6. Equitable – do work that improves the customer/citizen/planet well-being.

7. Be vigilant – eternal vigilance is the price of working with data.

If you create the conditions that enable your team to live their ethical values, you will have governance that people live by.

Notes

1 www.zdnet.com/article/swinburne-university-confirms-over-5000-individuals-affected-in-data-breach/ and www.itnews.com.au/news/deakin-university-reveals-breach-of-47000-students-details-582563

2 www.abc.net.au/news/2022-07-22/wa-arts-organisations-hit-by-major-data-breach/101262908

3 https://au.finance.yahoo.com/news/uber-avoids-prosecution-2016-data-breach-205134044.html

4 https://securityaffairs.co/wordpress/133593/data-breach/twitter-leaked-data.html

5 https://gdpr.eu/

6 www.tessian.com/blog/biggest-gdpr-fines-2020/

7 www.gpdp.it/web/guest/home/docweb/-/docweb-display/docweb/9782874#english

8 https://gdpr-info.eu/chapter-3/

9 www.oaic.gov.au/privacy/guidance-and-advice/what-is-personal-information

10 https://en.wikipedia.org/wiki/Automated_machine_learning

11 Although these are referred to as *AI* regulations and practices, they are essentially about what kind of *data* is used, how it is processed and how the results are used.

12 https://digitaleconomy.pmc.gov.au/fact-sheets/artificial-intelligence

13 www.whitehouse.gov/ostp/news-updates/2021/06/10/the-biden-administration-launches-the-national-artificial-intelligence-research-resource-task-force/

14 www.oaic.gov.au/privacy/guidance-and-advice/guide-to-data-analytics-and-the-australian-privacy-principles

15 www.standards.org.au/getmedia/ede81912-55a2-4d8e-849f-9844993c3b9d/R_1515-An-Artificial-Intelligence-Standards-Roadmap-soft.pdf.aspx

16 www.iso.org/standard/56641.html

17 www.digital.nsw.gov.au/policy/artificial-intelligence/nsw-ai-assurance-framework

18 https://digital-strategy.ec.europa.eu/en/library/proposal-regulation-laying-down-harmonised-rules-artificial-intelligence-artificial-intelligence

19 https://techcrunch.com/2022/04/01/ai-act-powers/
20 www.microsoft.com/en-us/ai/our-approach
21 https://hbr.org/2021/09/ai-regulation-is-coming
22 www.nist.gov/publications/trust-and-artificial-intelligence
23 In brief: *accuracy* = how close are the model results to reality; *reliability* = given the same conditions, does the model make the same predictions (repeatability); *explainability* = can the results be explained in a way that makes sense to humans.
24 www.capgemini.com/insights/research-library/ai-and-the-ethical-conundrum
25 www.innovationaus.com/ndis-robo-plans-test-algorithmic-transparency/
26 https://developers.google.com/machine-learning/glossary/fairness
27 Audit AI, Aequitas, AIExplainability360, fairml, parityfairness, ScikitFairness to name a few.
28 https://openethics.ai/canvas/
29 https://ethics.org.au/the-ethical-advantage/
30 www.forbes.com/sites/theyec/2019/08/20/do-ethics-really-matter-to-todays-consumers/?sh=359c5ca42d0e
31 https://insight.kellogg.northwestern.edu/article/consumers-care-if-your-product-is-ethical
32 www.atlassian.com/team-playbook/plays/sparring
33 https://theodi.org/article/the-data-ethics-canvas-2021/
34 www.oaic.gov.au/privacy/guidance-and-advice/guide-to-undertaking-privacy-impact-assessments
35 www.digital.nsw.gov.au/policy/artificial-intelligence/nsw-ai-assurance-framework

---

References

Chomiak, K. and Miktus, M. (2021), "Harnessing value from data science in business: ensuring explainability and fairness of solutions". arXiv preprint arXiv:2108.07714.

Culmsee, P. and Awati, K. (2012), "Towards a holding environment: building shared understanding and commitment in projects", *International Journal of Managing Projects in Business*, Vol. 5 No. 3, pp. 528–548.

Lee, M and Singh, J. (2021). "The Landscape and Gaps in Open Source Fairness Toolkits. In CHI Conference on Human Factors in Computing Systems (CHI '21)", May 8–13, 2021, Yokohama, Japan. ACM, New York, NY, USA, 13 pages. https://doi.org/10.1145/3411764.3445261

Mäntymäki, M., Minkkinen, M., Birkstedt, T. and Viljanen, M. (2022), "Defining organizational AI governance", *AI and Ethics*. https://doi.org/10.1007/s43 681-022-00143-x

Mehrabi, N., Morstatter, F., Saxena, N., Lerman, K. and Galstyan, A. (2021), "A survey on bias and fairness in machine learning," *ACM Computing Surveys (CSUR)*, Vol. 54 No. 6, pp. 1–35.

Mingers, J. C. (1995), "Information and meaning: Foundations for an intersubjective account". *Information Systems Journal*, Vol. 5 No. 4, pp. 285–306.

Schneider, J., Abraham, R., Meske, C. and Vom Brocke, J. (2022), "Artificial intelligence governance for businesses", *Information Systems Management*, pp. 1–21.

Suresh, H. and Guttag, J. (2021), "Understanding potential sources of harm throughout the machine learning life cycle," *MIT Case Studies in Social and Ethical Responsibilities of Computing* (Summer 2021).

9

Coda

The Principles of Emergent Design Redux

Early in Chapter 1, we critiqued of the notion of *strategic alignment*, making the point that it is based on fixed models rather than a changing reality. As Claudio Ciborra noted (see his quote in Chapter 1), reality is ever-changing and any attempts to build *fixed* bridges between a technical capability and the business will fail because the two "shores" continually shift. Now that you have travelled with us through this book, we hope you will agree that an emergent design approach *guarantees* alignment because the strategy emerges gradually via interactions with the business. It is through these interactions that the strategist gains a first-hand appreciation of how specific aspects of the business are likely to change and is thus able to build in the flexibility needed to respond to them. To be sure, it may well be that some changes cannot be handled gracefully (or even at all!) but at least one is aware of them and is able to warn management of potential issues ahead of time.

In Chapter 3, we presented eight principles of Emergent Design, which we then referenced throughout the book. As a reminder, the principles are:

- Be a midwife rather than an expert.
- Use conversations to gain commitment.
- Understand and address concerns of stakeholders who are wary of the proposed change.
- Frame the current situation as an enabling constraint.
- Consider long-term and hidden consequences.
- Create an environment that encourages learning.
- Beware of platitudinous goals.
- Act so as to increase your choices.

These principles *do not tell you what to do in specific situations*. Rather, they are about cultivating a *disposition* that looks at technology through the multiple, and often conflicting, perspectives of those whose work is affected by it. Put another way, they encourage practitioners to recognise that building

DOI: 10.1201/9781003260158-9

and embedding a data capability is a process of organisational change that is best achieved in an evolutionary manner. This entails starting from where people are – in terms of capability, culture, technology, and governance – and enabling them to undertake a collective journey in an agreed direction. The momentum for the journey comes from a shared understanding of the organisation's need to develop the capability.

How do the principles help? They do so by articulating ways to:

a. agree on interim goals,

b. identify potential issues enroute, and

c. address them in ways that are acceptable to all affected stakeholders.

In practical terms, the principles are aimed at encouraging people from across the organisation to participate in designing and building the new capability.

What is this if not strategic alignment!

Selling the Strategy; Choosing Your Adventure

There remains the question of how you sell the strategy to the executives in your organisation. By this point, we hope you see that there are several ways you can do this. Which one you choose depends on their mindset. If they are comfortable with the ambiguity associated with Emergent Design, go ahead and present it to them as we have presented it to you in this book.

However, if they are uncomfortable with the ambiguity associated with an emergent design approach, you can hand them a teddy bear (see Chapter 3) that will reassure them that you are not advocating chaos and anarchy (which, of course, you aren't). The teddy bear is essentially a framing of what you are going to do (which is Emergent Design) in a way that looks like a more conventional strategy. How you frame this is entirely up to you; you are free to "choose your own adventure". We offer a couple of examples to show you just how easy it is to present Emergent Design in a more "corporately acceptable" manner.

Example 1: As a Means to Enable Data-Supported Decision-Making

The starting point is with the four (or five) pillars of your data (science) strategy: capability, culture, technology, and governance/ethics (which can be split up into separate pillars if needed). These pillars, which we covered in detail in Chapters 5–8, support the aspirational goal of "embedding an organisation-wide data-supported decision making culture".[1] You might

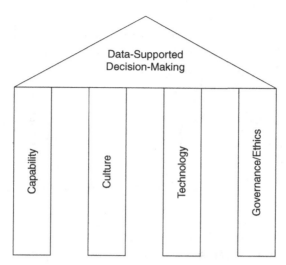

FIGURE 9.1
A possible "strategy on a page".

visualise this via a "strategy on a page" (SOAP) diagram that resembles the one shown in Figure 9.1.

You can customise this in several ways. For example, you may be aware – from experiences of interacting with the board – that the word "culture" can be contentious. If that is the case, you may want to fold it into the *capability* pillar and keep it out of sight. Alternatively, you could keep it as a separate pillar but call it *data literacy* instead of *culture*.

The possibilities are endless!

Example 2: As a Means to Support the Organisation's Strategy

If the board expects to see an explicit connection between the data capability and the organisation's strategy, you can recast the above very simply as shown in Figure 9.2.

The way we have shown it here is that the data capability supports the organisational strategy. You would replace the dotted horizontal box with your organisation's SOAP diagram. Again, our intent here is to show that the elements we have discussed in this book can be put together in many different ways to help you make your case to the decision makers.

We admit is ironic, even a tad rich, for us to advocate such diagrams after critiquing notion of strategic alignment. In our defence, we would like to point out that the diagrams are not a depiction of how the strategy will be implemented. Rather, it is intended as an aid to explain Emergent Design to the board and, more importantly, assure them that the approach is a principled one, not a license to "do as you please".

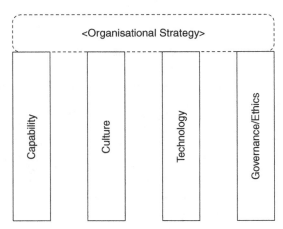

FIGURE 9.2
Another possible "strategy on a page".

Quo Vadis?

So, finally, it's time for us to sign off and for you to decide where to go from here. Before parting, there are a few points we would suggest you keep in mind as you venture into the exciting task of building a data capability for your organisation:

1. Your goal should be framed as a broad or aspirational statement rather than a detailed, fleshed out goal. Example: *"to enable data-supported decision making across the entire organisation"*.

2. Do not attempt to build a detailed strategic roadmap; focus first on working on proofs of concept that deliver value to the business and thus enable you to gain credibility. For your very first proof of concept, pick a quick win over a project that is going to take longer, even if the latter delivers greater value (unless the value is compelling).

3. For technology, start with what your organisation already has in place and build incrementally from there. Avoid wholesale changes as far as possible; they are a recipe for integration nightmares.

4. When it comes to choices, prioritise people over processes and/or technology. For example, when choosing a technology, pick the one that makes life easiest for your staff rather than one that is cool.

5. As your data capability matures, you will need to put in place the technology and skills to productionise models. However, in the early stages of your capability building efforts, it is perfectly fine to update and run models manually as needed.

6. Doing the right thing is as important as – if not more than – doing the thing right. Your models should be both ethically and technically sound.

In closing: keep in mind it is the journey that matters, not the destination.

Note

1 Our use of the word "supported" here is deliberate: data does not "drive" or "make" decisions, it can at best support them.

Index

Printed in the United States
by Baker & Taylor Publisher Services